THE JEWS IN THE TIME OF JESUS

An Introduction

by
Stephen M. Wylen

Paulist Press
New York/Mahwah, N.J.

Maps by Shane Kelley, Kelley Graphics

Book design by Jay Gribble, C.S.P.

Library of Congress Cataloging-in-Publication Data

Wylen, Stephen M., 1952-
    The Jews in the time of Jesus : an introduction / by Stephen M. Wylen.
      p. cm.
    Includes bibliographical references and index.
    ISBN 0-8091-3610-4
    1. Judaism—History—Post-exilic period, 586 B.C.-210 A.D. 2. Jews—History—168 B.C.-135 A.D. I. Title.
BM176.W95   1995   95-20928
296'.09—dc20   CIP

Published by Paulist Press
997 Macarthur Boulevard
Mahwah, NJ 07430

Printed and bound in the
United States of America

Contents

What Kind of Group Were the Sects?; Class Structure and Sects; Conclusion: Some Points to Remember About the Pharisees

To Fr. Rob Schwarz,
a Christian

Acknowledgments

This book developed out of a course I taught at the University of Scranton. I am grateful to Fr. J.A. Panuska S.J. PhD., president of the University of Scranton, for the opportunity to teach. As Hillel said: "Much I learned from my teachers, more from my colleagues, and most of all from my students."

I am grateful to Steven Casey, who carefully read the manuscript and made numerous valuable suggestions for improvement. Helpful suggestions also came from Fr. Richard Rousseau, Fr. Robert Schwarz, and John Downey, who advised me and guided me in the early part of my writing.

Much of the research for this book was conducted while I was a fellow of the Coolidge Colloquium of the Association for Religion and Intellectual Life. I am grateful to Katherine Kurs, Exec. Dir. of the A.R.I.L., and to Rabbi Larry Edwards, John Downey, Suzanne Stewart and Emilie Townes, and to all the 1994 Coolidge Fellows. You shared your wisdom and sent me in new directions. Thanks and greetings to "old boys" Jonathan, Rhett, Alan, Barry and Victor, and to Rabbi Rachel Sabath.

I am grateful to those who have helped me in my journey of the spirit—to David Rojay, Ronald Goodman, Chuck Broches, Charles Mabee, Susan and Tim Ettenheim, Tom Blomain, my old friends at B'nai Sholom Congregation and Temple Hesed, Joel Smith and Howard Kagan and my new friends at Temple Beth Tikvah. To my friend, colleague and mentor Fr. Rob Schwarz. To Fr. Jack Bendik, Fr. Joseph Quinn, and all the members of the Abington Ecumenical Ministerium and the Central City Ministerium of Scranton. I am grateful for my bicycle, and for the clarity that comes while riding it.

Most of all I am grateful to my wife Cheryl, a pure soulmate, a supportive friend and companion, and a person of immeasurable compassion and ability.

May this work be for the glory of God. You who create harmony in the heavens, may You create peace among Your children.

1 Adar 5755
February 1995

1

An Introduction

Why Learn About Jesus and the Times He Lived In?

Many people today want to know more about the world in which Jesus lived. There are many recent books on the subject, ranging from dense historical scholarship to novelistic biography. We intend this book to fill a gap between the scholarly and the fictional works on Jesus and his times. Our goal is to present the known historical facts about Jesus' life and times without an excess of scholarly detail. We shall reveal the significant historical questions about the world in which Jesus lived. We will explore the views of different scholars on these questions. We will ask ourselves in what way these scholarly debates are important to our own religious concerns.

Christians of today want to know more about Jesus as a person. This interest is unique to modern Christians. The earliest Christians were primarily interested in their own experience of the risen Christ. They presumably could have recorded a great deal of biographical detail about Jesus, but they did not wish to do so.

Later Christians, before the dawn of the modern age, were likewise more concerned about the Christ as a means to salvation. The life and teachings of the historical person, Jesus of Nazareth, did not much interest them. Only in the past two hundred years have Christians sought to gain religious direction from the earthly life of Jesus and the message he preached.

The modern interest in the person of Jesus is motivated in part by humanism, the belief in the importance of people as individuals. Traditional Christian doctrine teaches that Jesus was wholly human as well as wholly divine, but in the past little attention was paid to the human side of Jesus. Modern Christians, on the other hand, are confident that there are important lessons to be learned from an acquaintance with the person of Jesus.

The modern study of history has also led to greater interest in the historical person of Jesus. We have come to realize that one who reads the gospel accounts of Jesus' life is prone to make many wrong assumptions about the meaning of these texts. Our modern culture differs greatly from that of two thousand years ago. Times have changed. Literary styles have changed. The meaning of words and catchphrases has changed. We can only understand the story of Jesus and the preserved words of Jesus if we study the times during which Jesus lived. We must extend our minds back through two thousand years of continuous social and historical change if we are to truly understand the Christian scriptures.

As modern people we think historically. We ask ourselves the question, "What really happened in the past?" Premodern people did not ask this question, at least not in the same way. They remembered the past through myths. A myth is a story which encapsulates the essence of the events of the past. A myth contains symbolic elements which represent the meaning of past events. Ancient historical writers usually do not provide the answers to our modern questions. We try to answer our own questions by interpreting ancient historical writings to separate events ("that which actually happened") from myths ("the story which summarizes the meaning of the past"). Our historical thinking leads us to ask the question, "Who was Jesus?" in a new way. Not only do we want to know what Jesus means for the Christian, we also want to know what events occurred in the life of Jesus from his birth to his crucifixion. For people like us who think historically this new question can seem urgent and compelling. It is almost maddening to us that the ancients who had the information we vainly seek did not share our interests.

Many Christians of today want to return to the earliest forms of Christianity. This desire originates in a belief that the earliest church represents a pure form of Christianity which may re-inspire the Christian churches of the present age. Historical study may be a tool to renew the Christian spirit. This objective has brought Christians to the study of Judaism, for the earliest Christians were Jews. After some years the young Christian church departed from its Jewish home to find a new home in Hellenism, the Greek culture of the Eastern Roman Empire. A return to Christian sources requires peeling away the Greek culture of later Christianity to discover the original core, which expressed its creative impulse within Judaism. We can see that today's Christians have good reason to study Judaism in the time of Jesus.

Modern Jews, also, are curious to know more about Jesus. Jews have lived among Christians for two thousand years, more than half of all Jewish history since the time of Abraham. The modern spirit of free inquiry has made it possible for Jews to learn about Jesus while remaining secure and unchallenged in their own faith. Before the modern age any Jew who asked about Jesus would be expected, indeed compelled, to convert. In the modern spirit Jews may now fulfill their curiosity. Knowing that Jesus was a Jew, Jews want to know how it came about that Jesus became the basis for a new and different religion among the Gentiles. Jews wish to know how Jesus' Jewishness affects Christian attitudes toward Jews. Jews wish to understand more of the religious motivation of their neighbors. Also, as we shall see, Jews can learn a great deal about their own religion by studying the insights of Jesus scholars.

The Modern Study of Jesus

Since scholars of history and religion began to study the life of Jesus some two hundred years ago, we have learned much about how to conduct such a study. The study of the Jesus of history falls into three eras.

First came the "search for the historical Jesus" which occupied scholars, mostly German, throughout the nineteenth century. In this period scholars confidently composed detailed biographies of Jesus. Since the gospels and other sources presented many contradictions and left many questions unanswered, the scholars filled out their biographies with their own best guesses. The "search for the historical Jesus" came to an end when the great scholar Albert Schweitzer demonstrated that the biographers of Jesus were not really describing a first century Jew, but a nineteenth century German liberal philosopher. That is, the scholars were looking in the mirror and describing Jesus as if he were one of them.

Then began the "new search for the historical Jesus." This new search lasted until approximately the 1970s. The scholars of the new search tried to avoid the errors of the past by carefully analyzing their source materials for accuracy. Unfortunately, each generation of scholars discovered that the previous generation had made too many unfounded assumptions. After decades of carefully reading the sources, scholars came to the conclusion that there is almost nothing that we can say with complete confidence about the actual life and teaching of Jesus. We do not have enough information to write a detailed modern biography.

That would seem to bring us to a dead end, but a new approach brought us hope that we could learn more about Jesus. Scholars had come to recognize that Jesus of Nazareth was a man of his age. He was a Galilean Jew, of humble birth, living in the first third of the first century. The more we could discover about how such a Jew would have lived, the more we can know about Jesus. How would a carpenter's son from Nazareth spend his day? What would his home have looked like? What would have been his family's religious practice, their beliefs, their significant rituals? How would a child like young Jesus have been educated? What kind of leaders and teachers would have attempted to influence him? What were the overwhelming social, economic and political concerns of his friends and neighbors? The attempt to answer such questions may be called "Jesus research." It is the third and contemporary stage of the historical study of Jesus. It promises greater results than the earlier attempts to write Jesus' exact biography.

Jesus research leads us directly to the study of first century Judaism. This is not the same as Judaism as it exists now. Neither is it the same as the Judaism of the time of the Hebrew scriptures. Both modern and ancient Judaism have some relevance to our study, but we are primarily interested in Judaism as it existed in the time of Jesus. This was a period of great religious creativity in Judaism. Both Christianity and Judaism as we know them today grew out of the common root of first century Judaism.

The earlier search for the historical Jesus was often marred by a spirit of anti-Semitism. In the nineteenth century academic scholars of history carried over into the secular university the old religious prejudices against the Jews. The religious anti-Judaism that was characteristic of the Middle Ages had led to the isolation and persecution of the Jews. The modern age saw a shift to anti-Semitism, which had its basis in ideas of race and culture rather than religion. Anti-Semites distinguished Christians from others not by religion but as Aryans, people of European race and culture. They condemned Jews as Semites, an inferior people who could never be assimilated into European culture. Anti-Judaism had the conversion of the Jews as its goal. The goal of modern anti-Semitism was the elimination of the Jews.

The scholars of the search and new search were often divided between anti-Semites and philo-Semites. The latter group opposed the abuse of scholarship in the service of prejudice and hatred. All historians of Jesus were acutely aware that their work influenced contemporary Christian attitudes toward Jews. Some historians of Jesus helped pave the path to the Nazi gas chambers, while others foresaw and used their scholarship to actively oppose such a development.

In modern Jesus research the finest scholars distance themselves from the historic rivalry between Christians and Jews. They have joined in a search for historical truth. The common background of Judaism and Christianity promises to provide a basis for interfaith understanding and mutual appreciation. This book is composed in today's spirit of cooperation. We are confident that both Christians and Jews will benefit from this study. Their own faith will be challenged but ultimately strengthened. In honestly confronting history we may be forced to abandon some cherished notions. We may find this disturbing, but in the end our religion will stand upon a more firm foundation.

The lifetime of Jesus took up about 33 years, probably from 3 BCE to about 30 CE.[1] Jesus' lifetime lies within a broader era of Jewish history which modern historians call the Second Temple era. In this book we shall be studying Second Temple Judaism, with special emphasis on those aspects of Second Temple Judaism which are most relevant to Jesus' life and work.

Time Periods

A historical understanding of the time of Jesus requires us to have a good sense of chronology. We must be able to distinguish the relative time in which past events occurred. (For example, the relationship in time between the revolt of the Maccabees and the rise of the Pharisees.) A further complexity is that we must understand how our perspective on events has changed through time. For example, historians judged the revolt of the Maccabees one way in the time shortly after the event. Jews in the time of Jesus had a different perspective on the Maccabees. Today we have our own modern judgment of the Maccabean revolt. To keep our times straight we must keep track of five different places in time, four of which are important to our study in this book.

"A" is the time in which an event actually occurred. (For the preaching career of Jesus, this would be around 30 CE.)
"B" is the time in which the event "A" was first recorded in books that have come down to us. (For the life of Jesus, this would be from 50–200 CE, when the gospels were written and edited.)
"C" is the era when Christians and Jews did not subject their sacred writings to historical analysis (roughly 300 CE to 1800 CE). We shall not be speaking much of this era, but we must remember that it existed.
"D" is the time when historians began to analyze Christian and Jewish

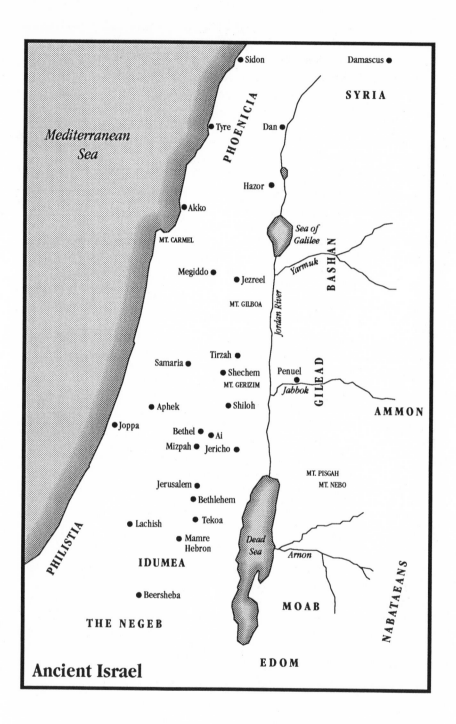

Ancient Israel

sacred writings using the standards of the modern science of historical research (1800–1980). We possess two centuries' worth of modern scholarly research about the historical Jesus and the origins of Christianity and Rabbinic Judaism.

"E" is our own time, right now. We want to know what the most recent, contemporary scholars are saying.

We note that historians are concerned with the relationship between the time of an event and the time when that event was recorded for history. We have no eyewitness accounts to answer most of our historical questions about Jesus' time, and the accounts we do have often come from highly prejudiced sources. The records that come to us from a later time represent a set of concerns that the actors in the original events may not have shared. For example, the events in the life of Jesus took place while the Jewish Temple in Jerusalem was still standing. Most of the gospels were written after the Romans had destroyed the Temple in the Jewish great revolt. To understand Jesus' life from our gospel sources we have to factor out all the great changes that followed upon the destruction of the Temple.

The Second Temple Era and the Meaning of "Biblical" Times

If you open a Christian Bible you will find in it the Hebrew scriptures (formerly called the Old Testament) and the New Testament. It is natural for a Christian Bible reader to think of these two Testaments as forming a single work—The Bible. From this it is natural to presume that the Hebrew scriptures and New Testament take place within a single era of time—"biblical times."

From a historical point of view, Old Testament times and New Testament times do not form a unit. We must overcome the idea that the Hebrew scriptures end where the New Testament begins. It is misleading to suppose that Judaism is the religion of the Old Testament, as if Jewish faith and practice never developed beyond their primitive origins.

There is, in fact, a period of many centuries between the end of the Hebrew scriptures and the beginning of the New Testament—roughly five to seven hundred years. This period, formerly called the "Intertestamental Period," is precisely the Second Temple era in which we are interested. As we shall see, it was a time of great religious development and change within Judaism. Judaism at the time of Jesus was quite different from "Old Testament Judaism." One can never know Jesus' Judaism only from reading the Hebrew scriptures.

There are three different "ends" to Old Testament times: (a) the final time about which the Hebrew scriptures speak; (b) the final time in which biblical books were written; and (c) the final time in which existing books were added to the Bible. The biblical period (a) ends early in the Persian Empire, shortly after the rebuilding of the Temple, about 500–450 BCE. This is five hundred years before the time of Jesus! The last biblical book written (b) is the book of Daniel, written about 169 BCE. For some reason, Jews decided that biblical writing had come to an end with the Maccabean revolt. The council of rabbis closed the Bible for good (c) about 100 CE, a generation after the time of Jesus. The rabbis voted on some old books that were still questionable, including some in the Bible and excluding all others. The book of Esther may have slipped into the Bible later, but basically the Bible was now closed. More than a century later the Christians added the New Testament to the scriptures. Jews, at the same time, added the Mishnah. The New Testament and Mishnah are not a mere continuation of earlier biblical writing. They represent a new beginning.

In Jesus' time the Hebrew Bible contained only two of its eventual three sections—the Torah and the Prophets. These were not considered a "Bible," a single book, but two separate collections of sacred scriptures. Thus the New Testament term for sacred scripture is "the Torah (or, Law) and the Prophets." The closing of the Bible in the second century completed the third section, the Writings. (Some Christians include a fourth section, the Apocrypha, in the Hebrew scriptures.) By Jesus' time Jews had generated a great body of interpretation on how to live by these holy books. The complete "Bible" that Jesus knew consisted of not just the Torah and the Prophets, but also five hundred years' worth of interpretation by Jewish sages. We only know Jesus' "Bible" if we know how Jews in Jesus' time interpreted the written words of the scriptures. Most Christians today outside the community of historical scholars are not well acquainted with this body of interpretation.

For example, the "lex talio"—"an eye for an eye and a tooth for a tooth." This verse is found in the Torah. Not many Christians today know that in Jesus' time Jewish law prohibited mutilation as a judicial punishment. Jews interpreted the "lex talio" to mean the payment of fines for healing, pain and suffering, and lost time. The idiom "eye for an eye" was understood to mean "equality before the law"—that the fine for injuring a peasant was the same as that for injuring an aristocrat. All people are equal in the eyes of the law! We only know Jesus'

Torah if we know that this is how Jews interpreted the Torah in his time. It is prejudiced and historically false to derive from the "lex talio" the message that Judaism in Jesus' time was a teaching of strict judgment without forgiveness. Jesus' message of divine love and forgiveness stands on its own. There is no need to highlight it with false contrasts to the Judaism of his day.

The Historical Method

Since our approach to our subject is the historical method, let us take a few moments to consider what is special about this method. How does it differ from earlier ways of studying sacred literature?

First, the historical method presumes that things change over time. Our times are not like former times. We cannot understand the past just by looking at how things are now. We have to see how things have changed.

God does not change. Looking only at the divine authorship of sacred scripture, we might feel that we have no need to study history. If God is unchanging, then God's word must be unchanging. God is speaking directly to us in the scriptures. Why bother to study history?

We use the historical method because we presume that humans also had a role in the writing of scriptures. Rabbis wrote the words of the Talmud. Paul wrote his epistles. Matthew, Mark, Luke and John wrote their gospels. These writers, being human, were subject to the forces of history. They wrote for the human understanding of their times, using the literary conventions of their times. Councils of learned humans voted on which writings to include in the Hebrew scriptures, the Talmud, and the New Testament. There is a human element that requires historical understanding, even in sacred scripture. In the words of the second century sage, Rabbi Ishmael: "Scripture speaks in human language."

A second important element in the historical method is the presumption of causality. If something happened, it happened for a reason that we can discover. There is cause and effect in human events, just as in the bouncing of balls on a billiard table. When we note an extraordinary event in time, we want to know what caused it. It is not enough to say, "it was God's will." That may be so, but there will still be specific causes. Jesus preached the coming of the kingdom of God. We want to know what generated this message in the events of the time, and what made Jesus' audience interested in hearing it.

The historical method does not deal with supernatural miracles, which have no discernible cause. Some historians do not believe in miracles. They look for historical causes for miracle *stories*. Other historians do believe in miracles but as historians, they still have nothing to say about them.

Historians do not just "make up" history. They must build history from good raw materials. The raw materials of history are of two types: texts (written materials) and archeology (physical evidence left behind by former people, such as the foundations of buildings and old pots). A good historian must know how to use the raw materials wisely. We must carefully analyze our materials in our search for truth. We do not presume something happened just because an ancient author said so. We need a method to interpret the ancient writings. Historians ask one or more of the following questions when they analyze scriptures and other ancient writings:

- What is the meaning of key words?
- Who were the original authors or sources of the information in the book? How did this information get to the final author or editor of the book? How did the editor adapt his received information to fit it into the final form of the text?
- What group or institution in ancient society might have preserved the information and generated the perspectives of a particular book?
- What literary genre or genres are found in this book?
- How do this author's views compare against the views of other ancient writers who discussed the same matter? What were the objectives and the personal prejudices of the author?

History is a science. As with natural science, we start with a commonsense hypothesis—an idea of what we believe to be historical truth. Then we test our hypothesis, using all of the evidence (texts and archeological data) at our disposal. We accept our original hypothesis only if the preponderance of the evidence supports it. We do not throw out a hypothesis because of a small amount of counter-evidence, as long as most of our evidence supports it. Neither do we adopt a hypothesis that has only a little bit of evidence to support it, just because it fits our religious beliefs or preferred idea of events. When the evidence is contradictory and balanced, it is better to withhold judgment pending further discoveries or a better analysis of our materials. In our study of history we are trying to find out what really happened. We are not trying to support our preconceived theological notions. Theology must come after historical study, not before it. As good scientists we must be skeptical about our data, maintaining objective distance and not being gullible about the truth claims of our sources.

Although history is a science, it is not a hard science like physics or chemistry. There is room for opinion in interpreting events. History is not just a list of events. That is mere chronology. History is a search for pattern and meaning in events. When our study is early Judaism and early Christianity, we must acknowledge that our own religious beliefs are going to affect our interpretation of history. We must keep our religious passions sufficiently in check so that we can conduct a good investigation. Our conclusions are valid only if we start with good raw materials and we analyze them with intelligence and a good method.

The Relationship of Judaism and Christianity

The greatest danger to historical objectivity in this study is the historic rivalry between Judaism and Christianity. We must confront this rivalry from the start. Only if we factor it into our analysis will we understand how Christians and Jews have interpreted the events of the past.

In the era when the gospels and epistles were being composed, Judaism was a widespread religion in the Roman world, while Christianity was a young upstart religion. The leaders of Judaism opposed all sectarian groups, which included the Christians. The Christians in this period felt greatly oppressed by official Judaism. They responded with the view that Judaism was the old, rejected covenant with God, while Christianity came, not just as a new religion, but as God's replacement for the rejected Judaism. This is the general view of the gospels.

In the early modern period anti-Semitic scholars wrote history from the prejudiced view that Jesus was surrounded by an evil, corrupt Jewish world. Hegel, the father of modern historical study, was a strong anti-Semite. He saw Judaism as a flawed religion superseded and replaced by the superior Christianity. He believed that Judaism should have died out with the rise of Christianity.

The early modern scholars more friendly to Judaism saw Christianity as an outgrowth of Judaism, a "wild branch grafted into the olive tree," to use Paul's imagery. In the eyes of these historians Judaism and Christianity were no longer to be perceived as rivals in conflict, but as a mother and daughter.

Among some of today's scholars the mother-daughter image still holds. However, many scholars prefer a different family image of Judaism and Christianity. Having recognized that Judaism in the first century was remarkably diverse and complex, they do not believe Christianity was born out of a fixed, more ancient Judaism. They see rabbinical Judaism and Christianity as two common outgrowths of the earlier first century Judaism, each adopting different aspects of the ancient religion. To these scholars, rabbinic Judaism and Christianity are two daughters of a single mother, biblical Judaism. Judaism and Christianity are sisters. This author is undecided whether the mother-daughter image or the two sisters image best describes the historical relationship between Judaism and Christianity.

The idea that Christianity came along to replace an outworn and divinely rejected Judaism is called "supercessionism." Early modern scholars used the terms Early Christianity and Late Judaism—late, because it was about to die and be replaced by Christianity. Today's scholars, having abandoned supercessionism, prefer to use the terms Early Judaism and Early Christianity to describe the first century outgrowths of the biblical Jewish heritage. The term Early Judaism acknowledges that Judaism, like Christianity, has continued its creative evolution over the past two millennia.

Is the Religion of Jesus Continuous with Judaism?

Does the religion of Jesus flow from the traditions of biblical Judaism, or did Jesus make a radical break from Judaism and found a new religion? That is a hotly contested question in modern historical study. Was Christianity an inheritor of the religion of the Hebrew scriptures? Or, was Christianity a brand-new religion that came into being in contrast to the older Judaism? One can find Christians who champion either view.

We can see what is at stake in this distinction by presenting two contradictory and extreme views, which we shall title "X" and "Y". The reader will want to keep these two statements in mind as we continue our study:

X: Everything Jesus said was new from his lips, the opposite of the Jewish teachings of his age.
Y: Jesus represents the true continuation of biblical Judaism, the unbroken line of prophecy.

Can you, the reader, discover in your own passions a preference for one or the other of the above statements? Are you able to see that if you prefer them both, you have adopted a contradiction?

Some Christians are pleased to adopt both statements, to think of Jesus as both the great originator of Christianity and the true extension of the biblical prophets. Some recent Christian historical scholars have attempted to encompass this pleasing contradiction in their theories by suggesting that Jesus represents a "radical" interpretation of biblical themes. For example, we can all agree that "love" is a central theme in the teachings of Jesus. Historical research refutes the idea that Jesus taught love in contrast to a Jewish teaching of hate (the "X" position). Did Jesus' love teaching flow from the contemporary Jewish teaching of love ("Y")? The historians who want to encompass both claims, "X" and "Y" claim that the Jews of Jesus' time taught love, but Jesus taught "radical" love. There were Jewish teachers who sought social justice, but Jesus sought "radical" social justice. The weakness of the "radical" thesis is that one cannot find or demonstrate anything in our evidence that distinguishes love from radical love, and so on. The historians who made the claims for Jesus' "radical" extension of Jewish teachings were, to all appearances, succumbing to a desire to have it both ways. They wished to see Jesus as both the great religious innovator and the representative of biblical continuity.

My own view is that statements X and Y are both untrue because they represent extreme and absolute judgments. Instead of making general statements we must compare Jesus' teachings to first century Judaism on an issue by issue basis. It then becomes apparent that Jesus was in some ways an innovator who taught new ideas or extended old ideas into new territory, while in other ways Jesus followed the Jewish teachings of his times. Generally speaking, Jesus' teachings can be placed in the broad context of first century Judaism in its many manifestations.

Placing Jesus' teachings in historical context neither strengthens nor weakens Christianity. But, it will please or disturb individual Christians and Jews depending on how they feel about statements X and Y.

Sacred Scripture as Historical Information

Another major issue that divides historical scholars is the historical reliability of sacred scriptures, Christian and Jewish. How much can we rely on the New Testament (written ca. 50–200 CE) to tell us about Jesus and his times (ca. 30 CE)? The sacred writings of rabbinical Judaism, considered scriptural by Jews, are the Mishnah (ca. 200 CE), the Talmuds (400–500 CE), and books of midrash (300–700 CE). The Mishnah and Talmuds and related rabbinical literature are our sources for information on the Jewish religious leaders who lived before and during the time of Jesus. Can we rely on this information?

Do the sacred writings of Christianity and Judaism tell us a lot about Jesus' time as they claim to do? Or, do they only tell us about the time, up to centuries later, in which they were written? Some scholars are willing to accept the pious view that the scriptures are exceedingly accurate in all they record. Other scholars are quite skeptical about using sacred scriptures as a source of historical information. We have very little outside information to either corroborate or contradict the claims of the scriptures. Internal comparisons are useful but inconclusive. Left with an open field, scholars allow their personal leanings to play a role in their historical judgments.

The "pious Christian assumption" is that the gospels accurately reflect the events of Jesus' life, his teachings, and his general surroundings.

The "pious Jewish assumption" is that the Talmudic literature accurately describes Judaism when the Temple stood.

The "skeptical assumption" is that the Christian and Jewish sacred writings reflect the times in which they were written, not the times about which they speak. According to the skeptical assumption, we have little direct information about early first century Judaism.

Many scholars take a position between the two extremes, granting some historical accuracy to the Christian and Jewish scriptures, but not total acceptance. These scholars then need to find some way to separate the kernel of historical fact from the shell of later legend.

Further complicating matters is the fact that we do have much Jewish religious writing from the first century, but in sectarian books that mainstream Jews[2] did not accept. These books were preserved (sometimes in obscure translations) by various Christian groups, or have been dug up by archeologists. Can we honestly compare first century sectarian texts, second century gospels, and fifth century rabbinic writings? The sectarian writings are often contradictory to Talmudic teachings about Judaism. Should we grant more historical accuracy to sectarian writings because they are written closer to Jesus' time? Should we rather ignore them because they are merely sectarian, while the Talmud is mainstream? Generally, Christian scholars are more willing to use the sectarian writings as a source of information on first century Judaism, while Jewish scholars grant more authority to the rabbinic literature. Among Jewish and Christian historians some lean toward the pious assumptions, others toward the skeptical view. We shall keep this in mind as we proceed with our study.

A related issue is whether our many textual sources may be used together to describe the totality of first century Judaism, or whether we must independently analyze each text. Do you describe a forest by describing every tree within it, or by describing the appearance and ecology of the forest as a whole? This writer takes the view that the latter approach creates a more holistic and probably more accurate view of first century Judaism. We do believe that the various source texts combine to paint for us a "big picture" of our subject.

2

The Biblical Background of Second Temple Judaism

The Geography of the Land of Israel

The land of Israel lies on the southeastern shore of the Mediterranean Sea. The land of Israel connects Africa to Asia and Europe. As the bridge between three continents the land of Israel is strategically important, though it is a small land, no larger than the state of New Jersey.

From west to east the land rises from the Mediterranean coastal plain to the hill country. The land goes up to a central spine, then down into the Jordan River valley. The major towns of ancient Israel lay on the crest of the hill country—Samaria and Shechem (Nablus) in the north, Jerusalem in the center, Hebron and then Beersheba in the south. South of Beersheba the hills flatten out into the Negev Desert. The desert reaches southward to the northern tip of the Red Sea, an arm of the Indian Ocean.

North of the hill country of Judea and Samaria is the great Jezreel valley. The ancient road from Egypt departed from the coast and went through this valley, across the Jordan River, and then up to the Syrian plateau, and on to Mesopotamia. This valley and its major town, Megiddo, was the site of ancient clashes between Egyptian and Mesopotamian armies. Thus Megiddo lent its name to the prophesied future battle between the forces of good and evil—Armageddon!

North of the Jezreel valley is the Galilee region. A series of parallel ridges runs west to east (perpendicular to the line of the Judean hills), from near the seacoast to the Sea of Galilee and the Syrian plateau. On the eastern boundary of the Galilee flow the headwaters of the Jordan River. The Jordan flows into the Sea (really Lake) of Galilee. The river continues south past Jericho and ends in the Dead Sea, the lowest point on the surface of the earth.

From the seacoast to the Jordan River valley the land goes from well-watered to semi-arid to arid. The Judean hills pull the water out of the clouds that come from the sea, leaving the eastern slopes a virtual desert, suitable only for nomadic sheepherding. The hill country is suitable for dry farming by small landholders, while the coastlands and valleys are suited for larger plantations. In ancient times the Jews lived mainly in the hill country, while the Philistines and others controlled the major cities of the coast and the great valleys. There was also a large Jewish population at times in the Galilee, and east of the Jordan River in Gilead, Bashan and the Golan. The northern hill country of Samaria was occupied by Israelites until the Assyrian Exile in 722 BCE. Afterwards a mixed people called the Samaritans lived there.

The land of Israel receives rain only half the year, from fall until spring. Grain is grown in the cool, wet rainy season, while fruits and vegetables are grown in the hot, sunny dry season. The desert turns quite green at the end of winter, is briefly covered with a carpet of beautiful wildflowers, and then dies to a barren brown in late spring and summer. The seeds of next winter's grasses and flowers hide in the desert soil. The cycle of dry and rainy seasons suggests the resurrection of the dead—a doctrine which arose in this very land.

The Name of the Country

Before the Israelites entered the land, it was called the land of Canaan. After the Israelites conquered the land and absorbed its Canaanite inhabitants into their own group the land was known as the land of Israel. In Second Temple times the name of the Jewish state was Judah. This was also the geographical name for that part of the land from Jerusalem south to the desert, and from the beginning of the hill country in the west to the Dead Sea in the east. Thus, in Second Temple times the term "Judah" designates both a geographical region within the land of Israel, and the political state of the Jews. In Second Temple times the area identified as the land of Israel had no political significance but it had religious significance. Jews living within this area were bound to bring agricultural sacrifices to the Temple; Jews living outside the land of Israel were free of this requirement. Whatever the current boundaries of their state, the Jews thought of the entire land of Israel as their promised land, a land dedicated to God.

When the Romans put down the Jewish rebellion in the year 70 CE they wanted to eliminate the names "Israel" and "Judea," which brought to mind Jewish claims of sovereignty over the land. The Romans renamed the land "Palestine" after the ancient Philistines, a people long gone. Each succeeding colonial power retained the name "Palestine" for this region. Jews never accepted this colonialist name, preferring always to call the land the land of Israel.

Summary of the History of Tribal and First Temple Israel

Ancient Israel was a confederation of twelve tribes who shared a common worship and traced their family tree to a common ancestor, Abraham. The Israelites remembered that at the beginning of their history they were slaves in Egypt. God redeemed them from Egyptian slavery and brought them to Mount Sinai. There, God entered into a sacred covenant with the Israelites. Then God brought them into the land of Canaan and gave it to them (c.1250 BCE). For this, the people owed God eternal and exclusive allegiance.

These twelve tribes eventually joined into a united kingdom. The first king of united Israel, Saul, died in battle. The next king, David (c.1000 BCE), had a long and successful reign, and was followed by his son Solomon. Solomon built a great Temple to God in the city of Jerusalem, which David had made the capital of the united kingdom. David and Solomon reorganized the hereditary priesthood around the Jerusalem Temple. The high priest under King David was Zadok. From this time on two dynastic leaders led the Jews. The king was a descendant of the House of David. The high priest, the religious leader (who also had much temporal power) was a descendant of Zadok. The Zadokite priesthood lasted until the year 170 BCE, a dynasty of about 800 years!

After the death of Solomon the kingdom split in two. The Southern Kingdom of Judah continued under the rule of David's descendants. The Northern Kingdom—variously called Israel, Ephraim or Samaria—suffered a variety of dynastic changes until the Assyrians destroyed it in 722 BCE. The Southern Kingdom of Judah lasted until 586 BCE. In that year the Babylonians conquered Judah, burned down her capital of Jerusalem, placed the Davidic king, Yehoyakin, in their palace dungeon, and forced most of the Judeans (Jews) into exile in Babylon. Thus, the era of the First Temple ended with a great destruction of the nation.

The kings of Judah had gradually centralized the worship of God in the Temple in Jerusalem. King Hezekiah, and later King Josiah, destroyed all the "high places" where sacrifices were offered to God. By the time the Babylonians destroyed the Temple in 586 BCE, Jews believed they could not worship God through sacrifice in any other location. This was a problem for the Jews in Babylon. They had to develop new ways of serving their God even as they hoped to return to Jerusalem and rebuild the Temple.

The leaders of the Jewish people—the priests, the royal and noble families, the wise men and elders—were all exiled to Babylon. Only the simplest peasants had been left in Judah by the Babylonians. It fell to the traditional Jewish leaders—and, to the charismatic prophets who spoke for God—to preserve the religion and identity of the Jews in the Exile.

The Return from Exile

The prophet Jeremiah had foretold that the Exile in Babylon would last seventy years. He was close to the mark. In about 539 BCE Cyrus the Great of Persia conquered Babylon. Cyrus considered himself the champion of all the gods whom the Babylonians had angered. Cyrus encouraged the Jews in Babylon to return to Judah and restore their worship. Most Jews remained in Babylon, where they had come to feel at home. A few waves of Jews did return to Judah. Returning priests hoped to restore the Temple, and with it their livelihood, since priests ate the sacrifices offered by the Jewish farmers and herders. Fortunately, the Babylonians had never resettled the country of Judah, and it was largely empty except for the few Jews who had not been exiled. In about 515 BCE, just about seventy years after the Babylonian destruction, the Jews rebuilt the Temple. There were old men present who remembered the First Temple from their childhood. The old men grumbled at the modest dimensions of the new structure compared to the grandeur of the First Temple, but the prophets reassured them that this Temple would eventually outshine the first. The prediction came true. The Second Temple was periodically rebuilt, each time on a grander scale. The Second Temple in the time of Jesus was one of the most magnificent buildings in the world.

The territory of the Persian province of Judah was tiny. It consisted only of the city of Jerusalem and the villages in the surrounding hill country. As we shall see, the Jews gradually expanded their territory over the centuries to eventually include the territory of the biblical twelve tribes.

Israelites Become Jews

Early in the Persian Empire era the term Israelite ("B'nai Yisrael"—Children of Israel) fell out of use. With the twelve tribes of Israel long gone, the remaining people came to be called Jews after their country of Judah. The Persians called the restored Jewish country the province of "Yahud" (Judah). The people who came from there, whether still in the country or in Babylon or living elsewhere in the 127 provinces of the empire, were called Jews. The Jews retained the term "Israel" as a poetic term for their collective group identity.

The Last of the Prophets

Early in the Persian period the institution of prophecy ended. The biblical prophets fall into two historical categories. Early in Israel's history came the charismatic prophets—including Samuel, Elijah and Elisha. Later came the classical literary prophets who left us writings— the biblical books of the prophets. The first literary prophet was Amos. The greatest literary prophets were Isaiah, Jeremiah, Ezekiel, and Second Isaiah (author of most of the book of Isaiah from chapter 40 on). The last literary prophets were Haggai, Zechariah and Malachi. The central interest of the last prophets was in rebuilding the Temple, reestablishing the priesthood as a pure and dedicated institution, and combating the cynicism and doubt that overcame many Jews as they struggled to rebuild their country.

Ezra and Nehemiah

The Jews went through a period of difficult struggle in their attempt to rebuild their devastated country. Their task advanced greatly under the guidance of two great leaders, Ezra and Nehemiah.

Nehemiah was a government minister in the service of the Persian emperor. He requested and was granted permission to return to his home country to restore her fortunes. Nehemiah rebuilt the city walls of Jerusalem, established honest local government, and defeated the local enemies of the Jews, most notably the Samaritans. The Samaritans were the occupants of Samaria, the former Northern Kingdom of Israel. The Assyrians, in intentionally mixing up their subject peoples, had brought in settlers from other lands. These mixed with the remaining Israelite peasants and, following ancient custom, adopted the religion of the land. Thus, the Samaritans were Jewish by religion, though not by descent. The Samaritans offered to help rebuild the Temple in Jerusalem. When the Jews rebuffed them they acted as enemies, attacking Jerusalem to foil the project. When Nehemiah successfully defended Jerusalem, the Samaritans built a rival temple to God on Mount Gerizim in the center of their country, near the city of Samaria. The Samaritans and Jews remained rivals throughout the Second Temple era, though by the time of Jesus the Jews had gotten the upper hand.

Ezra was a priest, a religious leader. He came from Babylon with a warrant from the Persians granting him absolute secular power to rule over the Jews. He is remembered as "Ezra the Scribe"—the first Jewish leader to be so titled. We do not know what the title "Scribe" meant formally in Ezra's time. Clearly it had something to do with his scholarly knowledge of ancient Jewish traditions from the First Temple period, knowledge preserved among the Jewish sages in Babylon.

Ezra found that the Jews of Judah were not careful in observing the Sabbath. He established strict Sabbath laws, closing down the shops in Jerusalem on the seventh day. Ezra was probably enforcing the Jewish custom of Babylon, where Sabbath observance had become a major feature of Jewish divine service.

Ezra also established a strict separate identity for the Jews. He rejected political union with the Samaritans. Ezra also prohibited intermarriage with the surrounding peoples. He even forced all Judean men married to foreigners to divorce their wives. The biblical book of Ruth, the story of a Moabite woman who came to Judah and became the grandmother of King David, was probably written in this time by Jews who opposed Ezra's exclusivist policy. We do not know why Ezra segregated Jews from Samaritans and other foreigners. He may have been acting on orders from the Persians, who did not want their subjects to unite against them. He may have been following the custom of Babylon, where maintaining bloodlines could have been a Jewish strategy for preserving group identity in the Exile.

Ezra's most important act was introducing to the people of Judah the scroll of the Torah (Teaching) of Moses which he had brought with him from Babylon. Ezra read from this scroll on the New Year's Day (Rosh Hashanah) after his arrival from Babylon. The event is recorded in Chapter 8 of the book of Nehemiah (here condensed):

> When the seventh month arrived—the Israelites being settled in their towns—the entire people assembled as one person in the square before the Water Gate (in Jerusalem), and they asked Ezra the Scribe to bring the scroll of the Torah of Moses

with which the Lord had charged Israel....He read from it...from the first light until midday, to the men and women and those who could understand; the ears of all the people were given to the scroll of the Teaching (Torah)....Ezra opened the scroll in the sight of all the people....Ezra blessed the Lord, the great God, and all the people answered "Amen, Amen," with hands upraised....They read from the scroll of the Torah of God, translating it and giving the sense; so they understood the reading.

Judaism Becomes a Scriptural Religion

The translation was necessary because the Jews now spoke Aramaic, the language of Babylon, rather than Hebrew. Aramaic remained the common language of Jews throughout the Second Temple era. It was the language of Jesus. Aramaic is similar to Hebrew, and Jews continued to know Hebrew, though we do not know how much. Jews who had schooling certainly knew enough Hebrew to understand the Torah. The translation in the public reading of scripture was not just a simple word-for-word translation, but a running commentary and explanation. From its first public introduction the Torah had two aspects to it—the written text, and the public explanation. By the time of Jesus, Jewish religious leaders had been explaining the Torah in public for five centuries. A vast interpretive tradition had built up around the Torah. The Jewish scriptures in the time of Jesus consisted of the written Torah, the books of the Prophets, and five hundred years' worth of accumulated tradition. We have in existence today several written Aramaic translations of the Torah from late Roman times. These translations are called Targumim (sing. Targum). The Targumim tell us a lot about the way people in Jesus' time understood the Torah. They include Jewish legends and commentaries intermixed with the translation.

When Ezra read the Torah in public and the people accepted it, the Torah became scripture to the Jews. This was the final event in biblical times. Jews in biblical times did not have a Bible—they were living what became the Bible! Once Jews had a Bible, they were no longer living in biblical times.

Jewish tradition—the pious Jewish assumption shared also by Christians—says that the Torah existed since the time of Moses, who brought it down from Mount Sinai, when God had dictated these five books. Historians doubt this. They believe that the Torah was edited in Babylon out of the earlier source texts preserved by exiled priests and elders. Ezra the Scribe brought the Torah from Babylon to Judah, where it was previously unknown. The Torah then went through a bit of final editing under Ezra's successors, reaching the form in which we know it, about 450 BCE.

The Religious Revival

One might think that the Jews who returned to Judah from Babylon would have been a very religious group of people. After all, they had seen their fondest hopes and the most optimistic prophecies fulfilled, beyond all reasonable expectation. The Jews had their country back, their Temple, their worship, their way of life. Though not politically independent, they were free to live as they wished. Would they not offer constant thanks to God?

One may think so, but just the opposite happened. Life was difficult for the returnees. The daily grind seemed to make a joke of their expectations. There was a terrible drought in those years, which caused in turn an incredible plague of locusts. Barely able to eke a living out of the soil, the Judean farmers were reluctant to pay their sacred dues to the Temple. The priesthood, for their part, cynically kept for themselves the offerings that were supposed to be burned on the altar. There was widespread doubt about the existence of a God in heaven who cared about human devotion or just and ethical actions.

In circumstances not entirely clear to us, that early cynicism was reversed. There was a great revival of devotion to God, a devotion so powerful it continued to be the central characteristic of Jewish life throughout the Second Temple era. The prophets of the First Temple complained bitterly about Israelites worshiping foreign gods. All such foreign worship now ceases, totally and forever. No Jews are ever again accused of bowing to idols. The Jews support their Temple and its newly devoted priesthood. They revere their holy leader, the high priest. Jews pray constantly to their God. The Jews try their best to fulfill God's will as revealed in the Torah of Moses. Ezra, Nehemiah and the last of the prophets seem to have played a great role in causing this religious revival.

The End of Prophecy

Haggai, Zechariah and Malachi lived around the time of Ezra and Nehemiah. After these three no more prophets arose among the Jews. Nowadays people ask "How come God does not speak to us through prophets, like in biblical times?" People already began to ask themselves that question early in the post-biblical era. Throughout Second Temple times people yearned for a return to prophecy. They asked themselves, "Why is God distant from us? Where are the prophets?" Jewish literature of the Second Temple era displays a consistent nostalgia for prophecy.

From our historical perspective it is easy to answer the question, "Why are there no more prophets?" The acceptance of the Torah as sacred scripture under Ezra the Scribe brought prophecy to a sudden and irreversible end. One people, one religion, cannot have both scripture and prophets. One goes to a prophet for a new message from God. Scriptures claim to be the complete message from God. What would one do if a prophet contradicted the word of the scriptures?

Once the Jews acquired the Torah as scripture, the sage replaced the prophet. The sage was a scholar who knew the Torah and how to interpret it. God now spoke through the sage rather than through the prophet.

This transition may be visible even within the words of the last prophets. Zechariah and Malachi sometimes write in a question-and-answer format. Is this just a literary device? Or, are the final prophets imitating the style of the sage, who receives a question and responds to it with a learned answer?

Jewish Self-Government in the Persian Period

When the Persians restored the kingdom of Judah as a province in their empire, they restored the Davidic and Zadokite dynasties to their places. Zerubabbel, a grandson of King Yohoyakin, was placed on the throne. The Persians appointed a certain Joshua as high priest. The prophet Zechariah describes his vision of the divine investiture of Joshua and Zerubabbel—a vision which must have occurred at the time of their earthly investiture. Kings and high priests in Judah were placed into office by a ceremony of anointing with oil. Thus they were called by the term *messiah*—"anointed one." The term *messiah* did not mean anything in this era except "rightful ruler."

Zechariah had some advice for King Zerubabbel: "Not by might and not by power, but by My spirit" shall you rule (Zech 4:6)! Zerubabbel could not hope for real power under Persian rule. He should instead try to be a good and just king, according to the ideal of the Torah and prophets.

It seems that Zerubabbel did not listen to Zechariah's advice. In circumstances unknown to us the Persians removed Zerubabbel from office and did not replace him. The royal line of King David ended after nearly six hundred years. The whole royal family must have been wiped out, for we do not hear of any claimants to the throne for centuries after, nor is any descendant of the royal line mentioned in any Jewish book. The next thing we know, the Persians are handling their affairs in Judah through an appointed governor. Ezra and Nehemiah seem to be among the appointees. The high priests, however, remained in office. For the next few centuries the high priest alone was the internal ruler of the Jewish people. Judah became a theocracy, ruled by its hereditary priests.

Messianism

We do not hear of any objections by the Jews to the removal of their king. They seem to have been quite content to be ruled by their high priest. The Jews even boasted of having a theocracy, which they considered a sign of direct divine rule. Only centuries later, when Jews become dissatisfied with their rulers, do we find the longing for a return to the Davidic kings. We find this longing among various sects of Jews in the time of Jesus. While messianic doctrine varied in detail from sect to sect, it generally represented a desire for a king who was appointed directly by God to perform supernatural wonders for the Jews. He was to remove from them all oppression and injustice, defeat all forces of evil, and usher in the true reign of God.

The biblical prophets, such as Isaiah, spoke of the Messiah as the human king of Israel. Isaiah spoke glowingly of King Hezekiah as the Messiah—Hezekiah was a "good" king who followed the teachings of the priests and prophets. In later centuries those Jews who desired a restoration of the monarchy took these messianic passages in the Prophets as a symbolic reference to a future time when the divinely appointed Messiah would make his appearance. This later symbolization of the messianic (royal) passages in the Prophets was the background for the Christian reading of these passages as predictions of the coming of the Christ. Later, Jews and Christians agreed that these passages were predictions of a future Messiah, though they obviously disagreed on its application to Jesus.

The Books of the Bible

We have seen how under Ezra the Scribe the first five books of the Bible were *canonized* (recognized as holy books) as the Torah. Some time later, in circumstances not known to us, the books of the Prophets

Comparison between the Jewish and Christian Canons

Jewish Canon	Protestant Canon	Roman Catholic Canon
TANAK	OLD TESTAMENT	OLD TESTAMENT
Torah (*Torah*)	**Pentateuch**	**Pentateuch**
Genesis	Genesis	Genesis
Exodus	Exodus	Exodus
Leviticus	Leviticus	Leviticus
Numbers	Numbers	Numbers
Deuteronomy	Deuteronomy	Deuteronomy
Prophets (*Nevi'im*)	**Historical Books**	**Historical Books**
Joshua	Joshua	Joshua
Judges ⎤ Former	Judges	Judges
Samuel ⎥ Prophets	Ruth	Ruth
Kings ⎦	1 & 2 Samuel	1 & 2 Samuel
Isaiah ⎤	1 & 2 Kings	1 & 2 Kings
Jeremiah ⎥	1 & 2 Chronicles	1 & 2 Chronicles
Ezekiel ⎥	Ezra	Ezra
The Twelve: ⎥	Nehemiah	Nehemiah
Hosea ⎥	Esther	*Tobit*
Joel ⎥ Four		*Judith*
Amos ⎥ Books of	**Wisdom**	Esther (plus *Additions*)
Obadiah ⎥ Latter	Job	*1 & 2 Maccabees*
Jonah ⎥ Prophets	Psalms	
Micah ⎥	Proverbs	**Wisdom**
Nahum ⎥	Ecclesiastes	Job
Habakkuk ⎥	Song of Songs	Psalms
Zephaniah ⎥		Proverbs
Haggai ⎥	**Prophets**	Ecclesiastes
Zechariah ⎥	Isaiah	Song of Songs
Malachi ⎦	Jeremiah	*Wisdom of Solomon*
	Lamentation	*Ecclesiasticus* (or *Sirach*)
Writings (*Kethuvim*)	Ezekiel	
Psalms	Daniel	**Prophets**
Job	Hosea	Isaiah
Proverbs	Joel	Jeremiah
Ruth	Amos	Lamentations
Song of Songs	Obadiah	*Baruch and Letter of Jeremiah*
Ecclesiastes	Jonah	Ezekiel
Lamentations	Micah	Daniel (plus *the Prayer of*
Esther	Nahum	*Azariah, Song of the Three*
Daniel	Habakkuk	*Young Men, Susanna, Bel and*
Ezra-Nehemiah	Zephaniah	*the Dragon*)
Chronicles	Haggai	Hosea
	Zechariah	Joel
	Malachi	Amos
		Obadiah
		Jonah
		Micah
		Nahum
		Habakkuk
		Zephaniah
		Haggai
		Zechariah
		Malachi

were organized as another class of sacred scripture. These books must have been publicly acknowledged by the populace, as was the Torah under Ezra. The Torah of Moses contained the books Genesis, Exodus, Leviticus, Numbers and Deuteronomy. The Torah was the constitution of the country of Judah. The Torah was the basis for all life and law. The Prophets contained the historical books of Joshua, Judges, Samuel and Kings, and the prophetic writings of Isaiah, Jeremiah, Ezekiel, and the Twelve Minor Prophets. The Prophets, though sacred, were not considered to be as sacred as the Torah. The law of the country was based only in the Torah, not in the Prophets.

There were other books which also had a claim to sacred status. Some of these were eventually included by the Jews in a third section of the Bible, the Writings. These include the books of Psalms, Proverbs, Job, Song of Songs, Ruth, Ecclesiastes, Esther, Lamentations, Daniel, Ezra, Nehemiah and Chronicles. The Writings were closed about a century after the time of Jesus (ca. 100 CE, by the Jewish high court of rabbis in Yavneh). Certain books considered holy by the Christians were excluded from the Bible by the Jews. These books are included in the collection called the Apocrypha. It includes First and Second Maccabees, the Wisdom of Jesus ben Sira (also called Ecclesiasticus), and other books. To Catholics, the Apocrypha constitutes a fourth section of the Old Testament.

There were other books that mainstream Jews and Christians rejected, which were considered holy by various Jewish and Jewish-Christian sects. Many of these books have come down to us. As a group they are called the Pseudepigrapha ("false autograph"), since most of these books are anonymous but claim authorship by various biblical heroes. Much of the Pseudepigrapha is in a style that we call apocalyptic.

The Transition from Prophecy to Apocalyptic

When prophecy ended writers who wished to transmit a literary "message from God" wrote in the style that we call "apocalyptic." The term "apocalypse" means to "uncover," to "remove the curtain." It is used in the sense that the reader gets to peek into heaven, to see what is happening in the divine realm that is usually hidden from human view. The reader gets a glimpse into the meaning of current events and God's plan for the future. In English usage the term "apocalypse" is used to mean a total breakdown of society with chaos and general destruction. This meaning comes from the fact that most apocalyptic works of the Second Temple era predict a cataclysmic end to history as we know it. God then initiates a new world order in which the righteous are triumphant and the doers of evil are punished.

Mainstream Judaism eventually rejected apocalyptic literature. The early Christians preserved much of this literature, whether written by Jews or Christians, apparently because they saw important elements of their own Christian belief in it. In modern times Jews and Christians have engaged in polemics over the value of apocalyptic literature relative to biblical prophecy.

There is a small amount of apocalyptic literature within the Hebrew scriptures, in the book of Daniel and in the last books of the prophets. The New Testament gospels contain apocalyptic sections (Matt 24:4–36, Mk 13:5–37, Lk 21:8–36). The final book of the New Testament, the book of John, is apocalyptic. We can see the emerging style of apocalyptic in the prophet Zechariah's vision of the restoration of the monarchy:

> The angel who talked with me came back and woke me as a man is wakened from sleep. He said to me, "What do you see?" And I answered, "I see a lampstand all of gold, with a bowl above it. The lamps on it are seven in number, and the lamps above it have seven pipes, and by it are two olive trees, one on the right of the bowl and one on its left." I, in turn, asked the angel who talked with me, "What do those things mean, my lord?" "Do you not know what those things mean?" asked the angel who talked with me; and I said, "No, my lord." Then he explained to me as follows....
> (Zech 4:1–5)

Whatever one's ultimate judgment on the value of apocalyptic literature as divine revelation, it is easy to distinguish it from the writings of classical prophecy. Among the distinctions of apocalyptic literature are:

1. A difference in content and style from biblical prophecy. This is difficult to quantify, but readily apparent to one who reads both types of literature.
2. The apocalyptic message is less concerned with improving social ethics, more with other-worldly solutions to contemporary problems. There is not much call for repentance; rather, humankind is divided into the "righteous" and the "wicked." God will sort them out in a future action.

3. Apocalyptic writers are more pessimistic than the prophets about the ability of humankind to correct social evils. Only a massive divine intervention can set things right. Although apocalyptic writers call for dependence upon God rather than human action, there is a sense of great urgency in their message. This may have the effect of generating social change, even active revolution or the establishment of utopian communities, among the believers. The sense is that there is very little time left before the coming cataclysm, and those who would be saved must act immediately to establish the forces of righteousness.

4. The authors of apocalyptic literature do not dare to speak for God in their own name. The authors apparently doubt their own prophetic credentials, although they are sure they have a divine message. Therefore the apocalyptic literature is ascribed to known biblical figures—it is pseudepigraphic. Popular figures for literary attribution are Enoch (the seventh generation descendant of Adam), Ezra the scribe, and Baruch (the prophet Jeremiah's secretary).

5. Consistent with item #4, the authors do not claim a direct revelation from God. There is always an angel who serves as intermediary. The angel takes the writer on a tour to heaven, displays wonders, and then explains them. Angels with personal names (Michael, Gabriel, Satan) are generally not found in prophetic literature but are common in apocalyptic literature.

6. The writers describe strange and wondrous visions which they themselves do not understand. The explanations provided by the angel are said to be "secret," not for revelation to any other human. The reader thus feels that he has entered an elite circle of initiates.

7. It is usual in apocalyptic literature for the writer to claim or ascribe to a biblical figure a journey into heaven. In prophetic literature heaven remains off-limits to human entry, though the prophet may receive a glimpse of the opened heavens. In apocalyptic literature heaven and earth are well-defined locations. The geography of heaven is known, and is parallel to earthly sacred geography—for example, there is a heavenly temple corresponding to the Jerusalem Temple.

Second Temple Jewish Attitude to Prophecy

The Jews themselves acknowledged the end of prophecy early in the Second Temple period. They clearly did not consider the apocalyptic preachers in their midst to be prophets—nor did the apocalyptics themselves, as is evident by their pseudepigraphy and their angelic intermediaries. Jewish expressions about prophecy in the centuries of this era reflect a wistfulness for prophecy—regret over its disappearance and a wish that it would return. There was a feeling that with the end of the biblical era God was less close to the world than before. We see this attitude in the Talmudic statement of Rabbi Jonathan (2nd C.) that "since the destruction of the Temple, prophecy has been taken from prophets and given to fools and children" (T. Baba Batra 12b—probably a sneering reference to the apocalyptic groups which arose after the destruction of the Temple), and in the earlier statement of the Maccabees (c.165 BCE) that the stones of the Temple altar which had been defiled by the Greeks should be set aside "until a true prophet should arise" (I Macc 4:46), for they did not know what should be done with them and feared to grant themselves the prophetic authority to decide. Generally, then, Second Temple era Jews fervently wanted prophets and were puzzled by their disappearance. They honestly evaluated the religious leaders of their age as inferior to prophets in divine authority. It is interesting to note in this regard that the rise of Christianity and Rabbinic Judaism, with their authorization of new holy books (the New Testament and the Mishnah, respectively), demonstrates a new self-grant of prophetic authority in the first and second centuries of the Common Era. Yet this grant was not accompanied by a restoration of the title of "prophet." The authors of the new scriptures assumed the mantle of prophecy but, unlike the authors of the apocalypses, they did not demand public acknowledgment.

Malachi—the Final Word of Biblical Prophecy

Malachi is the last of the prophets. He arises shortly after the time of Ezra. The Torah has by now been acknowledged as the divine revelation. The third and final chapter of the book of Malachi represents, as it were, a farewell statement from biblical prophecy. Malachi gives the final prophetic message to a future that would be dominated by interpreters of scripture rather than messengers of God. It would be good for the reader at this point to open a Bible and read Malachi chapter 3. It reads, in part:

> Behold, I am sending you My messenger to clear the way before Me, and the Lord whom you seek shall come to His Temple suddenly. As for the angel of the covenant that you desire, he is already coming. But who can endure the day of his coming, and who can hold out when he appears?...Bring the full tithe into the store house and let there be food in My

house, and thus put Me to the test—says the Lord of Hosts. I will surely open the floodgates of the sky for you and pour down blessings upon you...on the day that I am preparing, said the Lord of Hosts [those who revere the Lord] shall be My treasured possession...and you shall come to see the difference between him who has served the Lord and him who has not served Him....Be mindful of the Torah of My servant Moses, whom I charged at Horeb (note: Mount Sinai) with laws and rules for all Israel. Lo, I will send the prophet Elijah to you before the coming of the awesome, fearful day of the Lord. He shall reconcile parents with children and children with their parents so that, when I come, I do not strike the whole land with utter destruction.

If we might summarize Malachi's points:

1. In objecting to the religious cynics and doubters of his day, Malachi encourages the Jews to bring their sacred offerings to the Temple, and the priests to receive and use them with proper reverence.
2. Jews are to wait for the Day of God. The prophets of the First Temple presented this day as a day of divine retribution for social injustice (a prediction of destruction by Assyria and later Babylon). Malachi now interprets the Day of God as a day of personal vindication for those who obey God's laws, while those who cynically disobey and seek unjust advantage by illegal means shall be punished.
3. Jews who wish to be vindicated on this Day shall prepare themselves by living according to the laws given in the Torah. This rule becomes the essential rule of piety and devotion for Second Temple era Jews. The Torah, with its laws and commandments, is to be the ultimate determinant of God's will for God's people.
4. Jews should expect a return of Elijah the prophet. By the time of Malachi, Elijah is ancient history. Some 300 years earlier Elijah had flourished in northern Israel and, according to the biblical book of Kings, never died, but was carried up to heaven on a chariot. Malachi now teaches that Elijah shall return from heaven to set the world right before the day of judgment.

These four points remain important to Jews throughout the Second Temple era, well into the time of Jesus. Christians applied Malachi's predictions to John the Baptist and to Jesus. In Christian eyes, John is Elijah returned, while Jesus' appearance brings the awaited Day of God.

3

Hellenism

The Advent of Hellenism

Alexander the Great of Macedon conquered the Persian Empire around the year 330 BCE. Alexander carried Greek civilization into the lands he conquered. This civilization mixed with the civilization of the Ancient Near East (ANE) to create a new, hybrid civilization that we call *Hellenism*. From their beginning as a people the Jews had been part of the ANE civilization. Hellenism caused a great extinction of cultures which the Jews miraculously survived. It seems that the Jews were protected from disappearance by their exclusive worship of a single God. The "four walls of the Torah," the Jewish devotion to their unique practices, protected them from assimilation.

The Jews had been at home in the world of the ANE. Except for their imageless worship of a single God, Jews were culturally like other ANE peoples. Once Hellenism became the dominant culture of the eastern Mediterranean world the Jews stood out as a different people. In the Hellenistic era the Jews gradually acquired a consciousness of being a people that survives, while other nations rise and fall. To be Jewish is to be distinct from "the nations." This consciousness of a unique Jewish destiny has persisted to the present day.

Changing attitudes toward the Jewish ritual of circumcision (the ritual removal of the foreskin of the penis) is a good example of the shift to cultural uniqueness. Jews perform circumcision upon their sons eight days after birth to enter them into the sacred Covenant of Abraham. Despite the appeal to their particular history, the Jews were just like every other ANE people in circumcising their boys. The only people in biblical Israel's world who did not practice circumcision were the Philistines, a non-Semitic people who came to the land of Canaan over the sea, probably from the Greek isles. The biblical Jews contemptuously called their Philistine enemies *arelim*—"the uncircumcised."

The Greeks looked upon circumcision as a desecration of the beauty of the male form. Under Hellenistic influence other Near Eastern peoples ceased to circumcise. The Jews clung to their ancient sacred ceremony although the Gentiles made this a subject of ridicule.

By the time of Jesus the relationship of Judaism to Hellenism was a major issue for all Jews. Christianity began in the Jewish cultural world, but as it spread among the Gentiles, this new religion soon became part of the Hellenistic cultural world. The relationship of these two cultures is essential to our understanding of the birth and growth of Christianity.

The Historical Extent of Hellenism

Let us take a brief foray forward into time to see the full extent of the Hellenistic culture. Hellenism begins, as we see, with the conquests of Alexander the Great, which brought Greek rulers and Greek colonists in significant numbers into the eastern Mediterranean and Mesopotamia. After the death of Alexander his generals divided his empire into several Greek-ruled kingdoms. Over a period of a few centuries these kingdoms were all swallowed up by the rising Roman Empire. The coming of the Romans did not change Hellenistic culture. On the contrary, as the Romans conquered Greece, the culture of the Greeks conquered the Romans, so that they too became Hellenized. Greek, and not the Roman language of Latin, remained the language of government and culture in the eastern Roman Empire—and even in Rome herself.

In the fourth century of the Common Era the Roman Empire converted to Christianity. This conversion brought Hellenism to an end in many respects. However, Greek remained the language of the Christianized ruling classes in the eastern Mediterranean. Only with the Arab conquest of the Middle East in the 7th–8th century did the Arabic language displace Greek. The Hellenistic era from beginning to its conclusion spans about a thousand year period—a full millennium!

Hellenism Transforms the Near East

Socrates, the greatest Greek philosopher, lived about the same time as the prophet Isaiah. Though contemporaries, the two held completely separate worldviews. They would not have understood one another.

The prophet Isaiah was a priest in the Temple of Jerusalem. In his world it seemed as if God were watching closely the unfolding of human events, causing nations to rise or fall. Isaiah saw a vision of God sitting upon a throne, surrounded by angels, ruling over the earth (Isaiah 6). It seemed to Isaiah that God was the cause of all being and all events, rewarding and punishing according to human obedience to the divine command. Isaiah saw the rise of the Assyrian Empire as a reflection of God's will to punish the nations. Jerusalem survived the Assyrian siege because of Israel's repentance and God's love for his people.

The Greeks had developed a worldview and a system of education based upon logic and science. They developed a curriculum whose subjects are the basis of our modern education—grammar, literature, history, logic, mathematics, natural science, philosophy. The Greeks sought truth not only through tradition and divine inspiration, but through human reason and the study of the natural world. This great intellectual tradition was powerfully attractive to all people who came into contact with it. We might compare it to the power of western European—American culture to overwhelm all native cultures in the modern world. What ancient tribe retains its native lore and folkways once they come into contact with blue jeans, automobiles, fast food, and all the material splendor of western society? The Greeks did not set out to overwhelm or destroy the culture of their subjects. Greek culture so attracted the subject peoples that they inevitably abandoned their own culture. Alexander was not a missionary for Greek culture—in fact he adopted many of the trappings of an Oriental ruler before his early death. The Greek kings of Egypt became Pharaohs—for instance, they mummified their dead. Hellenism began as a mutual admiration between Greeks and Near Easterners, but eventually the culture of the Greeks dominated.

The primary vehicle of Greek culture was, naturally, the Greek language. The Greek rulers did not bother learning the language of their native subjects. They continued to converse and conduct business in Greek. The language of the Persian Empire was Aramaic, originally the language of the people of Babylon. The native peoples continued to speak Aramaic throughout the Hellenistic era, but many of their leaders and intellectuals learned Greek, studied Greek subjects, and imitated the ways of the ruling class. We do not know to what extent Greek language penetrated to the masses in the lower classes over the years. One theory of the disappearance of the ANE religions (except Judaism) under Hellenism is that the sacred writings of these religions were written and preserved in ancient languages that were completely forgotten once the small literate class adopted Greek as the language of culture.[3]

Hellenistic Society—the Polis

When the Greeks conquered the Persian Empire they left their subject peoples undisturbed in the ancient cities and villages. The Greeks built new cities for themselves and inhabited these cities with colonists from the overcrowded Greek isles. The Greek kings established military colonies, offering Greek people free land in exchange for military service. The Greek cities were set up with the constitution of a *polis*—that is, a Greek-style city.

The polis was governed by a council of its leading citizens. This council was called a *boule*. The council was democratic, though not in the modern sense—only very important people had the status of citizens. A properly ordered polis would contain the important institutions of Greek social life. It would have a *gymnasium*—a school for the education of the young. The students would learn the subjects of the Greek curriculum in the morning, and participate in athletics in the afternoon. Sports were conducted in the nude, and females were prohibited from viewing. An important city might contain an *academy*—a school for the philosophical training of the young aristocrats, perhaps under the tutelage of a famous teacher. The polis would have a *stadium* for athletics and a *theater* for the performance of plays. The Greeks were also fond of bathing, and the polis would have a public bathhouse for men. The Romans were great not only as rulers but as plumbers, and when they came along the bathhouse became quite elaborate, with hot and cold pools. The Jews disapproved of most Greek cultural institutions, which were dedicated to gods and a way of life that the Jews found pagan and alien, but the Jews were very fond of the bathhouses. When rabbis arose among the Jews the rabbis warned their people away from the Greek sporting events, schools and theaters, but they justified attendance at the bathhouses despite the statues of the gods that were found in them. The sage Hillel said that just as the king's servants washed his statues, so the servants of God must wash the divine image—the human body (Leviticus Rabba 34:3).

The Greek Rulers of Judah

When Alexander died his top generals divided his empire. Two of the new Greek empires are important for Jewish history. Ptolemy took control of Egypt, while Seleucus took control of Syria and Mesopotamia. Judah, on the border of these two Greek empires, was originally part of Ptolemy's kingdom. Later, around the year 200 BCE, the Seleucid kings grew more powerful and wrested Judah away from Egypt into their own empire.

The Greek kings of Egypt all took the name Ptolemy. Their wives took the name Cleopatra. The famous Cleopatra was the last of the Ptolemies, who lost her kingdom to Roman rule. The Greek kings of Syria-Mesopotamia mostly alternated between the names Seleucus and Antiochus.

Ptolemy and Seleucus built new capital cities. Ptolemy built the city of Alexandria, named after his patron Alexander. Alexandria, in the Nile delta, grew to become the greatest Greek city in the ancient world. It was even more a center of Greek learning than any city in Greece. Alexandria's library was the most complete and famous in the ancient world. Seleucus did not make his capital in Babylon but in Syria. Avoiding Damascus, he built the city of Antioch on the northern coast. This city would become a major center for the young Christian church. By that time Antioch was rivaled only by Constantinople and Alexandria as a great city of the eastern Mediterranean.

At the time of Alexander's conquests Jews were already living in Egypt, Syria and Mesopotamia. Jewish numbers now increased throughout the Hellenistic world. Syria acquired a large Jewish population. Alexandria had a thriving Jewish quarter. Many Jews settled in Asia Minor (modern Turkey, then part of the Greek world) and in the Eastern Mediterranean islands of Crete and Cyprus. Jews in Judah, Syria and Mesopotamia continued to speak Aramaic and learn Hebrew (a language very similar to Aramaic). Jews in Egypt, Asia Minor and the Greek islands adopted the Greek language and forgot Hebrew. Historians call the Greek speaking Jews "Hellenistic Jews."

Hellenism in the Land of Israel

The Greek rulers of Judah were segregated from their subjects by language and culture. The Jews spoke Aramaic. They lived by their ancestral custom—that is, the laws of the Torah. The Jews worshiped their own God and followed the high priest. Despite this, there was an unmistakable degree of assimilation to Hellenistic ways that increased over time. Jesus grew up in a Jewish village in Galilee. The land of Israel in his time was a patchwork of Greek cities, Jewish cities and mixed cities. Would a village Jew such as Jesus have grown up with any knowledge of Greek language and culture? Or, would he know exclusively Aramaic and perhaps the Hebrew of the Bible? We cannot be sure. Scholars would like to know the extent to which the Greek language had penetrated the general Jewish populace. That would give us a clue to the inner, intellectual life of Jesus and his followers. It would help us understand how Greek became the language of Christian discourse. It would also help us understand the extent to which Greek thought may have influenced early rabbinic Judaism. Those scholars who would like to believe that Jesus spoke Greek point out that Nazareth was only a few miles from the Greek city of Sepphoris. Those who see Jesus as living exclusively in the Aramaic-speaking Jewish world respond that according to the gospels Jesus visited only Jewish villages. As far as we know he never set foot in Sepphoris or Tiberius, the Greek cities of Galilee.

The Greeks established colonies in the land of Israel. The major cities of the seacoast were Greek, probably absorbing the remains of the Philistine population who were Greek to begin with. Scythopolis (Bet Shean), located where the Jezreel Valley joins the Jordan River valley, was a major Greek town. There were ten Greek towns in the highlands going up from eastern Galilee into Syria. These ten towns were called the Decapolis. In Jesus' time, Caesarea on the seacoast, built by King Herod, became the primary Greek city of the land of Israel and the center of Roman rule.

Jewish-Gentile Relations

For the Jews these Greek towns in the biblical land of Israel presented a particular problem. Any people would resent having their land colonized by foreigners, but most people seemed to accept the mixing of all the nations that occurred in the Hellenistic era. Jews also, after all, took advantage of this opportunity to spread to new lands. However, the Gentiles (Greeks, non-Jews) brought with them the worship of their gods. Jews believed that their covenant with God required them to keep the land free of the pollution of idols. They had striven to keep themselves pure in their devotion to the one God. Now these Gentiles planted their temples, holy places and idols throughout God's land. Would God be angry and withdraw the divine blessing from the people Israel? Jews worried greatly about what they saw as the spiritual pollution of their land, which was God's land.

Alexander's conquest initiated an "Era of Good Feeling." There was a sense that Alexander had caused a good and wonderful thing. It was terrific that the different peoples of the world had come together under one rule. There was much mutual admiration. The Greeks believed that they had not developed their own wisdom, but had learned it from extremely ancient sources in the East. They therefore looked up to the wise men of Egypt and Mesopotamia and to the Jews, much as many Americans of today admire the ancient sacred wisdom of India and China. Like modern anthropologists, Greek scholars came to the new lands to learn about the peoples of the Middle East. They sent home glowing reports about the wise and ancient peoples who lived there, including the Jews.

Hellenism grew by religious syncretism. Syncretism means the mingling of religions. The subject peoples and Greeks identified their gods with each other. Each religion had a royal god, a fertility goddess, a warrior god, and so forth, so this was easily done. Greeks attempted to syncretize with the Jews, as well. Many Greeks, not really understanding Jewish monotheism, saw Jews as a people especially devoted to Zeus, the king and father-figure of the gods. Greeks resented the refusal of Jews to exchange and worship one another's gods. This appeared to the Greeks to be a sign of anti-humanitarianism among the Jews, a refusal to participate in the universal goodwill. The prejudice that Jews are tribalistic, stand-offish and non-universal, which unfortunately persists to this day, derives from the Greek misunderstanding of the exclusive demands of Jewish divine service.

When the Roman general Pompey invaded Judah and added it to the Roman Empire, he used his right of conquest to brazenly enter the inner sanctum of the Jerusalem Temple. It was unusual in ancient times for a ruler to disregard the sanctity of any god, a general piety being more in order. When Pompey found no statue of the Jew's God in the Holy of Holies he came out and declared to the Jews that their religion was a fake. The priests were taking sacrifices under false pretenses, for there was no god in the sanctuary. The Jews were contemptuous of Pompey for his foolish incomprehension of imageless worship. This may be one reason that the Jews so fervently supported Julius Caesar in his civil war with Pompey for control of the Roman Empire.

Jews who lived in the great Greek cities of the world thought of themselves as citizens, in every way equal to the Greek inhabitants. The Jews expected and demanded equal treatment under the laws of the city. But the Jews would not participate in the public civil institutions and ceremonies, because all of these things were formally dedicated to the gods of the city. To sit on the city council or participate in the city's athletic games was the same as worshiping idols. To state the problem in memorable form: the Jews demanded *civil rights* without *civil rites*. This was a constant source of tension between Jews and Gentiles.

As time went by relations between Jews and Gentiles deteriorated. By the time of Jesus there was a great deal of tension in the land of Israel and throughout the Roman Empire between Greeks and Jews. One can feel this tension in the stories of the New Testament. The unsuccessful Jewish rebellion against Rome in 66–70 CE increased anti-Jewish feeling, as Jews now seemed seditious. In the years 115–17, during the reign of the Roman emperor, Trajan, a full-scale war broke out between the Jews and Gentiles in all the mixed cities of Egypt, North Africa, Crete and Cyprus. We know very little about this war except that there were pitched battles in the cities, and the Jews lost. There was a massacre of Jews in Alexandria and elsewhere. With the conversion of the Greek-speaking world to Christianity in the fourth century the Jews became subject to official government persecution. Jews did not then regain full citizenship status until modern times. It is unfortunate that relations between Jews and Gentiles continually deteriorated throughout the Hellenistic era, but not all Gentiles nor all Jews felt the same way. There were also Gentiles who admired Jews, and vice versa.

The Septuagint

The Greek-speaking Jews needed a way to learn the scriptures, since they had lost the knowledge of Hebrew. There arose in Alexandria a Greek translation of the Bible, called the *Septuagint*— "Seventy Elders." This translation gets its name from the legend of its origins:

> When King Ptolemy II "Philadelphus" (reigned 283–246 BCE) established the library in Alexandria he wanted to place in it all of the wisdom of all of the nations, translated into the Greek tongue. He was informed that he must have a copy of the sacred writings of the Jews. He sent away to the High Priest in Jerusalem, who sent him seventy of the finest sages in Israel who knew Greek. When they arrived in Egypt Ptolemy locked each of them in a cell with a copy of the Hebrew Scriptures and pens and blank paper. He provided for all their needs, but they were not allowed to leave their cells until they had finished a complete translation. After seventy days all of the elders had completed their work. When the seventy manuscripts were compared they were all alike, word for word! (Letter of Aristeas)

The story is clearly legendary. The Septuagint is the work of many hands over many years. Furthermore, it is not in any way a literal translation of the Hebrew Bible, but a highly interpretive one. Rabbi Akiva, the greatest Jewish sage of the second century, was so disturbed by the inaccuracy of the Septuagint that he commissioned a Gentile convert, Aquila, to compose a more literal translation into Greek. Aquila's translation is now lost, but, in an odd twist of history, his name was incorrectly attached to the most renowned ancient Aramaic translation of the Bible which is now called "Targum Onkelos" (the translation of Aquila).

The legend of the Septuagint serves an important purpose. The Jews believed that in the Torah and Prophets they had, quite literally, the word of God. A translation is no longer God's exact word—unless the translation comes from God directly! The story of the Septuagint gives divine validation to the use of a Greek translation. The Hellenistic Jews believed that they were using the Bible itself, even in Greek. The Septuagint became the official scriptures of the Christian church.

The use of the Septuagint by the early church had important repercussions. For instance, the Septuagint translated the word Torah as *nomos*, "law," rather than the more accurate "teaching" or "guidance." Paul's characterization of Judaism as "legalism" was clearly influenced by his use of the Greek scriptures. Paul seemed to have a speaking knowledge of Aramaic, but Greek was his primary language. (See Acts 21:37–22:2. The term "Hebrew" in this passage probably means "Aramaic.") In Isaiah, chapter 8, the Hebrew term *alma* ("young woman") is translated into Greek as *parthenos* ("virgin"). Thus it appears that Isaiah says a virgin shall give birth to a child, whereas in the Hebrew the divine sign lies not in virgin birth but in the child's name—*Emmanuel* ("God is with us"). The Septuagint is not the basis for the doctrine of the virgin birth of Jesus, but it did provide a scriptural prooftext for this belief.

Philo of Alexandria

The Hellenistic Jews of Egypt and elsewhere were very comfortable in the world of Greek thought. Their intellectual leaders learned Greek philosophy and thought as philosophers. They came to think of the Torah as a Jewish book of philosophy. They interpreted the Torah allegorically, finding in it the lessons they had learned from Plato and Aristotle.

The outstanding intellectual of the Hellenistic Jewish world was Philo of Alexandria (c.20 BCE–50 CE). The political and religious leader of Alexandrian Jewry in the time of Jesus, Philo was also a prolific writer. The Christian church preserved his allegorical interpretations of the Bible. From Philo's writings we can see that Hellenistic Judaism developed in its own way, and was different from the Judaism of the Aramaic-speaking Jews of Judah and Babylon.

In the following two passages we can see how Philo interprets Jewish beliefs and laws as lessons in philosophy:

> Moses tells us that man was created after the image of God and after His likeness. Right well does he say this, for nothing earth-born is more like God than man. Let no one represent the likeness as one to a bodily form; for neither is God in human form, nor is the human body God-like. No, it is respect of the mind, the sovereign element of the soul, that the word "image" is used; for after the pattern of a single Mind, even the Mind of the Universe as an archetype, was the mind in each of those who successively came into being molded. ("On the Creation of the World" #69)
>
> What our most holy prophet through all his regulations especially desires to create is unanimity, neighborliness, fellowship, reciprocity of feeling, whereby houses and cities and nations and countries and the whole human race may advance to supreme happiness. Hitherto, indeed, these things live only in our prayers, but they will, I am convinced, become facts beyond all dispute if God, even as He gives us the yearly fruits, grants that the virtues should bear abundantly. ("On the Virtues," 119–20)

In the first passage above we see how Philo interprets the divine image of God in humankind as the "mind." According to Greek philosophy the mind rules the body and is the person himself in the truest sense. In the second paragraph we see how, to Philo, the purpose of the laws of the Torah of Moses is to instill in society the virtues defined by Greek philosophers. As a divine law the virtues have a greater chance of being actualized than if they were wise human teachings only, as among the Gentiles.

The Fate of Hellenistic Judaism

Hellenistic Jews lived in great numbers in the Greek and Roman world, perhaps far surpassing in number the Jews of Judah. By the early Middle Ages there were no more Hellenistic Jews. What happened to them? Nobody knows. Did they all become Christian or were they reabsorbed into the rabbinic Judaism of Judah and Babylon? It is possible that the Hellenistic Jews offered their great numbers and their religious ideas to the young Christian church.

Lacking genuine knowledge, contemporary scholars have been contentious about the eventual fate of Hellenistic Jews. The old rivalry between Christianity and Judaism has affected the analysis of this historical question. Some Christian scholars triumphantly claim that all the Hellenistic Jews became Christian. Some Jewish scholars have defensively insisted that all of the Hellenistic Jews were reabsorbed into the fold of rabbinic Judaism. Some more Orthodox-leaning Jewish scholars have insisted that the Hellenistic Jews really did all become Christian. This seems like a warning to the Jews of today that those who worship in English rather than Hebrew will be lost to the Jewish people, like the Jews of antiquity who abandoned Hebrew for Greek.

If we can set aside these rivalries and contentious notions, we must admit our ignorance. The Hellenistic Jews disappeared over time, with many individuals making their own choices. Rabbinic Judaism may have reabsorbed some, while others became Christian. The preservation of Philo's work by the church suggests that Hellenistic Judaism was a significant factor among at least some groups of early Christians. Christianity surely represents to some extent the legacy of the Hellenistic Judaism that existed in Jesus' lifetime. As we can never know the exact fate of the Hellenistic Jews, we can also never know the true degree of influence that Hellenistic Judaism had in the early church.

Friends and Opponents of the Jews

The Jews were relatively much more numerous in the Greco-Roman world than at present. Jews in the time of Jesus may have represented as much as 10 percent of the population of the Roman Empire (7 million out of 70 million) and a similar percentage of the neo-Persian Empire in Mesopotamia and Persia. Nothing like modern anti-Semitism existed in the Hellenistic world, but the Jews had their admirers and detractors, friends and enemies.

The opponents of the Jews accused them of atheism because they had no divine image. This was a serious accusation in antiquity; it meant that one had no morals or culture at all. The enemies of the Jews accused them of being anti-humanitarian because they would not join in the common (pagan) rites of the empires, nor would they exchange gods with other nations. They mocked the Jews by claiming that the

Jews were not freed from Egyptian slavery by their God as the Bible says, but expelled from Egypt as a group of lepers. And, they mockingly claimed that Jews worshiped the head of a donkey as a divine image. These claims greatly annoyed the Jews.

The admirers of the Jews saw them as a nation of philosophers, with just laws, wise teachings and a true understanding of divinity. We know from legend—and the complaints of certain Romans—that many wealthy Roman matrons became patrons and students of Jewish sages. We might compare this phenomenon to the following acquired by some Indian Hindu gurus and Buddhist spiritual masters in contemporary America.

Many Gentiles adopted the Jewish faith in the one, indivisible God who is worshiped without idols. These Gentiles were called "God-fearers." They were numerous in the time of Jesus. God-fearers joined Jews in sending an annual half-shekel contribution to the Jerusalem Temple. This may have been the revenue source that allowed King Herod to rebuild the Temple into one of the wonders of the ancient world. God-fearers worshiped the God of the Jews, but they were not Jews. Jewish identity was based not just on a God-idea, but on living by the Torah. In ancient empires every nation lived under its own laws. The Jews lived by their Torah. The Greeks and Romans lived by their laws, and the various subject peoples by their laws. The God-fearers did not convert to Judaism because they wanted to continue as members of their own nation. They preferred to live by their own laws, with the social status of Greeks. Most particularly, God-fearers did not convert to Judaism because they opposed circumcision—a requirement for male Jews—and because they did not wish to observe the Jewish dietary laws. When Paul the apostle decided that Gentile converts to Christianity did not have to observe circumcision or keep kosher—a decision validated by the church after some internal struggles, as described in the book of Acts—Paul was reaching out to the God-fearers as potential Christian converts. God-fearers became an important element in the growth of the young church. A Christian could worship the God of Israel—with some distinguishing doctrines, to be sure—and remain Gentile!

After the Jews' failed rebellions against Rome (66–70 CE, 115–17 in the Diaspora, 132–35) the status of God-fearer became less attractive. The Jews were associated with sedition, which made them less attractive to Gentiles. Also, why would one join oneself to a people who kept starting wars and losing them? In the centuries after the time of Jesus God-fearers disappeared as a category.

Conversion

Many Gentiles did convert to Judaism in the Hellenistic world. The very idea of religious conversion evolved within Second Temple Judaism. Conversion could not exist in pagan religion, because conversion requires the rejection of one's former religion. Pagans took on a new religion by adding gods to their pantheon or by identifying their gods with similar gods. They never turned away from one religion to another. A necessary condition for conversion was the Jewish insistence on the exclusive worship of one God.

There is no conversion in the Hebrew scriptures. Religion in the Ancient Near East depended on geography. One worshiped the gods of a particular locale. When a foreigner came to the country of Judah or Israel he adopted the worship of that country, as the Samaritans had done. The biblical term for resident foreigner—"ger toshav"—became the later Jewish term for a convert. This makes sense when we see that conversion began with the idea of immigration.

In the Babylonian Exile the Jews segregated religion from locale— a first among humankind. The Jews believed that God, as creator of the whole universe, could be worshiped anywhere[4]. This made possible the idea of conversion as an inner turning, not just a geographical move.

Another prerequisite for the idea of conversion was the idea of religion as a personal expression of the individual human psyche—a matter of thought, belief, and personal deeds. Religious personalism was also a teaching of the exilic prophets—especially Ezekiel. In ancient times nations and peoples performed divine service as a collective. During the Exile and afterwards, Jews developed the idea of devotion to God as a personal matter. One could serve God independent of the priestly sacrifices and other collective forms of divine service.

Interfaith marriage was not a possibility in the Ancient Near East, because women did not bring personal status into a marriage nor confer it on their children. The woman's status was that of her husband. If a Jew married a foreign woman, her children were members of the Jewish nation. Many foreign wives did bring their gods into the household, as the biblical writers complain, but in terms of formal status the families of Jewish men were all Jews.

Our earliest hint of the developing idea of conversion is in the book of Ruth. As we have mentioned above, the book of Ruth was composed in early Second Temple times, probably opposing Ezra's requirement that Jewish men divorce their foreign wives. The book of Ruth is about a Moabite woman who not only marries a Jew, but becomes the ancestor of King David. Ruth converts to Judaism but the author of the book does not use any term for conversion. Probably in his time the idea was so new it had not yet received a name. Conversion could be shown but not yet conceived in the mind as an abstraction.

Two schools of thought developed in Second Temple Judaism. One school accepted, welcomed and actively sought converts to Judaism. The other school, probably more conservative in rejecting ideas that were not found explicitly in the Torah, rejected the idea of conversion. This school believed that one joined the Jewish nation only by birth. (We note that in America there are those who favor immigration and those who oppose it, each side believing that their view is for the good of the nation.)

In the time of Jesus, the Pharisees took the pro-conversion point of view. The Sadducees believed that there was no such thing as conversion. The Pharisees were known for their active mission to the Gentiles, seeking converts everywhere. Christianity became perhaps the most missionary religion of all time—to evangelize is one of the first duties of the Christian—but in the early church not all Christian groups took this position. The author of the gospel of Matthew opposed conversion. His Jesus preached only to Jews, and he claims that Jesus criticized the Pharisees for traveling far and wide to seek converts.

Christianity shared with Pharisaic Judaism a strong awareness of the inner, personal conviction required for true service to God, and a demand for exclusiveness in divine service. It is not surprising that in the end Christianity shared with Pharisaic Judaism its strong emphasis on seeking converts.

Once Christianity became the official religion of the Roman Empire, the emperors made it illegal for Jews to seek converts. The punishment for conversion to Judaism was burning at the stake for the convert and the Jew who performed the conversion. Stymied by restrictions and persecutions, the Jews turned inward. Today it is largely forgotten that Judaism in the time of Jesus was a missionary religion, with Pharisaic Jews hoping to eliminate paganism and idolatry from the whole world.

Judaism Adjusts to Hellenism

There was no clear line marking off Hellenistic Jews from unas-similated Jews. Every sect and branch of Judaism adjusted to Hellenism in one way or another. We should not adopt the simplistic picture,

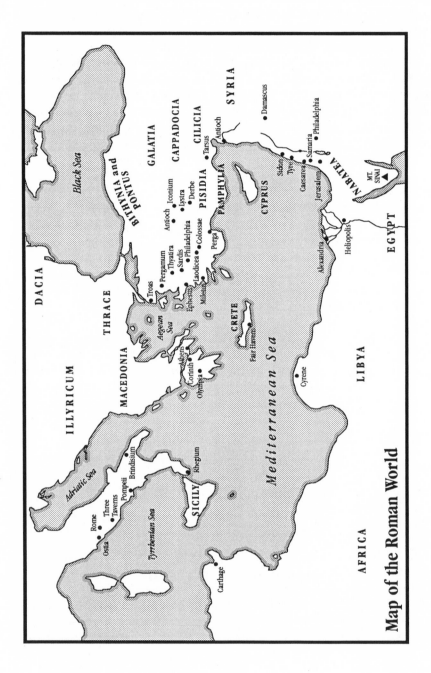

Map of the Roman World

ILLYRICUM

DACIA

Black Sea

THRACE

MACEDONIA

BITHYNIA and PONTUS

GALATIA

CAPPADOCIA

SYRIA

Damascus

CILICIA

Antioch

Philadelphia

Samaria

Tarsus

PISIDIA

Antioch
Iconium
Lystra
Derbe
Colossae

Philadelphia
Sardis
Thyatira
Pergamum

Sidon
Tyre
Caesarea
Jerusalem

PAMPHYLIA

Perga

Laodicea

Ephesus
Miletus

Troas

CYPRUS

NABATEA

MT. SINAI

Aegean Sea

Athens
Corinth
Olympia

CRETE

Fair Havens

Alexandria

Heliopolis

EGYPT

Mediterranean Sea

Cyrene

LIBYA

AFRICA

Adriatic Sea

Brindisium

Rhegium

SICILY

Pompeii
Three Taverns
Rome
Ostia

Tyrrhenian Sea

Carthage

often painted by historical writers, of assimilated Greek-speaking Jews cut off from their ancient traditions vs. Aramaic/Hebrew Jews who knew nothing of Greek. Inscriptions dug up by archeologists show that even in Judah Jews knew and used some Greek—how much is hard to say, but half of all Judean Jewish inscriptions from Jesus' time are in Greek. Jesus and his followers probably knew some Greek terms, phrases and ideas. Though the rabbis prohibited the study of Greek philosophy (which they would not have done unless Jews were studying it) it is clear from the rabbis' own writings that the concepts of popular Greek philosophy were known and accepted by all. Just as everyone today is a pop psychologist, everyone in the Hellenistic world was a pop philosopher.

Rabbinic Judaism represents a particular Jewish version of Hellenism. The "rabbi" is the Jewish philosopher. The *yeshiva* (school for training rabbis) is the Jewish academy, and the rabbis derive laws and traditions from the Torah, just as the Greek philosophers derived teachings from Plato and Aristotle and the literature of Homer.

The Language of Jesus and of the Early Church

Jesus, the Galilean Jew, spoke the Aramaic language. He preached in Aramaic. His teachings, his prayers, his religious terminology, all spoke directly to the relatively non-Hellenized Jews of the land of Israel. These Jews were insulated from Greek influence by their use of the ancient Near Eastern tongue.

Some twenty years later, when the first Christian writings appeared, these writings were in the Greek language. The epistles of Paul, all of the four gospels and the book of Acts were composed in Greek and therefore reflect the influence of Greek thought.

How did this transition take place, from an Aramaic-speaking Jesus and his followers to a Greek-speaking early church? The language shift is obviously of great significance. The fact that it took place so quickly and thoroughly is surprising. How did it happen? What does it all mean? We can never know for sure. Those twenty years of early Christian history are closed to us, since we have no sources of information. Historians sometimes attempt to understand this historical transformation by translating backwards from the Greek sources to what must have been the Aramaic originals. For instance, apparently the two versions of the Lord's Prayer in the gospels of Matthew and Luke result from differing translations of a single Aramaic original. The Lord's Prayer likely originated with Jesus, or at least his earliest followers. Paul's term "works of the Law" seems parallel to the Hebrew "ma'aseh Torah," a term known to us from the Dead Sea Scrolls. Other matters, such as Paul's musings on the meaning of the Christ, are difficult to imagine in Aramaic. They are suited to the more philosophical patterns of Hellenistic Greek thought. Untranslatable ideas must have arisen after the language shift in the early church and are probably not original to Jesus. If, as seems likely, the primitive church, consisting of Jesus' own followers, spoke Aramaic, then our research into the Aramaic sources of early Christian teachings will return us to the Jewish world of Jesus himself.

4

The Maccabees

From Alexander the Great to Antiochus IV

When Alexander the Great died his top generals divided his empire between themselves. Two of these Greek generals established kingdoms that are important to Jewish history—Ptolemy in Egypt and Seleucus in Syria-Mesopotamia.

Judah was on the border between the kingdoms of the Ptolemies and the Seleucids. From 301 to 200 BCE Judah was part of the Egyptian kingdom. During this period the Jewish population of Egypt expanded greatly. There was a large Jewish quarter in the capital of Alexandria.

Around 200 BCE the Seleucids took control of Judah, as their power waxed greater than that of the Egyptians. The Jews had quietly accepted the Ptolemies as their rulers, and now they acquiesced to the rule of the Seleucids.

During the centuries of Persian, Ptolemaic and Seleucid rule Jewish society was stable. The Zadokite High Priests ruled over Judah. From what we can tell the Jews were content. There was some destabilization of traditional faith and society because the of influence of Greek thought (perhaps represented in the cynicism of the biblical book, Ecclesiastes, which was composed early in the Hellenistic period). By and large Jews were content to live by their customary laws, grounded in the words of the Torah. The Jewish attitude of this period can be seen in the apocryphal book, The Wisdom of Jesus ben Sira, also called Ecclesiasticus. Ben Sira was a Jerusalem priest who lived around 200 BCE, about the beginning of the Seleucid reign over Judah. He wrote his book as wisdom for the guidance of his son. In this book Ben Sira praised the existing social order. Ben Sira spoke with pride and admiration of Simeon the Just, the high priest, who fulfilled his daily office with distinction. We understand from Ben Sira's description of life in Jerusalem that the Jewish farmers faithfully brought their offerings to the Temple. They traded agricultural goods for the crafts of the Jerusalem artisans. The people lived by the laws of the Torah, as taught by the priests. There was neither great wealth nor great poverty, and unity prevailed among the Jews. Parents ruled in the home, training the children in their traditions. God sat on his heavenly throne, watching over the people of Israel and rewarding the righteous with blessings. The Jews had grown accustomed to living under the rule of great empires, and we can detect no longing for Jewish sovereignty.

In chapter 35, Jesus ben Sira praises the one who lives righteously and brings sacrifices to the Temple. Note that to Ben Sira there is no distinction between "religious ritual" and "ethics, the love of neighbor," but that one goes hand in hand with the other:

> One that keeps the Laws brings offerings enough; he that takes heed to the commandment offers a peace offering. One that requites a good turn offers fine flour; one who gives charity sacrifices praise. To depart from wickedness is pleasing to the Lord, and to forsake unrighteousness is a propitiation. You shall not appear empty (i.e., without bringing a sacrifice) before the Lord. For all these things are to be done according to the commandment (i.e., of the Torah)....The sacrifice of a just man is acceptable, and its memorial shall not be forgotten. Give the Lord his honor with a good eye (i.e., be generous in offerings to the Temple) and diminish not the firstfruits of your hands....Give unto the Most High according as He has enriched you, and as you have received, give with a cheerful eye. For the Lord recompenses, and will give you seven times as much (Ecc'us 35:1–11).

In our next passage Ecclesiasticus praises the high priest:

> Simon the High Priest, the son of Onias...how he was honored in the midst of the people when he came forth from the Sanctuary. He was as the morning star in the midst of the cloud, and as the full moon, as the sun shining upon the Temple of the Most High, as the rainbow giving light in the bright clouds....When he put on the robe of honor, and was clothed with the perfection of glory, when he went up to the holy altar, he made the sacred garments honorable. When he took the portions out of the priests' hands he himself stood by the hearth of the altar, surrounded by his

brethren, like a young cedar of Lebanon surrounded by palm trees. So were all the sons of Aaron (i.e., the priests) in their glory, and the offerings of the Lord in their hands, before all the congregation of Israel (Ecc'us 50:1–12).

The world of Jesus ben Sira was so different from the Jewish world of Jesus, just two centuries later! There came an event which shook the Jews out of their contentment and initiated the era of creative change that culminated in Christianity and rabbinic Judaism. This event was the persecution initiated by King Antiochus IV and the ensuing revolt of the Maccabees.

The Persecutions of Antiochus IV

For reasons unknown to us, the Seleucid king, Antiochus IV, began interfering in internal Jewish affairs. In 175 BCE Antiochus overthrew the high priest Onias. Onias fled to Egypt and the protection of the Ptolemies. He was to be the last of the Zadokite high priests. Antiochus appointed a certain Jason as high priest, then a certain Menelaus. Meanwhile, Antiochus enforced a Hellenistic reform in Jerusalem. He granted Jerusalem the status of a *polis*. Jerusalem acquired a Greek school for the education of young aristocrats according to the Greek curriculum, and other Greek cultural institutions. A Greek-style acropolis was built for the defense of the city. (This acropolis is the site of the citadel of Jerusalem to this very day, and is now a museum of the history of the city.)

The Hellenization of Jerusalem created a sharp social conflict among the Jews. The upper classes welcomed their new status. Priests of the most aristocratic families sent their children for a Greek education instead of an education in the Torah. The common people, especially the pious farmers in the Judean villages, were scandalized and outraged by the Hellenistic reforms. The objections overflowed into an open revolt.

In 169 BCE Antiochus eliminated the high priesthood, rededicated the Jerusalem Temple to a Greek god, and outlawed the Torah. The Greeks made the Jews worship the Greek idol and eat pork sacrificed in its honor. Anyone who refused was executed. The Greeks killed anyone who circumcised a newborn boy, and also the child. To obey the law of the Torah was now to disobey the edict of the king.

No one knows why Antiochus tried to Hellenize the Jews. This was contrary to the Greek policy of leaving the native peoples to their own laws and customs. Jewish legend says that Antiochus was insane. This is not true, but turns on an old joke. Antiochus took the eponym *Epiphanes*—meaning "divine." In ancient times rulers were often thought of as gods incarnate. Antiochus' enemies mockingly called him *Epimanes*—"the madman."

Another theory is that Antiochus was Hellenizing his subjects out of fear of Rome. The Roman Empire was growing and encroaching upon Antiochus' western borders. He may have wished to unite his empire under the banner of Greek culture. This explanation seems unlikely, as the Hellenization was limited to the borders of Judah. It was not enforced on Jews elsewhere in the realm.

It is likely that Antiochus began his Hellenization program as a favor to the Jews. A polis had many social and economic advantages not shared by native cities. A polis paid fewer taxes and was licensed to engage in international trade. The citizens of a polis shared in the identity of the rulers—they were Greeks. Antiochus may have outlawed the Torah because he was outraged that his Jewish subjects were rebelling against what he perceived to be an extraordinary benefit—the right to be Greek and have the status of a polis for their capital city.

The Progress of the Jewish Revolt 168–65 BCE

When Antiochus outlawed the Torah, the dividing line between the pietists and the Hellenizers was sharply drawn. There was war between them, with the Greek garrison of Judah supporting and defending the Hellenizers. The *Hasidim*,[5] the "pietists," ran off into the hill country and hid from the Greeks. The Greek soldiers stayed in the safety of Jerusalem until the Sabbath. Then they came out and hunted down the Hasidim who, out of religious scruples, would not fight on the Sabbath. In one terrible case the Greeks found a few hundred Hasidim hiding in a cave. They built a fire at the entrance, suffocating the Jews inside. Those who tried to escape were slain by the sword. Meanwhile, the Greeks went from village to village, forcing the Jews to display their loyalty by bowing to an idol and eating a sacrifice of pork. Pious Jews became willing martyrs rather than succumb to this demand.

The Greeks came to the village of Modin in the western foothills of Judah. The leading Jew there was a priest named Mattathias (Matthew), of the Hasmonean family. Mattathias had five sons, named Johanan, Eleazer, Judah, Jonathan, and Simon. The head of the Greek garrison offered Mattathias a bribe and a noble title if he would set an example by worshiping the idol. Instead, Mattathias drew his sword, slew the Greek, and called out, "All who are loyal to the ways of our ancestors, follow me." He led his sons and followers out into the wilderness, and became head of the rebellion. The next winter, as he lay dying of old age, Mattathias appointed his middle son, Judah, as successor to lead the rebellion. Judah was chosen over his brothers because of his military brilliance. He was nicknamed, Maccabee, "hammer," and we remember his followers as "the Maccabees."

The Maccabees succeeded where the Hasidim had failed. This was due in part to Judah's brilliant conduct of guerrilla warfare. He smashed one Greek army after another, causing losses that Antiochus could not afford while he was simultaneously defending his borders against Roman and Persian incursions. Also, Judah made alliances with Sparta and with Rome. The Romans, seeking a pretense, threatened Antiochus with war if he should attack their ally, Judah Maccabee.

Another reason for the Maccabees' success was a new interpretation of the Torah—that it was permissible to fight defensively on the Sabbath. The Torah explicitly prohibits "labor" on the Sabbath, but the Torah does not define labor. The exact definition of prohibited Sabbath labor underwent continuous development throughout Second Temple times. For example, Ezra the Scribe introduced into Jerusalem the prohibition of shopping on the Sabbath. This was a new ruling to the surprised Judean farmers and shopkeepers, but it was probably standard practice among the Jews of Babylon. The Maccabees made a new interpretation of Sabbath law. They would not attack on the Sabbath, but they would fight to save their lives (I Macc 2:40–41). This ruling allowed the breaking of Sabbath ritual law to save a life. It was eventually stated in principles, such as, "The Sabbath was made for man, and not man for the Sabbath," and in the saying, "Let them desecrate one Sabbath so that they may sanctify many Sabbaths." (See Talmud Yoma 85a-b, Sanhedrin 74a, Tanhuma Buber Masa'ey 81a, N.T. Mark 2:27.) This ruling of the Maccabees is important to our understanding of Judaism in the time of Jesus, for this may be our first sighting of the "legal traditions of the Pharisees." This became the "Oral Torah" of rabbinic Judaism—a way of living by the Torah that was more flexible and liberal than the older priestly traditions.

The Peace

In 165 BCE King Antiochus sued for peace. He granted the Jews the right to live by their ancestral customs. The Jews, in turn, pledged

HELLENISTIC KINGS WHO SUCCEEDED ALEXANDER THE GREAT

SYRIA (SELEUCIDS)

Seleucus I Nicator	311-281 BCE
Antiochus I Soter	281-261
Antiochus II Theos	261-246
Seleucus II Callinicus	246-225
Seleucus III Soter	225-223
Antiochus III the Great	223-187
Seleucus IV Philopator	187-175
Antiochus IV Epiphanes	175-164
Demetrius I Soter	162-150
Alexander Balas	150-145
Demetrius II Nicator	145-140
Antiochus VI Epiphanes	145-142
Antiochus VII Sidetes	138-129
Demetrius II Nicator	129-125
Cleopatra Thea	126
Cleopatra Thea and Antiochus VIII Grypus	125-121
Seleucus V	125
Antiochus VIII Grypus	121-96
Antiochus IX Cyzicenus	115-95
Seleucus VI Epiphanes Nicator	96-95
Demetrius III Philopator	95-88
Antiochus X Eusebes	95-83
Antiochus XI Philadelphus	94-83
Philip I Philadelphus Antiochus XII	87-84

EGYPT (PTOLEMIES)

Ptolemy I Soter	304-282 BCE
Ptolemy II Philadelphus	285-246
Ptolemy III Euergetes	246-221
Ptolemy IV Philopator	221-205
Ptolemy V Epiphanes	205-180
Ptolemy VI Philometor	180-145
Ptolemy VII Neos Philopator	145
Ptolemy VIII Euergetes II	170-116
Ptolemy IX Soter II	116-107
Ptolemy X Alexander I	107-88
Ptolemy IX Soter II (restored)	88-81
Ptolemy XI Alexander II	80
Ptolemy XII Neos Dionysos	80-51
Cleopatra VII Philopator	51-30

loyalty to the king. Judah and his followers gained control of the Temple, but the Hellenizers retained the citadel for their protection. The Maccabees went up to the Temple, which they found abandoned and in disarray. They removed the idol, the altar, and everything tainted with pagan sacrifice. They placed the altar stones in an isolated place "until a true prophet should arise" to tell them how to properly dispose of the desecrated stones. After cleansing the Temple they observed an eight-day festival of dedication that they called *Hannukah*, the Jewish name for a dedication ceremony. The eight days were a late observance of the fall festival of Sukkot, which was the traditional holiday for a temple dedication. The first day of the holiday was three years to the day (by the Greek calendar?) from the day of the Temple's desecration—the 25th day of the first winter month (December 25 in the Gregorian calendar, Kislev 25 in the Hebrew calendar).

By decree of Judah Maccabee, Hannukah became a holiday for all Jews. Originally celebrated with bonfires, by the time of Jesus Jews observed Hannukah by lighting oil lamps in the windows of their homes. A later legend gave a reason for the eight days and eight lights of Hannukah. According to this legend the Maccabees found in the Temple a vial of oil with the seal of the old high priest, Onias, so they knew it had not been desecrated. They used this oil to rekindle the menorah, the sacred lamp in the Temple. The oil was sufficient for only one day. By divine miracle it burned for the full eight days of the festival. The miracle showed God's pleasure with the newly rededicated Temple and the self-sacrifice of the Maccabees.

After the War

Now that they were free to live by the Torah, the Hasidim went back to their homes and farms. Judah Maccabee had greater plans. He wanted to fight on for complete independence for the country of Judah. Now supported only by his personal following of a few hundred soldiers, Judah died in battle not long after the first Hannukah, preceded in death by his brother Eleazar. Greek armies again marched victoriously in Judah, though the Greeks never again outlawed the Torah.

Onias expected to come back and resume his office as high priest, but the Hasmoneans did not allow him to return. Onias eventually built his own Temple in Leontopolis, Egypt, despite the Torah's prohibition against alternate temples. This temple lasted until the Romans destroyed it after the Great Jewish Revolt of 66–70 CE.

Two different families now clashed as they sought to usurp power and authority from the Zadokites—the Hasmoneans and the Tobiads. In the factional clashes Yohanan and Jonathan were assassinated. Ultimately Simon the Hasmonean, the youngest and only surviving brother, triumphed over all his enemies. He defeated the Tobiads, the Hellenizers in the Jerusalem citadel, and all other enemies. In 142 BCE Simon became the high priest. In 140 he called himself *Nasi*—"prince," a royal title, and he minted coins by permission of the Seleucid emperor. Judah was now a sovereign state, and Simon was the king. Later he or his descendants dropped the pretense of the humble title, Nasi, and used the title of "king."

The Hasmonean triumph was not due to Judah's victories but to the political cleverness of his surviving brothers. The Seleucid empire was crumbling under an onslaught from the Romans to the west and the neo-Persians, or Parthians, to the East. Multiple pretenders arose to claim the Seleucid throne. The Hasmoneans showed impeccable judgment in always siding with the eventual winner in these dynastic struggles. The pretenders to the throne needed Hasmonean support more than the Hasmoneans needed them. Simon was in a position of great potential power. He and his successors made good use of their opportunities.

Significant Results of the Maccabean Conflict

The revolt of the Maccabees initiated the era of Judaism into which Jesus was born, an era of conflict and creativity. Below are seven results of the Maccabean conflict that are essential to our understanding of Judaism in the time of Jesus.

The holiday of Hannukah

Jews celebrated the Hasmonean victory every year in the holiday of Hannukah, which became an important Jewish festival. The message of Hannukah is, as stated in the Jewish liturgy, "the victory of the weak over the strong, the few over the many, the righteous over the arrogant" (Daily Prayer Book, addition to "Modim" prayer in the Tefilah). This celebration encouraged Jews to bravely persist in opposing later oppressors. The result of this Jewish self-confidence was a mixture of triumph and disaster. Judaism survived, but Judah Maccabee's victory too often inspired the Jews to hopeless rebellion against the power of Rome. Probably due to the political consequences of the Hannukah story, later rabbis suppressed the memory of Judah's victory. The rabbis emphasized the "miracle of the oil"—a more spiritual, less political message.

The end of the Zadokite line

Having lost the royal dynasty of King David some centuries earlier, the Jews now lost the high priestly dynasty of Zadok. Future high priests never held full legitimacy in the eyes of the Jewish people. This generated an era of disunity and continuous conflict among the Jews, as different factions promoted their own preferred leaders. Later high priests, such as Caiphas (the high priest who condemned Jesus), were considered by many Jews to be little better than usurpers. Jews continued to revere the office of high priest, but not necessarily those who held that office. The Hasmoneans kept the office of high priest for about eighty years, until the Roman takeover of Judea. The Romans auctioned the high priesthood to the highest bidder from among the aristocratic priestly families, selling the office for a two-year term. Herod, and after him the Romans, held the high priestly vestments in the royal palace. The high priest had to come each morning to receive his vestments from the ruler as a symbol of submission to higher authority.

The end of biblical writing

For reasons not known to us Jews became self-consciously aware after the victory of the Maccabees that they were now living in different times. They believed that the era of holy inspiration for writing sacred books had now passed from the world. The rabbis who closed the biblical canon considered any book written after the revolt of the Maccabees to be too late to get into the Bible. The book of Daniel just beat the deadline. This book was composed after Antiochus outlawed Judaism, but before the Maccabees took control of the Jewish revolt. It represents the despair of the persecuted Jews before there was any intimation of a possible military victory. The Babylonian and Persian kings mentioned in the book of Daniel are really code names for Antiochus IV. The "abomination of desolation" that the Babylonian king forced the Jews to worship according to the book of Daniel was, in reality, the idol that Antiochus IV set up in the Jerusalem Temple. The book of Daniel shows us the Jews' devotion to prayer, keeping kosher, and monotheistic worship, and their hope that God would intervene to protect Jews who remained true to the Torah. Daniel is the one truly apocalyptic book in the Bible. In secretive imagery it gives hints of a future transformation planned by God. In the anticipated future time the wicked shall be punished, the righteous shall triumph, all the world will acknowledge God's sovereignty, and the victims of Antiochus' persecution shall be resurrected to glorious life. The book of Daniel has always held special importance for Christians, who interpret many passages in this book as support for various Christian doctrines.

The rise of sects

With the elimination of the Zadokite high priesthood different leadership groups arose. Each claimed to possess the true interpretation of the Torah and the true understanding of the priestly office. The sects best known to us from ancient writings, including the New Testament, are the Pharisees, the Sadducees, the Essenes, and the Zealots. There were probably other sects as well. The era of sects begins with the revolt of the Maccabees and ends with the Roman destruction of the Temple in 70 CE. The high point of the sects is around the time of Jesus. The earliest Christians were a sect within Judaism, and may have had much in common with other Jewish sects. Sects arose in part because of the loss of legitimate leadership. The sects began to fade as the rabbis gained central control over Jewish affairs after the Roman destruction. Another reason the sects faded after the year 70 was that, with the Temple gone, the debate over its proper conduct and leadership became academic. Christians and rabbinic Jews survived the destruction in part because, unlike the other sects, they had a symbolic system that was not dependent on the actual conduct of animal sacrifice.

New religious doctrines

The most popular sect among the Jewish populace was the Pharisees. The Pharisees had two doctrines which became central to later Judaism and to Christianity—a belief in the oral interpretation of scripture, and the doctrine of bodily resurrection. Both doctrines arose out of Jewish piety during the revolt of the Maccabees.

The "traditions of the Pharisees," which evolved into the "Oral Torah" of the rabbis, was a set of laws and rules for living by the Torah. The Pharisees claimed to possess these laws as a living tradition, handed down from sage to sage since the time of Moses. Pharisaic tradition became the basis for the Mishnah and Talmud, the laws of rabbinic Judaism. The Pharisees were renowned among the Jews for their knowledge of the law, and it seems that people accepted Pharisaic authority in the legal interpretation of scripture. The Sadducees rejected the Oral Torah. They held to priestly traditions that, in their own eyes, hewed more closely to the literal meaning of the Torah.

Most historians doubt that the oral traditions of the Pharisees really go back to Moses, though they may be based in part on ancient Jewish traditions. Most historians perceive the Oral Torah as a post-Maccabean innovation, a flexible response to difficult and changing times. The traditions of the Pharisees were an attempt to update the Torah for the "modern" world of their time. The new interpretation of Sabbath rest mentioned above may be our first example of the Oral

Torah of the Pharisees in action. The Mishnah and Talmud name the sages associated with various legal traditions. The named sages, or "tradents," go back to the era of the Hasmoneans, none earlier. Some rules are not associated with any tradent and are called "a law that God gave to Moses on Mt. Sinai." Traditionally pious Jewish historians believe these to be the most ancient traditions of the Pharisees. Other historians believe that these laws are actually the newest and most innovative of Pharisaic rulings. The rabbis granted them the authority of Moses precisely because they had no tradition history.

It makes sense that every body of written laws includes a set of unspoken assumptions which make it applicable to society. Biblical Jews must have had an "Oral Torah," as did the Zadokite priests and every sect of Judaism in Second Temple times. The "traditions of the Pharisees" stood out from the other oral traditions—perhaps because it was radical and innovative, perhaps because the Pharisees themselves emphasized their "chain of tradition."

To summarize the opposing views on the Oral Torah of the Pharisees: the claim of traditional Jewish piety is that the Pharisees preserved the true traditions of Jewish law, while the Sadducees veered off to establish a new path. The more accepted historical view is that the Sadducees attempted to preserve the more ancient teachings of the traditional priesthood, while the Pharisees were innovative.

The doctrine of bodily resurrection

The Pharisees taught that sometime in the future everyone who ever lived will return to bodily life on earth. Each person will rise from the grave. Then God will judge every human being according to his or her earthly deeds. The wicked will die again, this time forever, while the righteous will receive a grant of a thousand years of life, followed by the indescribable "World to Come." This belief is called the doctrine of bodily resurrection (in Hebrew t'hiyyat ha-may-tim).

We must not think of resurrection as a "return of the spirit." It is a return to actual bodily life. There is no separation of human body and spirit in this doctrine; to be human is to both body and mind-soul. This can be confusing to modern people because we have adopted the Greek view that people have a mortal body and immortal soul as two distinct aspects of self.

The belief in a separate body and soul was a teaching of the ancient Greek philosophers. Socrates believed that the true "human" was the soul, which was imprisoned in the body. At death, the soul was released from its prison to return to a more pure, spiritual existence.

Biblical Judaism had no belief in an afterlife. Upon death people went down to "Sheol," the underworld, a concept similar to the Hades of Greek mythology. In Sheol the shadows slept for eternity with their ancestors. There was no reward or punishment after death. Good and bad alike slept in the underworld. When King Saul ordered the witch of Ein Dor to conjure the shade of the prophet Samuel, Samuel criticized Saul for waking him up from his sleep in Sheol. (I Sam 28:15). When the prophet Isaiah gloated over the death of the evil king of Babylon, who thought he would become a god in the afterlife, Isaiah said: "Once you thought...`I will mount the back of a cloud. I will match the Most High.' Instead you are brought down to Sheol, to the bottom of the pit" (Is 14:13–15). The righteous Samuel and the wicked pagan king both endure the same fate in death—eternal sleep in the underworld. We cannot call this "afterlife."

Our first hint of the doctrine of bodily resurrection is in the book of Daniel. In the final chapter of Daniel we find: "At that time your people will be rescued, all who are found inscribed in the book. Many of those that sleep in the dust of the earth will awake, some to eternal life, others to reproaches, to everlasting abhorrence" (Dan 12:1b–2) This is the only mention of afterlife, other than Sheol, in the Hebrew scriptures.

The first explicit argument for the doctrine of bodily resurrection is in the second book of Maccabees, a book in the Apocrypha. The first book of Maccabees is the official history of the revolt, commissioned by the Hasmonean rulers. The second book of Maccabees retells the history of the revolt, but its primary concern is to tell tales of pious martyrs and promote the beliefs for which they died. Second Maccabees was composed by a group with a religious agenda, possibly the early Pharisees. Second Maccabees, chapter 7, tells the tale of a mother and her seven sons who were executed in turn on a single day before the eyes of Antiochus because they would not bow to his idol nor eat his pork. Each son, and the mother, give brave speeches in which they express their faith that by forfeiting life now they are gaining eternal life in the resurrection of the dead.[6]

If we read the speeches separately from the story we see that we have here an essay. Its purpose is to convince Jews of this new doctrine and to answer possible objections. "Who will be resurrected?" "Those who live by the Torah." "What happens to wicked people?" "They will die forever." "Why is God allowing the loyal Jews to die?" "We are being punished for our sins, but God will more than make it up to us after the resurrection. There is true justice and retribution." "What of people who are mutilated before death?" "They shall be resurrected whole, with all of their limbs." "Isn't the doctrine of resurrection too far-fetched to be believed?" "It is no harder to believe than the miracle of conception and birth itself, yet we know this as a reality. As God places the child in the womb and protects it until birth, so shall God cause a new birth at the resurrection."

The Pharisees argued that though the doctrine of resurrection is absent from the Torah, they could use exegesis (interpretation) to derive it from every verse if they had to. This exaggerated claim seems defensive.

The Sadducees vigorously opposed the new doctrine of bodily resurrection. They held that "when you're dead, you're dead." Some see the doctrine of the Sadducees as a concession to Hellenistic thought, but more likely the Sadducees were clinging to more ancient Jewish beliefs.

Jesus is said to have firmly believed in and preached the doctrine of bodily resurrection. He is reported to have debated with the Sadducees over this issue (Mk 12:18–27 et al.). Christians obviously affirmed the doctrine of bodily resurrection. It is necessary to their faith that Jesus experienced a special resurrection three days after his death on the cross. Christians shared with rabbinic Jews the faith in the general resurrection in the time to come. Where the New Testament is especially favorable or complimentary toward Pharisees, this is often in appreciation of the Pharisaic preaching of the doctrine of resurrection.

Eventually Jews and Christians adopted the Greek belief in the eternal soul and added it to their belief in bodily resurrection. The two doctrines have coexisted in Judaism and Christianity for two millennia, though they are distinct in origin. This collation of Greek and Jewish concepts of afterlife may have already taken place in the time of Jesus. Originally they were quite distinct, with Jews affirming one doctrine and Greeks the other.

Many modern Jews and Christians, tending toward scientific rationalism, prefer the doctrine of the eternal soul over that of bodily resurrection. Reform and Conservative Jews, and most secularized Jews, have abandoned the doctrine of bodily resurrection. If they look for eternity at all, it is only in heavenly life. Many modern Christians conflate the idea of the bodily resurrection of Jesus with the idea of Jesus who is risen in the spirit. Originally, these were two separate versions of Jesus' fate after the crucifixion.[7] To understand the doctrine of resurrection in Jesus' time we must somehow ignore our evolved Christian and Jewish tradition. We have harmonized the concepts of Greek philosophy with our biblical faith. Back in Jesus' time the doctrine of bodily resurrection was new, distinct from Greek ideas, and a matter of passionate debate among different sects of Jews.

The synthesis of Hellenism and Judaism

The revolt of the Maccabees was a civil war between those Jews who wanted to adopt Greek ways and those who wanted to remain true to their ancestral ways. Ultimately neither side won. Judaism evolved as a synthesis of Judaism and Hellenism. Before the revolt of the Maccabees one had to be either a pious Jew or a Hellenist. After the revolt of the Maccabees one could be both. The Hasmonean kings adopted many trappings of Greek monarchs, yet they remained loyal to Judaism and served also as high priests in the Temple. The various sects of Judaism in the post-Maccabean era represent different ways of adapting Judaism to Hellenism. The survival of Judaism was ultimately assured not by Judah Maccabee's ephemeral military victories, but by the Jews' creative adaptation of their tradition to the wider culture of Hellenism.

5

From the Maccabees to the Procurators: Political History

The Hasmonean Kings

The important successors to Simon the Hasmonean were his son John Hyrcanus (reigned 134–104 BCE), John's son Alexander Yannai (reigned 103–76 BCE), and the Queen Regent Salome Alexandra, widow of Alexander Yannai (76–67 BCE). After Salome's death her two sons Aristobulus II and Hyrcanus II contended for power until the Roman general Pompey came and claimed Judea for the Roman Empire. The Romans gradually drew power away from the Hasmoneans. They eventually appointed their own man, Herod, as ruler of Judea (c. 37 BCE). Herod's father had been an advisor to the last Hasmonean rulers, using his position to lobby with the Romans to advance the cause of his own family. Herod married Mariamne, "the last of the Hasmoneans," but later had her killed along with their two sons.

We shall deal with the reign of John Hyrcanus and Alexander Yannai as a unit. This was an era of expansion for the kingdom of Judah. The Seleucid empire was crumbling into multiple ministates. The Hasmonean kings were clever at politics and judicious in warfare, expanding their boundaries as opportunity allowed. They conquered Samaria and razed the Samaritan temple on Mt. Gerizim, thus completing the subjection of their old rivals. They captured and briefly held various Greek cities on the seacoast.

After some early expeditions to Galilee to save the Jews there from attack, the Hasmonean rulers conquered Galilee and added it to their kingdom. They also conquered Idumea, the ancient kingdom of Edom east of the Dead Sea. John Hyrcanus forced the Gentile

Galileans and the Idumeans to convert to Judaism—the only forcible mass conversion in the history of Judaism. In the time of Jesus Galilee contained many Jews whose ancestors had only been Jewish for about a century.

It does not seem that the Galileans and Idumeans resisted their conversion. During the Great Rebellion (66–70 CE) the Galileans and Idumeans were the most adamant fighters against Rome. They fought the Romans to the death when many Judeans were ready to accept peace terms.

The Galileans were fiercely loyal to Judaism. They undoubtedly were meticulous in fulfilling the essential demands of Judaism, such as Sabbath observance. The Pharisaic scholars of Judaism, centered in Jerusalem in Judea, found the Galileans to be insufficiently concerned about the details of Jewish observance—for example, the rules of Sabbath rest. The Talmud says that Yohanan ben Zakkai, a great Pharisee of the first century, was assigned to a post in Galilee during his training. In eighteen years he was asked only two questions of Jewish law, causing him to lament "O Galilee, O Galilee, in the end you shall be filled with wrongdoers!" (Jerusalem Talmud Shabbat 16:7, 15d). The Pharisaic criticism of Galileans is mirrored in the New Testament, in which Galilean religious passion in compared favorably against the minute concerns of the Judean legal scholars. There was rivalry between Galilee and Judea, the former representing a passionate approach to religion, the latter an intellectual approach. This was at heart a friendly "crosstown" rivalry which was contained within a shared devotion to Judaism and a higher sense of Jewish national unity. This regional rivalry is essential to our understanding of many stories and passages in the gospels.

As John Hyrcanus and Alexander Yannai continued their conquests east of the Jordan they expanded the boundaries of their kingdom to those once held by King David. Nevertheless, Jews did not believe they were living in a return to the golden age of King David. The Jews did not love John and Alexander. The kings' political expansionism did not necessarily benefit their Jewish subjects.

John and Alexander established themselves as Greek-style absolute monarchs. They hired non-Jewish mercenary soldiers to protect themselves. They were brutal to their opponents, adopting the Greek habit of crucifying political foes. Pietists did not approve of the Hellenizing tendencies of the monarchs that we can see from their names—half Hebrew, half Greek.

The Rise of the Sects

During the reign of John Hyrcanus and Alexander Yannai the major competing Jewish sects, the Pharisees and the Sadducees, first appear on the stage of recorded history. These sects must have arisen in the Hasmonean revolt, but we find no historical trace of them until they appear in the Hasmonean court vying for power.

Even the origin of the names of these sects is shrouded in mystery. "Sadducees" probably means "Zadokites," supporters of the ancient hereditary priesthood. "Pharisees" means "separatists." This may refer to their religious practices, or it may have the meaning of "Protestants." The proto-Pharisees may have been the Hasidim, the pious Jews who provided the bulk of the rebel forces in the time of the Maccabees. Though Judah Maccabee and the Hasidim were allies, the Pharisees and the Hasmonean kings were bitter enemies.

The Pharisees Oppose the Hasmoneans

The Hasmoneans disapproved of the way that the Hasmonean rulers had centralized their power, ruling as both king and high priest and maintaining mercenary forces. Legend tells that at a banquet Alexander Yannai (or John Hyrcanus, sources differ) forced the Pharisees to reveal their true feelings. When they urged Yannai to forgo the high priesthood he turned against them and killed many of them (Talmud Kiddushin 66a). From that time on Yannai supported the Sadducees in the rivalry between the two parties. On another occasion Yannai turned his mercenary forces loose against the people of Jerusalem after they pelted him with citrons while he was officiating (incompetently) as high priest at the festival of Sukkot. Many thousands of Jews were killed. Another time he crucified in one batch thousands of Pharisees who opposed him, while he callously rejoiced at their demise.

Legend says that on his deathbed Alexander Yannai repented of his persecution of the Pharisees. He told his wife Salome Alexandra that she must honor the Pharisees and grant them authority, for due to their popularity with the masses no one could effectively rule without their support. Whether or not the legend of the deathbed confession is true, Salome did support the Pharisees.

The Pharisees, once in power, took vengeance on those who had persecuted them during Yannai's reign. On the positive side they enacted their program of piety for the Jewish people, promoting observance of the Torah laws for which they were famous. Queen

Salome was herself pious and observant. She approved of the religious agenda of the Pharisees.

According to the Talmud's reconstruction of history (the "pious Jewish assumption") the Pharisees gained control of the institutions of Jewish self-rule during the reign of Salome Alexandra. They never relinquished that control. They accomplished this by replacing Sadducees in the Sanhedrin, the Jewish high court of seventy-one elders. The Pharisees made themselves a majority in the high court. As a result, the Sadducees, and even the high priests, had to obey the Pharisees' commands and live by their legal rulings.

Historians doubt the veracity of the Talmudic reconstruction of history. It seems more likely that after their brief period of power during the reign of Salome, the Pharisees fell out of power. They were powerless in the time of Herod and the Roman procurators. They returned to power only after the destruction of the Temple.

It also seems unlikely that the primary instrument of Pharisaic leadership at the time of Salome was membership in the Sanhedrin. The Pharisees controlled the government through Queen Salome's personal patronage, rather than through their control of institutions like the Temple or the Sanhedrin.

The Innovations of Simon bar Shetah

The leading Pharisee of this time was Simon bar Shetah. He may have been a brother of Queen Salome. The Talmud credits Simon with two innovations—the *ketubah*, or marriage contract, and the establishment of schools for the universal public education of Jewish boys. These innovations are important for our understanding of the world of Jesus.

Contemporary feminist theologians have paid particular attention to Jesus' relationship with women and his concern for their role in society. Too often feminist New Testament scholars have discussed the matter without a proper appreciation of the concern for women's well-being that existed among other Jewish leaders at the time. The social and economic burden of Jewish women was significantly eased by Simon bar Shetah's innovation of the ketubah. Biblical law allowed a man to divorce his wife at will. A divorced woman was sent out with no possessions, plunging her into dire and immediate poverty. The Pharisees now decreed that no Jewish man could marry a woman without providing her with a ketubah. This was a written document which guaranteed a woman a certain considerable sum of money in

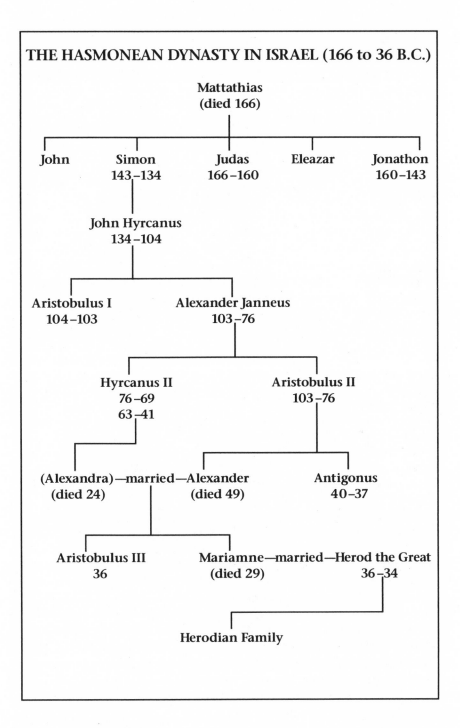

THE HASMONEAN DYNASTY IN ISRAEL (166 to 36 B.C.)

Mattathias
(died 166)

John   Simon   Judas   Eleazar   Jonathon
143–134   166–160   160–143

John Hyrcanus
134–104

Aristobulus I   Alexander Janneus
104–103   103–76

Hyrcanus II   Aristobulus II
76–69   103–76
63–41

(Alexandra)—married—Alexander   Antigonus
(died 24)   (died 49)   40–37

Aristobulus III   Mariamne—married—Herod the Great
36   (died 29)   36–34

Herodian Family

case of divorce or upon the demise of her husband (no less than 200 silver zuzim for a first marriage). The ketubah provided for a woman in case of divorce. It also provided a powerful economic incentive for a husband to work things out with his wife and remain married.

Simon bar Shetah established universal education for Jewish boys from the age of five so that all Jewish males would be literate in the Hebrew scriptures. The Pharisees held the ideal that the Jews were to be "a kingdom of priests, a holy nation," as the Torah promised. For this to come true, every Jewish man had to be literate in the scriptures, in the manner of a priest. (Subject to the limitations of their times, the Pharisees could not imagine literate women.)

Some historians doubt that Simon bar Shetah and the Pharisees really established universal education. Their argument is based on the conviction that no ancient society provided education to anyone other than aristocrats and a small scribal class. Literacy was power, which the tiny privileged elites of the ancient world would not have willingly shared. It is, of course, entirely possible that Pharisaic idealism overcame this ancient scruple. Jews in the Middle Ages were unique in their universal literacy—could they not have been similarly unique in late antiquity?

At stake, for Jesus scholars, is a major understanding about the mind of Jesus. If the Talmudic story is true, then Jesus received a formal education. If the story is not true, then a carpenter's son from Galilee would surely have had no formal education. He would have been familiar with scripture only aurally, from hearing the lesson and preaching in the synagogue on the Sabbath.

Our Jewish sources tell us that boys began formal schooling at the age of five. The children sat before the teacher all day. He read them a verse from the Bible, translated it and explained its meaning. The children repeated after the teacher, in this way learning the text, its translation, and how to live by it. At the age of ten children completed their education in scripture and were apprenticed in their future jobs. A fortunate few, mostly the children of the wealthy but also some dedicated scholarship students, went to a higher academy to study the laws and teachings of the sages.

Some Christians of today prefer to think of Jesus as formally educated, even as having spent hidden years studying intensively with the sages of Israel. Other Christians prefer the image of Jesus without formal education, a simple man of the people whose words were directly inspired by the holy spirit. If one looks at pre-modern Christian paintings of the gospel scene of Jesus debating with the Pharisees (Lk 2:41–52) one sees a historic Christian preference for the latter view. In these paintings the scholars are depicted poring over texts, while the boy Jesus sits enthroned above them preaching directly to them. A book is open before him but young Jesus does not need to look into it. We are to understand that the message of the book is embodied in him. Which picture is historically accurate, that of a schooled Jesus or that of an inspired Jesus? It depends on the veracity of the Talmudic account of Simon bar Shetah's accomplishments.

The Roman Occupation of Judea

The Romans were opportunists. They preferred to expand their empire by expedient action rather than outright conquest. In 63 BCE the Roman general Pompey was in the Near East with his army. Salome's two sons, Hyrcanus II and Aristobulus II, were engaged in a civil war over the throne. Hyrcanus invited Pompey to come to his aid. Pompey marched into Jerusalem, and the Kingdom of Judah became the Roman province of Judea.

Pompey entered the Temple's inner sanctum, the Holy of Holies, infuriating the Jews with his impiety. When Pompey and Julius Caesar engaged in a civil war for control of the Roman Empire the Jews supported Julius Caesar, the eventual winner. The affection of the Jews for Caesar was genuine, and for his part he respected the Jews. When he became emperor, Julius Caesar made Judaism a legal religion. He excused Jews from agricultural taxes during the Sabbatical year (the Seventh Year when Jews neither planted nor reaped). He excused the Jews from emperor worship, which he understood was impossible for monotheists. Instead, the Jews were to offer an additional morning sacrifice to God in honor of the emperor. This remained the Jewish practice as long as the Temple stood. When Julius Caesar was assassinated in 44 BCE, all the Jews of Rome mourned his passing.

Jewish Self-Rule under the Romans: Herod, High Priest, Sanhedrin

The political situation in Judea underwent a period of uncertainty that lasted some decades. The Hasmoneans were weak, and their control of the country was crumbling. The Persians conquered and briefly occupied the country until expelled by the Romans. In the decade of the '30s BCE the Romans appointed an Idumean (from the land of Edom, conquered and converted by Hyrcanus) named Herod as king of Judea. Prepped for power by his father Agrippa, Herod used brave and desperate means to achieve his goals. He resorted as necessary to war, to diplomacy and to trickery. He backed Mark Antony, then went over to Octavian, during the Roman civil war that followed the assassination of Julius Caesar. When Octavian became Caesar Augustus, the Emperor of Rome, Herod had favor and power at the court. Herod was ruthless and brutal, clever and intelligent. He designated himself Herod the Great, and by this name he has gone down in history. His period of rule over Judea was approximately 37 BCE—4 BCE. His death coincided approximately with the birth of Jesus.

While the Romans ruled through Herod, the Jews maintained their own institutions of social control. Ancient empires did not impose their laws and customs on subject peoples. The Jews retained their own customary institutions. Most important of these were the Temple and the Sanhedrin.

The high priest presided in the Temple. Though the king held power over affairs of state, the high priest remained the head of the Jewish people, as he had been for centuries. Herod appointed high priests at will, but he could not usurp the authority of the high priest as the ultimate arbiter of Jewish affairs. The high priest had under him a large priestly bureaucracy. Priests of noble lineage held various offices in the Temple administration. The Temple was not just a place of worship as moderns conceive of it; it was the central institution of Jewish self-government.

The Sanhedrin was a high court or cabinet of ministers. It stood at the head of the Jewish court system. Ancient societies like that of the Jews did not have legislatures. Kings ruled by decree but law was traditional, handed down from God through the generations. New situations were handled not by legislation and amendment but by new interpretations of the law. While the Sanhedrin was the Supreme Court of Judea, it held many functions that in America today would be held by the Congress. Membership in the Sanhedrin gave one great influence over Jewish internal affairs.

We do not know the origins of the Sanhedrin. The word "Sanhedrin" is Greek, so the Sanhedrin must have arisen during Greek times, perhaps during the time of the Ptolemaic and Seleucid kingdoms. It probably arose among the Jews of Jerusalem as the parallel to the Greek *boule*, the council of leading citizens which ruled the polis, or as a parallel to the *gerousia*, the council of elders who ruled the Jews in each Diaspora city.

There are two versions of the function of the Sanhedrin, that posited by Jewish tradition and that proposed by modern historians. According to the Talmud the Sanhedrin held the highest authority in Judaism. It even supervised the activities of the high priest. The

Sanhedrin met in the Chamber of Hewn Stones, a dedicated room in the Temple compound. The Sanhedrin's seventy-one members were drawn from the leaders of the major sects, the Pharisees and the Sadducees—a sort of Parliamentary system. The two leaders of the Sanhedrin were the President, titled Nasi (Prince, Patriarch) and the Vice-President, titled Av Bet Din (Father of the Court). The leading party appointed the Nasi. From the time of Hillel and Shammai, and perhaps their predecessors Shamaiah and Avtalion, the Pharisees made up a majority in the Sanhedrin and controlled its offices. Hillel was Nasi in his time. Using their advantage as the majority in the Sanhedrin, the Pharisees oversaw the ritual functions of the high priests. The high priests were Sadducees, but they dared not defy the rulings of the popular Pharisees. The Pharisees also appointed the judges, teachers and civil administrators throughout the country, who judged according to the Pharisee's interpretation of Torah law.

Historians doubt the veracity of the Talmud's reconstruction of the ancient Sanhedrin. It is more likely that the high priest retained his authority in Jewish affairs as long as the Temple stood, until the year 70. The Sanhedrin was probably not a parliament or court but a privy council for the high priest. Its members were aristocrats, noble and powerful priests and laity. The members were chosen because of their power which derived from wealth and position, not because of their membership in any particular sect, fellowship or party. In Judean society, as in all ancient societies, power lay in the hands of a small group of hereditary aristocrats. The notion of a high council of scholars, appointed for their wisdom despite humble origins, is appealing but unrealistic.

The Sanhedrin posited by the Talmud did not exist in the time of Jesus, but something like it did exist in later times. After the destruction of the Temple the Jews reconstituted their self-government in the village of Yavneh, near the Mediterranean coast. The Sanhedrin of seventy-one members that met in Yavneh did contain a majority of Pharisees. As old sectarian issues lost meaning the Pharisees disappeared from the scene. The members of the Yavneh Sanhedrin came to be known as rabbis; the Nasi was addressed as Rabban (Our Rabbi). The rabbinical Sanhedrin under the rulership of the hereditary Nasi flourished from the year 70 until about the year 350 or 400. It moved from Yavneh to the Galilee after the Bar Kochba Rebellion of 132–35. Eventually the Sanhedrin settled in the city of Tiberius on the shore of the Sea of Galilee. The Talmud's reconstruction anachronistically reads this later rabbinic Sanhedrin back into Temple times, the time of Jesus.

Herod the Great

King Herod was always fearful, and for good reason. He had many enemies. He had no hereditary right to be King of Judea. He was not even of Judean ancestry, his Idumean ancestors having been among the forcible converts of John Hyrcanus. He was said to have been "half-Jewish," though what is meant by this is unclear. Herod worried about his two sons by Mariamne, who had royal Hasmonean blood thanks to their mother. Herod had the three of them killed. Then, in remorse and sorrow for his loss, he built three beautiful towers in the citadel of Jerusalem and named them after his wife and sons. He killed another son as well, leading one contemporary Gentile chronicler to joke that "it was better to be Herod's pig than his son," since Herod observed Jewish dietary laws and would not slaughter a pig. He killed many other rivals as well. Herod also was fearful because Cleopatra, Queen of Egypt, was powerful in Rome, and she coveted Herod's territory for her own kingdom. Herod worried about an Egyptian invasion, sponsored by his masters the Romans. Herod was not popular with his unwilling subjects, though like many a tyrant he wanted to be loved. Though he had blood on his hands, Herod never ordered the death of all the babies in Judea, as told in a New Testament story (Matt 2:13–23). That is a legend based on the Moses story. (Jews in the time of Jesus told a similar legend about the nativity of Abraham [Bet haMidrash 2:118–196]). The ancient historians who recorded every detail of Herod's evil deeds surely would have mentioned it had Herod ordered the slaughter of babies. All our sources are silent on this.

Herod was famed for his building projects. He built on a grand scale indicative of his imagination, his self-aggrandizement, and his sources of tremendous wealth. He built himself many residences. One of his finest palaces was in the city of Caesarea on the Mediterranean coast. Herod built this city as the Roman capital of Judea and named it after his patron, Caesar Augustus. The Judean coastline is swept by the sea and has no natural harbor. Herod built an artificial harbor for Caesarea, a massive project that brought the kingdom new possibilities for trade. Herod built Caesarea primarily for his Gentile subjects. He built a pagan temple there. He sponsored the construction of other pagan temples outside his kingdom.

Herod built three "escape" palaces in the desert between Jerusalem and his homeland of Idumea. The first of these was Herodian, which is visible from Jerusalem to the southeast. The second was Masada, atop a small plateau on the Western shore of the Dead Sea. The third, Machaerus, was in Idumea, in modern Jordan.

For his Jewish subjects Herod built a magnificent building atop the Tomb of the Patriarchs, the holy site near Hebron where Abraham and Sarah, Isaac and Rebecca, Jacob and Leah are buried. The building stands to this day, with a later mosque constructed before the entrance.

Then Herod turned to his grandest building project, a reconstruction of the Jerusalem Temple. The Jews feared to let Herod knock down the existing structure, so he spent years gathering all the building materials in advance to show his good intentions. Herod enlarged the top of the Temple mount by building up a wall of stones around all four sides and filled the space with dirt to make a broad platform. Multiple courses of Herod's retaining wall are visible to this day, including the famous Western Wall where Jews pray. No one knows how Herod's engineers moved the enormous stones into place. Herod then had the Temple built in the center of the courtyard. It was surrounded by porticos, outbuildings and purification pools as necessary for the conduct of sacrifice and Temple business. One approached the Temple by two arched stairways from the main city to the west, or from a triple stairway that rose inside the Temple mount from the south. There was a passage from the north end of the Temple Mount to the Antonia Fortress, Herod's palace in Jerusalem. The Temple building was faced with marble; it glistened in the sun from a great distance. Its beauty was said to be unsurpassed. This was the Temple that Jesus visited when he came to Jerusalem, the Temple whose beautiful stones were admired by the disciples (Mk 13:1). The project took many decades and was not completed until well beyond the death of Herod. The last decorated stones on the upper courses were just being set into place when the Jews rebelled and the Romans destroyed Jerusalem. The Romans burned the Temple and tossed all of its stones down into the valley below the Mount. The jumble of stones can be seen today in the archeological dig at the Southern Wall.

When Herod was on his deathbed, he ordered the arrest of many Jewish leaders. He left orders to murder them upon his own death so that there would be mourning rather than rejoicing in Judea at the news of his death. The order was not carried out.

The Romans found no one son of Herod worthy to inherit his kingdom so they divided it into three parts. Herod Antipater became ruler of Galilee. Jesus of Nazareth was one of his subjects. Judea itself was, in 6 CE, placed under direct Roman rule. The Roman governors of Judea held the rank of prefect, later raised to the rank of procurator. Among these governors was Pontius Pilate, the Roman prefect who presided over the crucifixion of Jesus. The prefect in Judea reported to the Roman governor of Syria, in Antioch.

Evaluation of the Reign of Herod

Historical opinion is divided in the evaluation of Herod as a ruler. It is hard to be objective since our sources, including the New Testament, but especially the historian Josephus, delight in dwelling on the evil deeds of this man. We can agree that Herod was a despicable human being. But, how was he as a ruler?

Some historians have viewed Herod's building projects as an enslavement of the populace for the aggrandizement of the king. Others have perceived Herod's undertaking as a great social welfare program, a way of employing the most desperate people, the unlanded peasants. This writer takes the latter view, that Herod worked for the good of his subjects. The end of the Temple construction project, long after Herod's death, generated economic disaster. Thousands of workers were laid off, adding to the general desperation that culminated in the Great Revolt. During the reign of Herod the country was relatively well off. People benefitted from the general social order, though at the cost of great repression and increasing disparity between rich and poor.

Perhaps Herod's greatest achievement was his ability to maintain the peace between his Jewish and Gentile subjects. No one after him was able to do this in all the regions of Judea, Samaria, Galilee, the Mediterranean Coast, and Trans-Jordan, all of which were calm once Herod pacified them early in his reign. Was Herod a Jew or a pagan? The best answer is that he presented himself as a Jew to his Jewish subjects, and as a pagan to his Gentile subjects.

The murders and intrigue conducted by Herod are typical of the court politics of Hellenistic rulers. We just know more details of Herod's depredations, and pay them more mind because he lived on a great cusp of history. Herod probably had no more or less blood on his hands than rulers who came before him or after him, from the other petty kings of the East all the way up to the Roman emperors themselves.

Roman Rule after Herod

The division of Herod's kingdom took place in 4 BCE, probably the year of Jesus' birth. The Roman prefects who ruled Judea after the death of Herod were, mostly, neither good nor capable men. Their desire was not to serve the needs of their subjects, but to advance their political careers and to enrich themselves. Appointments to government office were acquired in Rome by intrigue and bribery. Individuals paid great sums to be appointed to office, hoping to regain those sums many times over through oppressive enforcement of taxation. The governors in Judea, as elsewhere, paid a set sum of tax money to Rome each year. Any sum collected in excess of this went into the ruler's pocket. The Romans auctioned the right to collect taxes to the highest bidder. These "tax farmers" used every means at their disposal to regain their investment and make a profit. No wonder the tax collectors of Jesus' day were so despised!

Sadly, many of the prefects added needless cruelty and insensitivity to their cupidity. They displayed contempt for the native customs, oppressing the Jews beyond the requirements of maintaining public order and collecting taxes. Among the most cruel, according to our historian Josephus, were Pontius Pilate (26–36 CE) who condemned Jesus, and Felix (52–60) who was involved in the trial of Paul.

Roman governors ruled Judea continuously from 6 CE to 66 CE except for a period of three years when Agrippa I, a grandson of Herod, ruled Judea as king (41–44 CE). The Jews loved Agrippa because he was a genuinely pious Jew. They mourned when he was assassinated by poison under mysterious circumstances.

Rebellion

The era of the procurators was an era of increasing rebelliousness among the Jews. There were numerous peasant uprisings. People could no longer bear Roman oppression, the arrogance of the privileged upper classes, and the rulers' contempt for Jewish piety and ancestral custom.

In Galilee a group arose in revolt against the Roman census of 6 CE. Led by a certain Judas of Galilee, forebear of the leaders of the Great Revolt, their slogan was "no ruler but God." Galilee was known for its gangs of "bandits," rural peasants driven by poverty to desperate means. Like Robin Hood of medieval England, rural bandits were friends and heroes to the local poor, dangerous criminals in the eyes of the upper classes and those responsible for social order. The bandit groups in Galilee took on an increasingly political coloration after the census revolt. Eventually these Galileans, among them the party famed as Zealots, became the core of the militia who fought the Romans in the Great Revolt.

In the city of Jerusalem urban revolutionaries conducted a program of assassination against Jews whom they accused of collaborating with the Romans. Called *Sicarii*—"daggermen"—they stabbed their victims in the crowded market streets, then melted into the crowd.

The Jews were nearly driven into revolt during the reign of the mad Emperor, Caligula (37–41 CE). Caligula insisted on universal emperor worship, and ordered that a statue be set up in Jerusalem. (Romans generally respected the Jewish prohibition of idolatry. Roman troops sheathed their "idolatrous" standards before entering the Jews' holy city). Thousands of Jewish peasants gathered peacefully, offering their lives in passive resistance rather than submit to the emperor's decree. The Syrian legate Petronius, a compassionate man, appealed to the emperor in Rome. The reply came; Petronius was ordered to commit suicide. Fortunately, Caligula was assassinated soon after. His successors rescinded his orders, and all were saved. Sadly, this was just a momentary respite in a spiral of increasing conflict.

In 66 CE a violent peasant protest met with such surprising success that the Roman garrison was expelled from the country. The peasant rebel leaders found themselves in control of the country. The Jews repulsed a Roman invasion from Syria. The great Jewish revolt had begun—not through any organized plan but as a result of escalating political violence, intensified Jewish dreams of freedom, and by the accident of success.

Unprepared for their early success, the rebel leaders set about organizing the country for the Roman response. The official leaders of the Jews in Jerusalem tried to take control of the rebellion. The Jerusalem leaders dispatched Josephus to be general of Galilee, the key region since the Roman invasion would come from the north. Josephus was not able to gain more than nominal control over the rebel bands with their local leaders. The Great Rebellion was not only a revolt against Rome, but also a rejection by the masses of the "tainted" Jewish self-government. Before the war was over the rebels killed many Jewish aristocrats in a reign of terror.

Three Roman legions—regular armies which fought the empire's foreign wars—entered Galilee. Their commander in chief was Vespasian, a most capable general. The rebels soon lost their strongholds, and Josephus went over to the Romans. He became Vespasian's advisor on Jewish affairs. Josephus was not exactly a traitor, though he has been portrayed in this light. Seeing that the war would be lost, Josephus wanted to win the peace that would follow. This, at any rate, was his self-justification.

The remnants of the rebel army fled to Jerusalem, where they were joined by all who wished to fight the Romans. Three rebel armies from Galilee took over the city—one in the citadel, one in the Temple, and one on the city walls. The terrified people of Jerusalem wanted to surrender the city to the Romans. To make them desperate enough to fight, one of the rebel armies burned all of Jerusalem's food stores, which may have sufficed for a decade under siege.

Vespasian's army surrounded the city for two years. The rebel groups in the city exhausted themselves with fighting against one another. In March of the year 70 there were no more live sheep in Jerusalem, and the Temple sacrifices ended. In the spring and summer of 70 the Romans breached the walls and conquered the various sections of the city. They massacred the inhabitants and burned down every home and public building. In July the Romans took the Temple Mount and burned down the Temple. (Jewish tradition says this happened on the 9th day of the month of Av, the same date as the Babylonian destruction of the first Temple.) The Romans took the stones from the Temple structure and tossed them into the valley below, expending enormous labor to destroy every trace of this symbol of Jewish sovereignty.

The year 69 was the "Year of the Four Emperors" in Roman history. One Roman general toppled another in the dynastic battles that followed the death of Nero. Vespasian went to Rome to take the crown, leaving his son Titus in charge of the Roman armies. After Titus' victory Vespasian gave him a triumphal parade through the streets of Rome and built a great arch in his honor. (The arch still stands, a site for tourists. Jews, by tradition, do not walk under it.) These were unusual honors to grant a general who had not conquered new territories or defeated external enemies of the empire, but had suppressed a mere rebellion. It shows how seriously the Romans took the threat generated by the Jewish rebellion (and also the insecurity of a usurper to the throne who lacked noble blood).

The Roman armies took a few years to mop up the rebels. The last holdout was a group of Sicarii on top of Masada, King Herod's old fortress on the shores of the Dead Sea (70–73). The Romans took two years to build an earthen ramp up the mountainside, using Jewish slaves. They brought a siege engine up the ramp and attacked the walls, burning the gate. Before the Romans could storm the fortress all the defenders, with their wives and children, committed suicide. They preferred death in freedom over slavery to Rome. The ruins of Masada are today a favorite archeological site for visitors to Israel. One can still see the Roman encampment, the earthen ramp, the magnificent palace of Herod, and the modifications made by the Zealots who cared nothing for luxury but needed simple living quarters and Jewish ritual spaces. Masada, as the last stronghold of Jewish independence in antiquity, is a symbol of national significance to modern Israelis.

The Great Revolt of 66–70, Evaluation and Aftermath

How could the Jews have hoped to win a rebellion against Rome at the height of her power? They may have held an apocalyptic hope that God would intervene to save them if they showed faith by initiating a rebellion. They may have hoped that their many fellow Jews in Babylon would gain them the assistance of the Parthian (neo-Persian) empire. The rebel leaders may have hoped to inspire a general revolt with the assistance of Jews throughout the empire. As it happened, Jews outside the land of Israel offered no assistance to the rebels. The rebels may have been inspired by the example of Judah Maccabee, misreading the message and meaning of Jewish history. Most likely the rebellion simply happened, one event snowballing into another until an avalanche swept everything away. In retrospect it is easy to see that the rebellion was a colossal mistake, one that almost destroyed Judaism. The Jews have been few and relatively powerless ever since the failure of the Great Revolt, right up to our own day. Had the Jews been more patient, more tolerant of their sufferings, history may have turned out differently—but that, of course, is useless speculation. At any rate, the Jews rejected fiercely and reject to this day any suggestion that their defeat in the Great Revolt represents the rejection of the Jews by God. The Jews saw the destruction of the Temple as the chastisement visited upon the beloved children by a concerned Father. From our modern perspective we may say of the rebellion, as one of Napoleon's generals is reported to have said after a defeat: "It was worse than a sin—it was a mistake."

Judaism Goes On—Pharisees and Christians

The Romans were brutal and oppressive but they were not anti-Semites. Vespasian and Titus in particular were kindly disposed toward the Jews. Titus endured criticism to maintain a romance with Berenice, the famed beautiful sister of King Agrippa II of Galilee. Compared with Rome's infamous suppression of rebellious nations, they let off the Jews with a mere hand-slap. After the initial massacres and the imposition of a punitive tax, the *fiscus Judeaus*, the Romans sought a return to normality. They placed Judea under the close supervision of the Syrian legate.

Having handled matters of administration and public order, the Romans needed someone to handle internal Jewish affairs. They turned to Yohanan ben Zakkai, a leading scholar of the School of

Hillel, a branch of the Pharisees. Jewish legend says that Yohanan slipped out of Jerusalem during the siege, feigning death and his own funeral to get past the Zealot guards. He was the first to greet Vespasian as emperor. (Josephus claims this honor for himself.) As a reward Vespasian granted him a wish. He requested the preservation of the lives of the Sages, particularly the family of Gamaliel, the hereditary leaders of the Sanhedrin. He requested the right to reestablish the Sanhedrin under Pharisaic rule in the village of Yavneh. All of this was granted.

The legendary meeting is unlikely, but Vespasian had good reason to leave Yohanan ben Zakkai and the Hillelite Pharisees in charge of Jewish affairs. The Pharisees were untainted by collaboration with the Romans, and so they enjoyed popular favor as leaders. They had opposed the rebellion, which made them acceptable to Rome. Now the Pharisees ruled the Jews. Beginning with the new Sanhedrin at Yavneh after the year 70, the priestly hegemony over Judaism faded and the newly evolving rabbis set the direction of Judaism. (The actual process may have taken decades, even centuries, until rabbinic leadership was complete.)

Judaism, like all ancient religions, was constructed around sacrifice to God. The rabbis in Yavneh completely reformed Judaism around the Pharisaic program of symbolic priestly living, which did not require sacrifice. This reform, more than the ancient priestly customs reflected in the Hebrew scriptures, created the Judaism we know today. That is the reason that historians today call this the era of early Judaism, parallel to early Christianity.

Sectarianism ended with the destruction of the Temple. Most sects of Judaism could not endure the cessation of sacrifice. The revolutionary sectarians had been killed off by the Romans. Two sects survived the Great Rebellion intact—the Pharisees and the Christians. Fleeing Jerusalem, the Jewish Christians passed the rebellion in Antioch. They avoided the general slaughter, though their avoidance of the common fate may have been one significant wedge in the break between Judaism and Christianity.

A historian may not comment on the will of God in the preservation of Judaism and Christianity. Regardless of divine initiative, there were two historical causes for the success of the Pharisees and the Christians in surviving the war. These were: (a) the symbolization of sacrifice, which enabled these sects to serve God without the Temple; and (b) the benign neglect of the Romans, who tolerated sects that did not join the rebellion.

Rabbinic Modifications of Judaism

The Sanhedrin at Yavneh thoroughly reformed Jewish practice. Jews were now to serve God through sacred rituals in home and synagogue and through obedience to the law of the Torah, as decided by the rabbis. Table fellowship at home, following the kosher laws of ritual purity, became a substitute for sacrifice, along with liturgical worship and study of sacred scripture.

Yohanan ben Zakkai died, and Gamaliel II succeeded him. He was the grandson of Gamaliel I, who is mentioned in the book of Acts as the Sanhedrin leader who benignly recommended against active suppression of the Christian sect. Gamaliel I was the father of Simeon, mentioned by Josephus as an aristocrat in the Sanhedrin and a leading Pharisee. The Sanhedrin continued for centuries under the hereditary leadership of Gamaliel's descendants, who in turn claimed descent from Hillel, the greatest early Pharisee.

With sects fading away, rabbinic Judaism and Christianity grew. The religion of the rabbis became the religion of the entire Jewish people, while Christianity moved away from its Jewish origins to become the religion of the Roman world.

6

Jewish Religion in the First Century

What We Mean by "Religion"

In modern America when we speak of a "religion" we mean a set of beliefs and a set of voluntary institutions and rituals that teach and reinforce those beliefs. Religion of this sort did not exist in ancient Judaism. First century Judaism consisted of "the ways of our ancestors"—that is, doing things in the traditional way. The service of God was continuous with the agricultural and pastoral cycle of the land of Israel; the festivals and sacrificial offerings corresponded to planting and harvest and the birthing of domestic animals. The best available analogy for moderns may be the "Way" of the American Plains Indian. The religion of the Plains Indian was in no way separate from the buffalo hunt and the planting of corn and tobacco; the religion and the way of life are inconceivable without each other. Judaism also was a "Way." The terms *Torah* and *halakha*, too often misunderstood as a dry and arid law divorced from living reality, really mean, respectively, "Instruction" and "Way," inseparable from the life of the Jew. The earliest Christians similarly called their religion *The Way*—the Way of Christ.

On the other hand, first century Judaism was in some respects on its way to becoming a "religion." Expanded Jewish settlement and social change removed Jewish rites from their original life-setting. This forced Jews, especially the learned elite, to self-consciously ask themselves "what must we do to serve God?" Many Jewish practices came to seem symbolic and purely spiritual now that they were observed as distinct from peasant life in Judea. This led to a "religion" of doctrines and practices, though not in the modern sense. The service of God was never separate from daily living in early Judaism. The Jew believed himself or herself to be serving God at home, in the fields, and in the market square as much as in the synagogue, the schoolhouse or the Jerusalem Temple.

God

The unity of God is the central idea of first century Judaism. Jews in this period were avid monotheists. They avoided all physical representations of the divine, all foreign worship, all "other" gods. Jews would not perform public rites associated with pagan worship, even if not required to take the gods themselves seriously. The biblical prophets constantly complained about Israelite backsliding into idol worship. This was never an issue in Second Temple Judaism. Jews were prepared to lay down their lives rather than serve idols. They opposed syncretism—that is, they refused to identify Jewish worship with other peoples' worship of their gods. Early in the Second Temple period Jews began the custom, universally observed from then until now, of reciting twice a day the verse from Deuteronomy, chapter 6: "Hear, O Israel, Adonai is our God, Adonai is One." Jews acknowledged this recitation as the essential doxology (faith statement) of Judaism.

Although Jews were determinedly monotheistic, they were willing to allow for the existence of subordinate powers in heaven. Perhaps inevitably, the enormous space between lowly earth and a transcendent God in the highest heaven was filled with a profusion of angels. The angels were immortal creatures generated by God at the beginning of creation for service and praise. In most of the Hebrew scriptures angels are amorphous beings. Only in the latter biblical books do we find angels with names, character traits and specific roles to play, angels like Michael, Gabriel and of course Satan. Named angels are a unique creation of Second Temple Judaism, an innovation that has persisted to this day in Judaism and Christianity. Viewed historically, the angels resemble the ancient pantheon, the council of the gods, converted now by monotheism into subordinate heavenly beings. In another way we may say that the angels are the heavenly equivalent of government on earth, which in the Roman Empire contained multiple layers of bureaucracy.

There was also room in Jewish belief for the demonic. Jews had no clearly defined notion of hell, but many believed that evil demons inhabited the earth and presented constant danger to human beings. Some sects of Jews, especially the apocalyptically oriented, believed in fallen angels and evil spiritual forces who opposed God. There were many variations on the belief in the demonic and the forces of evil.

Satan

Satan is the first named angel to appear in biblical literature. He represents a special case in the development of angelology. Satan appears in the book of Job and some of the last books of prophets, all composed in the Persian period (ca. 500–350 BCE). The Persians believed in two gods, a god of good and a god of evil. The good god ruled over the heavenly world; the evil god created and ruled over the earth. This dualistic religion in its various forms is given the name "Gnosticism" by scholars of religion.

Gnosis is "knowing," the secret knowledge that removes the initiated believer from the material power of evil and elevates him into the spiritual world of goodness and blessing. In the Gnostic faith the material world and the spiritual world, the human body and the human soul, are hostile and opposed to one another.

Gnostic beliefs exerted a powerful pull on Jews, yet Judaism could not tolerate the belief in two powers rather than one. Monotheistic Jews converted the evil god of Gnosticism into Satan, literally the "Prosecuting Attorney." Satan is a loyal servant of God whose task is, as in the book of Job, to prosecute humans for their sins in the divine court of justice. In some forms of Judaism the Gnostic element became stronger. Satan became the Devil, a fallen angel who opposes God and tries to seduce the world into evil. The rabbis actively opposed Gnosticism. Many early Christians were Gnostics, but ultimately the church, too, declared Gnosticism a heresy. Nevertheless, Gnostic beliefs continue to exert an influence in Western religion to this very day. They were a greater force in the first century. Not every Jew saw Gnosticism as a threat. Some sects saw as perfectly Jewish the belief in the heavenly combat between God and Satan—the forces of good and evil, light and darkness. The Devil plays no role in the Hebrew scriptures but a large role in the New Testament. The New Testament was written in a time when Gnosticism was a major religious force in the Jewish world.

Logos

The Greeks served multiple gods, but Greek philosophers had a higher conception of a single divinity, as described by the philosophers Plato and Aristotle. Greek philosophical monotheism was radically different from Jewish monotheism. For one thing, the Greek philosophers still served all the gods and their statues in public life. More significantly, the one God of Greek philosophy did not create the world and demonstrated no concern for it. The God of Israel was a creator who lovingly watched over the creation, even every bird and flower and blade of grass. The God of Israel spoke to humankind and demanded obedience leading to love, justice and goodness. The "providence" of God—God's loving concern for every person—is a major and very Jewish theme of Jesus' preaching.

One branch of Greek philosophy suggested that the unmoved God of the philosophers related to the lowly earth through an intermediary, the "logos." Logos, literally "word," contains the mind and intention of divinity and sends these flowing down to earth. Jewish sages associated this idea with the pre-existent "Wisdom," mentioned in the book of Proverbs. And what could be Wisdom if not Torah, the word of God? So, the sages concluded that there was a heavenly Torah, the logos of the world.[8] Similarly, the gospel of John calls Christ the logos.

Worship

The service of God was called Avodah. Worship is an inadequate translation. Avodah means to do divine labor, to be literally a servant of God. This was accomplished through the sacrifices that were offered in the Jerusalem Temple. Every ancient religion in the Roman Empire and the Near East had a sacrificial cult; the Jews were no exception. Sacrifice was performed by a special caste of Jews, the priests. To be a priest one had to be born into the priesthood, and careful genealogies were maintained. The priests were the natural aristocrats of the Jewish people. They did not have to work the land for a living; they ate the sacrificial offerings of the Jewish people, as prescribed in the Torah. Ordinary Jews were allowed to approach only as far as the outer edge of the Temple courtyard. The priests took the sacrificial offerings of the Jews, slaughtered them and offered the parts to be burnt on the altar. Inside the Temple they tended the incense altar, the table of show-bread, and the menorah—the seven branched oil lamp. The inner room of the Temple, the Holy of Holies, was empty. It was the place where the invisible God of Israel resided on earth.[9] The high priest, the ruler of the Jewish people, performed the most important sacred functions himself. Lower priests vied for the right to perform any of the multiple daily tasks of the Temple service. It was an honor even to set the wicks in the lamp or shovel the ashes from the altar. All was done in the prescribed way, as necessary to maintain the constancy of Israel's relationship with God. A lower sacred caste, the Levites, performed secondary service like singing in the Temple choir and maintaining a guard at the gates.

Each day, morning and afternoon, the priests sacrificed a sheep in the name of the entire Jewish people. This animal was purchased from the half-shekel, an annual Temple tax paid voluntarily by every Jew in the world. This gave every Jew an equal share in the offerings, even those who lived in distant lands who could not come to observe the worship. There was also a daily sacrifice on behalf of the emperor. On Sabbath and holidays there was an extra morning sacrifice, and each holiday had its own sacrifices. On Sukkot, the harvest festival, there was a plentiful offering of bulls, rams, lambs and goats. Every Jew who could come to Jerusalem for Passover brought a lamb to be slaughtered at the Temple. There were offerings of grain, wine and oil as well. After the daily morning sacrifice Jews could bring individual offerings as atonement for sin, for special rites, or simply in gratitude to God. The poor could substitute inexpensive pigeons or doves for lambs.

On some level Jews were aware that their concept of a transcendent, single universal God obviated the need for sacrifice. Pagans sacrificed to literally feed the gods, who needed to eat. Sacrifices were believed to propitiate the capricious rulers of heaven. The gods would punish humans who did not supply them with their needs, but would favor those who fulfilled their desires. Jews believed that the God of Israel needed no food. God justly distributed reward and punishment based on human obedience to God's universal will as expressed in the Torah. Nevertheless, as children of the ancient world in which they lived, Second Temple Jews could not imagine divine service without sacrifice. The daily offerings confirmed the constancy of the relationship between God and God's people, Israel.

Sacrifice was universal, but first century Jews were unique in the establishment of daily liturgical prayer. (Liturgical meaning, following a set repetitive pattern.) The service of daily prayer was an innovation, a contribution of first century Judaism to the religious life of the western world.

Prayer

In the First Temple era there was no regular prayer service. Prayer was an accompaniment to sacrifice. Jews prayed spontaneously on occasions of great trouble or great joy. (See Hannah's prayer in I

Samuel ch. 1, and King Solomon's prayer at the dedication of the
Temple in I Kings ch. 8). The biblical term for prayer was "lifting up the
hands," the physical posture of prayer. The sages called prayer
"Tefilah." This word comes from a root meaning "to make an account
of oneself."

We do not know the origins of liturgical prayer. It may have
begun in the Exile in Babylon, where Jews could not offer sacrifice. The
book of Daniel (6:11), composed just before the revolt of the
Maccabees, depicts Daniel among the exiles in Babylon, piously
praying toward Jerusalem three times a day. The reference in Daniel
shows us that the Jewish custom of regular daily prayer must have been
well established by the time of the Maccabees. Jews did not pray in
a synagogue, but wherever they stood when the time for prayer
approached. The synagogue in the time of Jesus was for scripture study,
preaching and teaching, and public assemblies; only later in the first
century did it begin to take on the function of a house of prayer.

If prayer was well established by the first century, the words of
Jewish prayer were still in a state of development. Judaism has two
liturgies, the Shema and the Tefilah. The liturgy of the Shema centers
on the paragraph in Deuteronomy 6 which begins, "Hear, O Israel,
Adonai is your God, Adonai is One. You shall love Adonai your God
with all your heart, with all your soul, and with all your might...." The
priests recited this liturgy in the Temple along with the morning
sacrifice. It underwent further development after the Temple was
destroyed. Jews say it every morning and evening. The second liturgy,
the Amidah, was established after the destruction as a substitute for
sacrifice, though it may have had earlier roots. It contains nineteen
prayers, constructed in the pattern of a loyal subject approaching a
great king with a list of supplications. According to rabbinic legend the
two liturgies were composed by the Men of the Great Assembly, a
mythical council that existed early in the Second Temple era.
Historians believe the themes of Jewish prayer were developed by the
first century, but the wording underwent continuous development for
a long time after that.

Prayers of the Masters

There were no books of daily prayer in Jesus' time. The leaders of
prayer spoke in their own words, as the spirit moved them. Great
teachers and leaders composed short set prayers expressing their own
concept of ideal piety toward God. Many such prayers are recorded in

the Talmud (Berakhot 17). One, the prayer of Mar bar Ravina, is so popular with Jews that today it is printed in every prayer book.

It was natural for Jesus' disciples to ask him for his prayer, so they could recite the prayer of the Master. Jesus' response, the Lord's Prayer, expresses themes typical of Jewish piety in the first century: sanctifying God's name, acknowledging God's rule, requesting forgiveness of sins, faithfully presenting our simple needs before the gracious provider. There is no Christology in this prayer, a matter of historical significance. Jews do not recite the Lord's Prayer because of its Christian associations, but the content alone is very Jewish.

The Form of Benediction

The earliest liturgical form of Jewish prayer, well established by the time of Jesus, was the form of benediction. Every Jewish blessing began with these (six) words (in Hebrew): "Blessed are You, Adonai our God, ruler of the universe...." So established was this form that in rabbinic literature various blessings were identified only by their endings. The opening was so well known it did not require mention.

The Synagogue

Jewish literature before the revolt of the Maccabees does not mention the synagogue. By the time of the Great Revolt, Jerusalem alone contained over a hundred. We can see that the synagogue underwent an explosive development. After the destruction of the Temple the synagogue evolved into the Jewish house of prayer, study and assembly. The church and the mosque are Christian and Moslem names for this Jewish innovation, the house of prayer.

The origins of the synagogue are shrouded in mystery. The primary function of the first century synagogue was for a scholar to read scripture and explain its meaning to the public. The Torah reading evolved into a regular cycle of Sabbath and festival scriptural readings from the Torah and Prophets. This would be the type of synagogue in which Jesus read from scripture, the synagogue in which Paul preached. Incidentally, Jesus' visit to his hometown is the first instance in recorded history of the custom of Haftarah—reading a selection from the Prophets that relates to the weekly Torah portion.

In the Diaspora the synagogue served as an assembly hall in which the Jewish community would gather to conduct their own affairs. The synagogue also served as a hostel for Jewish travelers.

Sabbath Observance

Sabbath observance was an outstanding aspect of Jewish religion, eliciting comment by many Gentile writers of the era. Jews were extremely proud of their Sabbath, and noted that many non-Jews observed the day in imitation of Jewish practice. Jews refrained from all work on the Sabbath, from sundown Friday until sundown Saturday. They did not travel about, carry items abroad, or light fires. Jews did not fight, except in direct defense of life, although this law gave great military advantage to their enemies. Jews did no labor and did not buy and sell, but the exact details of Sabbath rest probably varied according to many factors, including local and family custom. Sects had their own laws of Sabbath rest which they carefully observed. Far from objecting to the stringencies of Sabbath law, many Jewish sects added new ones. The Essenes did not defecate on the Sabbath! The laws of the Pharisees were stringent in some ways, and in other ways represented a major liberalization. For example, the Pharisees allowed movement outside the city or town to a distance of 2,000 paces. They permitted, in fact required, the lighting of lamps on Friday before sundown so that the home would be filled with light on Sabbath eve.

There is no evidence that Jews found the Sabbath laws burdensome. On the contrary, the universal observance of the day of rest shows how dear it was to Jewish hearts. Jews were willing to lay down their lives for the right to observe the Sabbath with all of its laws, just as they were ready to give their lives rather than worship idols.

Sabbath was a day for joy. People ate their finest meal of the week and socialized with one another. Sabbath morning was spent in the synagogue, learning scripture. The Sabbath elevated the otherwise humdrum life that was the lot of ordinary people in ancient times. The Sabbath enabled people to commune with God via obedience to divine law and through the contemplation and worship made possible by the enforced leisure of the day.

Ritual Purity

Ritual purity was a significant category of ancient sacrificial Judaism. It does not play a role in modern religion, and there is, in fact, no word in English that can contain the concept. Bible translators use the terms "clean" and "unclean," though physical cleanliness is not directly relevant to ritual purity. "Pure" and "impure" are also inadequate terms. A person or thing which was *tahor*—"ritually pure"—

was suitable to enter the sacred precincts of the Temple, to approach the divine. A person or thing which was *tah-may*—"ritually impure," could not come near to God and so could not enter the Temple precinct. The rabbis later replaced the biblical terminology of tahor and tamay with their own preferred term—*kosher*.

Primary sources of impurity were eating unkosher food, contact with the carcasses of unkosher creatures, experiencing flows from the genitalia, certain skin diseases and, most severely, contact with the dead. An impure object gave second degree impurity to anything that touched it, and that could in some circumstances transmit third degree impurity to what touched it. Since everything touches everything ultimately, the attempt to remain in a state of ritual purity was a constant battle.

The primary mode of removing impurity was *mikvah*—full immersion in a body of living (unpiped) water. After immersion one bathed and washed one's clothes and waited until nightfall to be tahor. Death impurity required the performance of special rituals during a full week of purification.

In earlier ages only priests tried to remain in a state of ritual purity, since they went daily to the Temple. Ordinary Jews purified themselves only when they visited the Temple. The Temple complex was surrounded by mikvah baths so that Jews could purify themselves on the way up the Temple mount.

In the first century ritual purity became a major aspect of Jewish piety. Pietists of various sects attempted to remain in a constant state of ritual purity. Ordinary Jews may not have been sticklers on details of secondary impurity, but it seems that they, too, observed ritual purity laws. This may have been linked to the Pharisees' teaching of the universal priesthood of all Israel, though other sects were even more stringent about ritual purity. Jews in the Diaspora observed their own version of purity laws despite their distance from the Temple. Philo of Alexandria in Egypt mentions the custom of sprinkling oneself from a bowl of water after intercourse. Many Diaspora Jews washed their hands in the sea before dining.

Some Jews began to see a higher spiritual significance to ritual purity. It represented a state of nearness to God, as if one were actually present in the Temple. Since sin generates distance from God and atonement generates nearness, just like impurity and purity, there was by analogy an aspect of penitence in the act of ritual purification.

This correspondence between ritual purity and atonement was made explicit in the career of John the Baptist. We must remember that John was not a Christian but a Jew. His immersions in the Jordan River were not baptisms into faith in Christ but Jewish ritual immersions. He might better be called "John the Mikvah-man." John gave ritual immersion heightened spiritual significance. John was popular with Jews of all stripes. Even rich Jerusalemites, the representatives of the very society John had rejected by moving to the wilderness, went down to the Jordan to be immersed by John. These aristocrats also wanted a share in the spirit offered by John.

Archaeologists have discovered that first century Jews who could afford it used only stone plates and cups instead of much cheaper and more practical pottery. The reason is that stone was not susceptible to ritual impurity. Stone utensils could not be made impure by an accident such as the unintentional serving of unkosher food or the death of a mouse in the kitchen cabinet. The wealthy also had mikvahs in the basement of their own homes, often next to a bathing pool for physical cleanliness. These can be seen today in the "Burnt House" and the "Herodian Mansions" under the streets of the Jewish quarter in old Jerusalem. There were many public mikvahs for the masses.

Jesus and the early church seem to have had mixed feelings toward Jewish ritual purity. On the one hand the gospels present a consistent picture of Jesus as being unconcerned with details of ritual purity, even critical of those who placed too much emphasis on certain purity rites. On the other hand, Jesus' public career began with his immersion by John, and baptism early became a central Christian rite. It was only some decades after the crucifixion that Christianity permitted unkosher food, and then only after heated debate as recorded in the book of Acts. Had Jesus outrightly rejected the ritual purity laws there would not have been so much objection to Paul's innovation in granting Gentile Christians permission to eat unkosher food. Those modern scholars who presume that Jesus' dining with sinners demonstrates his disdain for the "outwardness," "legalism," and "unspirituality" of purity laws, presume too much. We now know that purity rites varied from group to group among first century Jews. Jesus' own practices most likely fell within the broad range of pious Jewish practice.

Circumcision

Jews circumcised the foreskin of the penis on the eighth day after the birth of a boy, as required by Torah law. The Greeks despised circumcision. Because of this, in the Hellenistic era fulfilling the law of circumcision acquired added significance as a sign of adherence to

Jewish values. Some Jews, embarrassed to be different or desiring to pass over into the Hellenistic world, had the sign of circumcision reversed through the operation of epispasm. When Paul allowed Gentile Christians to forgo circumcision and to dispense with most Jewish food laws, he removed the two major obstacles that prevented many Gentile worshipers of the God of Israel from converting to Judaism. Paul's innovation seems to have resulted in the Christian conversion of many of the Yir-ay Elohim, Gentiles who worshiped the God of Israel without conversion to Judaism.

Dress

Ancient Jewish men wore *tzitzit*, fringes, on the four corners of their skirts, in fulfillment of the Torah law. Roman styles of dress made this cumbersome. The tzitzit were transferred to the tallit, a shawl worn only during worship.

Ancient Jews also wore *tefilin*, "phylacteries," a headband containing four compartments for the placing of scriptural phrases written on parchment, and a matching armband. In the first century many Jews wore their tefilin only for morning prayer, removing them for daily work. Some Jews made a mark of piety by wearing their tefilin all day long or by wearing extra-wide tefilin. Jesus was sharply critical of such outward shows of piety. Ultimately Jewish teaching came to the same conclusion, and it became Jewish practice to remove tefilin after morning prayer. Today's tefilin are large square boxes. To imagine the discussion in Jesus' day we must realize that tefilin in that time were flat, resembling a leather version of a kerchief worn tied around the head.

We do not know whether Jews in the first century kept their heads covered or uncovered. Our sources are silent on the issue.

Financial Support of Religion

Every Jew donated the half-shekel to the Temple each year. Jewish farmers in the land of Israel owed a multitude of agricultural offerings to the Temple each year. The harmonization in Second Temple times of a variety of biblical rules of priestly offerings resulted in a great expansion of agricultural dues. These included first-fruits, firstborn animals, a tithe (one tenth) of all produce, and a second tithe to be given to the poor or consumed in Jerusalem on a rotating schedule.

Jews took great pride in the way their people voluntarily supported the Temple, giving their offerings without duress despite the heavy additional burden of Roman taxation. On the other hand, there were those among the pious elite who suspected the ordinary folk of cutting their tithes a bit short. We know of a group called *haverim* (companions) who ate only among themselves. They only ate produce that they knew beyond a doubt was properly tithed. The haverim had contempt for the *am ha'aretz*, the common folk, who were not equally cautious. Historians commonly presume that there was a close, if not well understood, relationship between haverim and Pharisees, who were known to have many laws about tithing. Jesus condemned those who seemed to him to be too concerned with tithing. Perhaps Jesus disliked their contempt for the common folk, or perhaps he thought they were taking details of observance too far.

Jews were also renowned for charitable giving. Josephus boasts that no Jew depended on outsiders for charitable support, since the Jews cared for all of their destitute and disabled brethren.

Afterlife

Most first century Jews believed devoutly in the afterlife. Every Jew desired to earn "eternity in the World to Come." The World to Come appears thousands of times in rabbinic literature but, curiously, it is never defined. Apparently the details did not matter. What mattered was that the good would achieve this eternity, while the wicked would not. The parable of the sheep and the goats in the gospel of Matthew (Matt 25:31–46) is a very Jewish perspective on the future world. One reason that Jews were so willing to lay down their lives rather than transgress the Torah is that they were not willing to forgo eternity in the World to Come for the sake of a few more years or a few creature comforts in this world.

> Seven classes of people will stand before the Blessed Holy One in the Hereafter. Which is the highest of them to receive the presence of the Shekinah? It is the class of the upright, as it is said (Ps. 11:7): "The upright shall behold their face," referring to the Shekinah and her retinue.
>
> (Midrash Psalms ad loc.)

> Rabbi Jonathan said: Every prophet prophesied only for the days of the Messiah, but as for the World to Come, no eye has seen what God has prepared for those who wait for Him.
>
> (Talmud Berakhot 34b)

Repentance: Personal and Communal Religiosity

The heart of biblical Judaism was the covenant relationship between God and the people, Israel. The service of God was performed by the nation as a whole. The high priest offered the daily sacrifice. He offered the atonement sacrifices of Yom Kippur on behalf of the nation as a whole, bringing down divine forgiveness upon every Jew. The Jews believed that they received reward as a people when their service was acceptable, and suffered as a group when they disobeyed God.

In late Second Temple Judaism there was a growing awareness of the importance of individual relationship with God. The individual could draw closer to God or withdraw to distance from God, independent of the communal covenant. Relationship with God required more than the public performance of the rites which identified one with the Jewish community (sacrifice, Sabbath rest, purity immersion). It also required an inner turning to God, a devotion that was not visible to the community but made the worshiper known before God.

This growing personalism is illustrated by the doctrine of *teshuvah*—"repentance." The ideal of repentance is that by regretting and repudiating one's past evil deeds one could find divine forgiveness. Change of heart generated change in one's relationship with God. The doctrine of repentance, so vital to first century Judaism, is also central to Christianity. It lies at the heart of the Christian sacrament of reconciliation.

The doctrine of repentance is unknown in the earlier layers of biblical writing. There, reward and punishment is only communal and trans-generational. Repentance appears forcefully in the teachings of Ezekiel, early in the Babylonian Exile. Ezekiel teaches (ch. 18) that the individual who repents does not suffer for the evil deeds of the ancestors, nor even for one's own former evil deeds. There is no historical determinism; everything depends upon the inner turning of the will toward God, a turning which is always received with love, grace and forgiveness. "It is not the death of sinners God wants," says Ezekiel, "but that they should change their ways, and live" (18:32).

Not every sect of first century Judaism accepted the personalism and interiority (what we moderns would call "spirituality") of the doctrine of repentance. Certain apocalyptic groups, such as the authors of the Dead Sea Scrolls, saw the world divided between "the Elect" and "the Wicked," the forces of Light and the forces of Darkness. Everyone belongs to one group or the other. The course of history is predetermined and inevitable. God would soon act in the world to punish the forces of evil. A call to repentance, to change the course of the future, is virtually absent.

Other sects, most notably the Pharisees, strongly emphasized the doctrine of repentance. To Pharisees, especially of the School of Hillel, the inner turning of the heart is of utmost importance. Performance of the law was necessary, but for many laws the mere observance did not fulfill the divine will. The law had to be fulfilled with *kavannah*—"intention," "directedness," "will." Kavannah means both consciousness that one is fulfilling the will of God in observing the law, and consciousness of the higher purpose of the law. Kavannah means fulfilling the law with all of one's will, without divided thoughts.

Jesus' teaching on repentance is similar to that of the Pharisees. The essence of Jesus' teaching is "Repent, for the kingdom of God is at hand!" Jesus, like the Pharisees, called the Jews to repentance, but his message had a tone of special urgency because he taught that there was not much time left. God's rule over the world was about to come, and if one did not repent fully and immediately one might not have another chance. One must change one's whole life immediately with no regard to future consequence, turning wholeheartedly to God. Jesus' apocalypticism was non-deterministic; every individual, no matter how evil up to the present moment, could still change sides and be on God's side when the judgment comes. The gospels highlight this point in Jesus' outreach to tax collectors and prostitutes, the very symbols of the evil man and woman in need of transformation.

Jesus' emphasis on kavannah is clear in many teachings attributed to him—the prohibition of anger and lust, the teaching that one should pray and fast privately rather than before the crowd, the teaching that what comes out of a person is more important than what goes in. Without judging the historical validity of each attribution, there is a consistency in these teachings that is compatible with Jesus' central message of urgent repentance.

Contrary to the claims of some New Testament scholars, Jesus was not criticizing nor invalidating the law. He did not oppose the fulfillment of the commandments of the Torah. In saying that what comes out is more important, Jesus was not invalidating the laws of ritual purity, any more than Jesus was invalidating the prohibition of murder in teaching against anger. The consistent point of Jesus' message is that the outward observance of the law should be matched by an inner turning to God. The law is divine service only when fulfilled with kavannah.

The Jewish doctrine of repentance presumes that God is loving, gracious and forgiving. Jesus taught that love is the central commandment—love of God and love of one's fellow. This teaching of Jesus is consistent with the Judaism of his time. Jesus' teaching that God who feeds the birds and clothes the flowers will surely respond to human prayer, an exquisite sentiment, was typical of the first century Jewish belief in a providential God. In general, Jesus' teachings about God's love and the importance of human love find many parallels in rabbinic teachings on the subject. Hillel the Elder and Rabbi Akiva, to name two of the most prominent exemplars of rabbinic ethics, are also said to have identified "love your neighbor!" as the chief commandment.

It is entirely inconsistent with the teaching of love to make invidious comparisons. Those who love do not say "my love is better than your love!"—that is the very opposite of love! Some scholars have suggested that historical study reveals a new, radical teaching of love and divine intimacy in Jesus' preaching. This is a new form of the old anti-Jewish doctrine of supercessionism, the teaching that Christianity came into the world to replace an inferior Judaism. Jesus taught love and the rabbis taught love. Love does not admit of invidious comparison.

Law and Ethics

Jews applied the teachings of the Torah to every area of human life—not only the cultic and ritual service of God, but also agriculture, business, family relations, sexuality, the intellect, personal relationships, and more. Jews perceived the extension of Torah law into every realm of life and being as a divine benefit, not a burden. God had graced the Jews with a clearly defined way of living, one that provided multiple opportunities for divine service. In the words of a later sage, "Rabbi Hananiah ben Akashya said: The Blessed Holy One was pleased to make Israel worthy, therefore God gave them a copious and extensive Torah, as it is said (Is 62:21) `It pleased Adonai for the sake of His righteousness (i.e., to justify the righteous ones) to make the Torah great and glorious'" (Mishnah Makkot 3:16).

There is no truth in the accusation of some anti-Jewish historical scholars that the laws of the Pharisees are dry, devoid of spirit and the breath of life. Judaism was not mere "legalism"; the law at the center of Judaism was a reflection of the life and the spiritual concerns of the people. There must have been some individuals, then as always, who paid attention to the outward forms of religion without comprehending the higher meaning. These individuals were the subjects of Jesus' criticism. There were many others who saw observance and performance as a reflection of the inner relationship with God. They fulfilled the spirit of the law as they fulfilled the law. They understood the difference between what was critical and what was peripheral.

First century Jews did not distinguish between ethical requirements of the law and cultic requirements. They attempted to fulfill them all. While doing so they strived to treat others with love, charity and concern. Many rabbinic statements show that the Jewish sages were aware of higher principles that must animate the law. According to the sayings attributed to the sages by the Talmud, these higher principles included faith, the equality of humankind as children of Adam, justice and mercy, and love for one's neighbor.

7

The Festivals

The Three Festivals

The Torah commands three festivals in the year. These are Pesah (Passover) in the spring, Shavuot (Pentecost, Feast of Weeks) on the fiftieth day after Passover, and Sukkot (Tabernacles, Feast of Booths) in the fall. Many Christian symbols, rites and holy days are drawn from the Jewish festivals observed by Jesus.

The festivals are called the *Shalosh Regalim*—the Three Pilgrimages. On these three occasions of the year the Torah commands every Jew in the land of Israel to go up to the Temple in Jerusalem, bearing the appropriate agricultural offerings for sacrifice. In Jesus' time many of the Judean Jews went up for every festival. Many went at least on Pesah. Jews in Galilee and Syria went as often as they could. Jews from distant lands attempted to make pilgrimage to the Temple at least once in their lives, usually for Passover. The population of Jerusalem multiplied greatly on these occasions. The craftspeople and shopkeepers of the city depended on the trade of pilgrims for their livelihood, keeping the city prosperous. Jerusalem was not on any trade routes and had no major industry; her significance (even to this day) was as a sacred center.

Pilgrimage and the Life of Jesus

How often did Jesus go up to the Temple? Sources disagree. The book of Luke suggests that Jesus' family went regularly to the Temple. The gospel of John gives Jesus a preaching career of two or three years during which he attended the Temple on several occasions for Passover and Sukkot. The passion story in the synoptic gospels gives the distinct impression that Jesus went to the Temple only once in his life, the

Passover of his crucifixion. There is much to support this view. If Jesus had been to the Temple before then it is difficult to imagine his outrage at the animal dealers and the moneychangers. He would have come to expect this scene. We rather get the impression that Jesus was disappointed in what he found when he came to the Temple. It did not live up to his image of his people's holiest shrine.

The Three Festivals in the Jerusalem Temple

The cultic rituals were a major aspect of the festivals. Sacrifice kept Israel close to God. More sacrifices meant more intimacy with the divine. The extra sacrifices with their attendant rituals made festivals special.

On Pesah each family group or group of men (we do not know how many women and children participated) brought a lamb or goat to sacrifice in the Temple on the eve of the holiday. The Jews then went out into the courtyards of the city to roast the lamb over an open fire. As the Jews ate the lamb with unleavened bread and bitter herbs they retold the story of the Exodus from Egypt.

Shavuot, the Feast of Weeks, was the celebration of the grain harvest and the firstfruits. Farmers came in procession. They brought baskets of grain and firstfruits as offerings. As each pilgrim handed his basket to the priest he recited a litany thanking God for bringing the Jews out of Egyptian slavery into this land of plenty.

Passover had become the most popular holiday, but Sukkot was the main Temple observance. The Mishnah calls it *HeHag*, "The Festival"—that is, the festival par excellence. During the eight days of the Sukkot festival the priests sacrificed seventy animals, each with its accompaniment of grain mixed with oil and a wine libation. On Sukkot the Jews came to Jerusalem with palm branches twined with willows and myrtles, and carrying an etrog (a citrus fruit resembling a large lemon). The people waved these in celebration as they prayed *Hoshiana* (Hosanna!) meaning, "God save us." After the ceremony parents gave the etrog to the children to eat. On one infamous occasion the Jews were unhappy with the religious performance of the royal high priest Alexander Yannai. They pelted him with etrogs. He unleashed his mercenary guard on the people, killing thousands of worshipers. Such incidents were not usual, but crowd feelings could run high at any festival. The Romans always brought soldiers into Jerusalem to control the mob. The governor came up from Caesarea to keep an eye on things.

Sukkot, the main harvest festival, took place in the fall at the beginning of the rainy season. A highlight of the festival was the water-drawing ceremony. The priests drew a pitcher of water from the Pool of Siloam, Jerusalem's ancient spring, and passed it by a "fire brigade" of priests up to the altar for a libation. This ceremony was followed by great rejoicing that lasted all night until dawn. The purpose of these rituals, including the Hosanna's, was the prayer to God for abundant rain. Without rain the land would know drought and there would be much suffering, even mass starvation. Sukkot was a time of nervous anticipation as well as joy in the harvest.

Two holy days preceded Sukkot. The first day of the month was Rosh Hashanah, the New Year. The tenth day of the month was Yom Kippur, the Day of Atonement. This was the busiest day of the year for the high priest. He performed multiple sacrifices and rituals to acquire forgiveness of sins for himself, all the priests, and the entire household of Israel. Thanks to the high priestly rite on Yom Kippur, the Jews would enter Sukkot free of sins that might impair the prayers for rain and plentiful harvest.

The Spiritual Meaning of the Festivals

In the time of Jesus the spiritual significance of the festivals was outstripping the agricultural celebration. The Torah tells us the spiritual meaning of the Passover. The Passover is a reminder of the Exodus from Egypt. In observing the Passover, Jews acknowledge God as the redeemer.

Shavuot (Pentecost) has only an agricultural significance in the Torah. Later Jews identified Shavuot as the date that God spoke to Israel at Mount Sinai. The Torah says that the revelation occurred in the third month after the Exodus, and Shavuot falls in the third month (the 6th day, by rabbinic calculation). The festival of Shavuot became the day for Jews to acknowledge God as revealer, as "Giver of the Torah."

Sukkot was the most agricultural holiday, and its connection to the archetypes of Jewish sacred history is weaker than for the other two festivals. The sages associated Sukkot with the forty years of wandering in the desert. On Sukkot they praised God as creator of the universe. This association probably dates back to early antiquity. We know that other ancient Near Eastern religions had a creation festival in the fall.

Between them the three festivals proclaimed three messages through rite, celebration and re-experience. God created the world;

God gave a teaching to the Jews which leads to earthly perfection and personal salvation; in the end God will redeem the Jews and the world. This triple acknowledgment of God as creator, revealer and redeemer is the essential theology of first century Judaism. Jews learned of God's deeds through their celebration of the festivals.

Festivals without the Temple

After the crucifixion of Jesus, but before the composition of the gospels, the Romans destroyed the Temple. The festivals then evolved into something new and yet not new, based on the growing spiritual interpretation. Passover was observed through the ritual meal, without sacrificial lamb. The new emphasis was on telling the story of the Exodus and relating it to the present and future age. God who redeemed Israel from Egypt still redeems and someday will redeem the Jewish people for good. On Shavuot Jews celebrated the giving of the Torah. Shavuot lacked non-sacrificial rites, a difficulty which placed Shavuot in the second tier of Jewish celebration when sacrifices ended. On Sukkot Jews continued to build harvest booths and to wave the palm branch with the willow, myrtle and etrog. The prayers for salvation once recited around the Temple altar were now recited around the reading table of the synagogue. After the destruction of the Temple, Sukkot became less significant than the preceding holy days of Rosh Hashanah (New Year) and Yom Kippur (Day of Atonement). The priestly atonement rituals of the Temple evolved into a private rite of intense introspection, prayer and confession designed to elicit personal repentance. Atonement was still communal to some extent. The confessional prayers of the synagogue liturgy are in the plural, recited for the Jewish people as a whole. But Rosh Hashanah and Yom Kippur became the most individual and personal of Jewish holidays, relating to the psyche and one's personal relationship with God rather than to the events of Jewish history.

Christianity Adopts the Festivals

Early Christian documents show how Christians appropriated the spiritual message of the festivals and reinterpreted them using Christian symbols. This is a point of connection between early Judaism and early Christianity. The resemblance between Christian and Jewish holiday celebrations, rooted in common origins, persists to this very day. Christians made Passover into Easter, the Christian celebration of Christ as redeemer. Christians adopted Pentecost, the celebration of divine revelation, as the day of the descent of the Holy Spirit into the congregation of Christian believers.

We note that Christianity did not adopt Sukkot nor its adjuncts, Rosh Hashanah and Yom Kippur. Sukkot is the only sacred season found in the Torah that was not adopted by the Christian church. It is interesting to speculate why this may be so.

One result of the elimination of Sukkot from Christian observance is that a Sukkot story about Jesus is turned into a Passover story in the gospels. We are told (Matt 21:8-9, Mk 11:8-10, Lk 19:37-38 with differences) that as Jesus entered Jerusalem for the Passover his followers greeting him with palm branches, praying Hosannah. It is very unlikely that Jesus' followers, in their joy at seeing his entry into Jerusalem, decided to celebrate by observing Sukkot on the eve of Passover. This gospel story may be a retelling of an earlier Sukkot story about Jesus. Or, it may represent an attempt to draw the symbolism of Sukkot into Christian observance. If this was the intent it was successful, since Christians celebrate with palms on Palm Sunday before Easter.

The Passover Meal and the Eucharist

The seder, the Passover meal, became the focus of Jewish Passover observance after the destruction of the Temple. Even before the destruction the seder[10] had grown to such importance that it probably overshadowed the Passover sacrifice in religious significance. There is evidence that this was so in the time of Jesus, three decades before the destruction. When Jesus came to Jerusalem for Passover he left the animal sacrifice to a few unnamed disciples. Jesus himself went to the room in the garden of Gethsemane to prepare the seder. This suggests that in the time of Jesus the sacrifice was already perceived as a mere preparation for the seder liturgy.

The seder in the time of Jesus was organized like a Greek banquet. The Hellenistic banquet was a well-established institution with its own etiquette, as formal and elegant and imitative of aristocracy as the "dinner party for eight" in our modern society, which imitates the court at Versailles of King Louis XIV. At the Hellenistic banquet the participants sat on sofas around a low table, dining at leisure. Meanwhile, they discussed a prepared topic. Each guest was expected to make a clever speech on the chosen topic and then offer a toast, which introduced a round of wine drinking. A banquet of this type was called a *symposium*. The seder evolved as a symposium on the topic of the Exodus from Egypt. There were four toasts, two before dinner and two after. These toasts were dedicated to the four terms for redemption found in Exodus 6:6–7. The banquet consisted of the required paschal lamb, unleavened bread and bitter herbs, and Greek delicacies like lettuce dipped in sauce (haroset) and greens dipped in salt water. These delicacies also entered the ritual of the seder. Though not an aspect of the ritual, the Roman custom of initiating a banquet with hard-boiled eggs is practiced by many Jews to this very day. The symposium banquet was the type of seder celebrated by Jesus as the last supper, according to the synoptic gospels of Mark, Matthew and Luke.

Christian Symbolism in the Seder

The synoptic gospels say that Jesus himself established the symbolic link between the redeeming symbols of the Passover seder and the redeeming symbols of Christian faith, the wafer and wine of the holy eucharist. These gospels say that Jesus arose and held up the matzoh, the unleavened bread eaten on Pesah, saying, "This is my body." He held up the cup used for drinking the four cups of wine and said, "This is my blood." Jesus explained to the twelve disciples at the last supper the Christian meaning which these Passover symbols would acquire once he had fulfilled his mission.

Christian historical scholars are divided over whether Jesus really established these rites, or whether the early church attributed these words to Jesus once the sacrament was established. The debate is grounded in theology. Those Christians who believe that Jesus established an actual church—that is, not just a new teaching but an organization to promote it—are prone to believe that Jesus initiated the sacraments of the church. Those Christians who believe that Jesus rejected all hierarchies, institutions and rituals of organized religion believe that Jesus would never have established a formal ritual. It is not possible to convincingly prove either side of this debate, which is really a debate, not about history, but about the proper constitution of the Christian church of today.

The gospel of John gives an entirely different version of the events of the passion in their relationship to the Passover holiday. According to John, the last supper was an ordinary meal, not a Passover seder. John depicts the last supper as an extended discussion between Jesus and the disciples, relating to the doctrines but not the rites of the church. Jesus is crucified the next day, which is the eve of Passover. He dies in mid-afternoon, at exactly the hour when the Passover lambs were sacrificed in the Temple. To John, Jesus is the paschal lamb, whose sacrifice takes away the sins of the world.

In all Jewish sources the paschal lamb is not an atonement sacrifice, but this is not a problem. The paschal lamb may have been understood by Jews in Jesus' time, though not by later Jews, to have an aspect of atonement. Or, it may have been enough for John that atonement was one of the major themes of Jewish sacrifice. By "atonement" we mean that human action which results in the divine forgiveness of sins.

Historical scholars have debated which version of the passion narrative is more historically accurate, that of the synoptics or that of John. It is generally agreed that the synoptic gospels are more biographical, but in this case there is no way to argue over historical events. What lies behind the different versions of the story is not two different remembrances of the events of Jesus' arrest and trial. We have here two different versions of the meaning of Passover symbols for Christian faith. In the synoptics the matzoh and wine of the seder are the important symbols, while to John the paschal lamb is the important symbol.

8

Source Texts for
First Century Judaism

Most of what we know about Judaism in the time of Jesus comes to us from the library of books that were written or were in popular use in that era. Unfortunately for our historical research the authors of these ancient books were generally not interested in the same questions and issues that excite us. These ancient books require much interpretation by experts before we can recover from them the historical information that we want.

Three Types of Sources

We can divide our source texts into three types which we shall call canonical, sectarian and non-canonical. The word *canonical* means "included in sacred scripture." We include here the writings which are considered scripture by either Jews or Christians. Jewish canonical sources include the twenty-four books of the Hebrew Bible and the texts of rabbinic Judaism which are considered extensions of biblical teaching. The canonical rabbinic texts include the Mishnah (3rd C.), the Tosefta (4th C.) and the two Talmuds (5–6th C.) which extend the teachings of the Mishnah. The extended Jewish scriptures includes the various works of *midrash* (homiletic explication of the Bible, 4–7th C.). We are also interested in the ancient translations which reveal to us how Jews understood the Hebrew scriptures. These translations include the Greek Septuagint and the various Aramaic translations called *Targum* (plural Targumim).

Canonical Christian source texts include the Hebrew scriptures and the New Testament (late 1st–2nd C.). The Christians also preserved in their Old Testament certain late-era Jewish books known as the Apocrypha (2nd C. BCE—1st C. CE). These books are vital sources of information on Second Temple Judaism. The writings of the church fathers contain occasional bits of information useful to our study.

Sectarian texts are books which were not accepted as scripture by the main streams of Judaism or Christianity but were revered as scripture by various sects of Jews or Christians. Many sectarian writings have been preserved to the present day, often in obscure translations, by small and isolated groups of Christians. In recent times much of this literature has been collected and analyzed by scholars who have scoured the world's most distant libraries looking for lost works. The collected sectarian writings are called the Pseudepigrapha. The title derives from the fact that many of these works claim for themselves authorship by biblical characters. Another important collection of sectarian writings is the Dead Sea Scrolls, an ancient library discovered in Judean caves in 1947. Another collection of sectarian writings is the Nag Hammadi library, containing the writings of an ancient Gnostic Christian group in Egypt. Most important of these works is the gospel of Thomas, a Gnostic gospel containing sayings attributed to Jesus.

Non-canonical texts are books written for purposes other than the explication of the laws and teachings of scripture, "secular" purposes in modern terms. Our most important non-canonical source is the works of Josephus. His two history books and his other writings give us most of our information about political events in the time of Jesus. Also valuable are the writings of Philo. Philo was a great leader of the Greek-speaking Jews of Alexandria, Egypt. In his many books, written in Greek, Philo explained the meaning of Judaism in the terms of Greek philosophical thought. Philo is our greatest source on the beliefs and practices of Hellenistic Jews. Also important to our study are remarks about Jews and Judaism which are scattered through the works of ancient Greek and Roman writers.

The Problem of Language and Genre

It is virtually impossible for one scholar alone to master all of the source texts for first century Judaism. One would have to know many different languages. Jewish sacred scriptures are in Hebrew and Aramaic. Many of our sources were written in Greek or preserved only in Greek translations. Some sectarian literature is preserved only in various languages such as Ethiopic or Old Slavonic. Hellenistic writings are in Greek or Latin. To read the modern scholarly literature on these works the scholar must know German and French as well as English. The ideal scholar would have to know Hebrew, Aramaic, Greek, Latin, German, French and English. This is a lot to ask, and few have been up to the task. Most scholars must specialize in a particular area of the ancient texts. One of our difficulties in this field of study is that scholars of early Christianity specialized in Greek, while scholars of early Judaism studied Hebrew and Aramaic. The result is that there was less cross-fertilization of ideas than one would hope for. This situation has improved considerably in recent times with a more interdisciplinary and cooperative approach. Scholars of early Judaism and Christianity have come to realize that they are studying the same subject.

Another problem for the historical scholar is that rabbinic literature exists in genres that are strange to modern Christians, and even to most modern Jews. Even if one knew Hebrew and Aramaic well, it takes many years to learn the techniques of studying rabbinic literature before one can decipher the meaning of the texts. Because of this problem many Christian New Testament scholars have ignored the rabbinic parallels. Too many have depended upon selected translations that are inadequate or even intentionally twisted toward an uncomplimentary presentation of Judaism.

Since few of us can master so much material, we are dependent upon a small group of top scholars who have built their insights upon firsthand knowledge of our source texts. (See the bibliography at the end of this book.)

Fortunately for the rest of us there has been an explosion of good translations into English. The nonprofessional student can now study most of the relevant materials in fluent translations. (Again, please see the bibliography.)

Mishnah

Naive laypersons, uninformed preachers and incompetent scholars attempt to compare Christianity and Judaism by comparing the New Testament to the "Old" Testament. Such a comparison is historically useless and usually comes out unflattering to Judaism. The Hebrew scriptures are centuries older than the New Testament. Much of the Hebrew Bible was written before what we know as Judaism had evolved. It is unfortunate for the proper study of history that the Hebrew scriptures and the New Testament are bound together in the same volume, as if they represented a continuous tradition.

THE BABYLONIAN TALMUD

Made up of the **Mishnah** (systematic legal opinions about the laws of the Pentateuch) and the **Gemara** (supplementary opinions after 200 A.D.). The Talmud is arranged in 63 **Tractates** in 6 major *Orders:*

Seder ZERA'IM ("Seeds")

Berakoth ("Blessings")
Pe'ah ("Corner")
 Lev 19, 23; Deut 24
Demai ("Doubtful cases")
Kilayim ("Two mixtures")
 Lev 19; Deut 22
Sheb'ith ("Sabbath year")
 Exod 23; Lev 25
Terumoth ("Wave
 Offering")
 Num 18; Deut 18
ma'aseroth ("Tithes")
 Num 18
Ma'aser sheni ("2nd Tithe")
 Deut 14
Hallah ("Cakes")
 Num 15
'Orlah ("Tree operations")
 Lev 19
Bikkurim ("First Fruits")
 Exod 23; Deut 26

Seder MO'ED ("Feasts")

Shabbath (Sabbath)
 Exod 20, 23: Deut 5
Erubin (Mixtures)
Pesahim (Passovers)
 Exod 12, 13; Num 28
Sheqalim (Shekels)
 Exod 30
Yoma (Atonement Day)
 Lev 16, 23
Sukkoth (Booths)
 Lev 23; Num 29
Besah (Egg)
Rosh hashana (New Year)
 Num 10, 28
Taanith (Fasts)
Megillah (Purim scroll)
Moeq qaton (Small feast)
Hagigah (Festivals)
 Deut 16

Seder NASHIM ("Women")

Yebamoth (Sister-in-law)
Kethuboth (Wedding
 deal)
Nedarim (vows)
 Num 30
Nazir (Nazirites)
 Num 6
Gittin (Documents)
 Deut 24
Sotah (Infidelity)
 Num 5
Qiddushin (Sacred things)

Seder NEZIQIN ("Damages")

Baba qamma (Civil law)
Baba mesi (property)
Baba bathra (real estate)
Sanhedrin (Criminal law)
Makkoth (punishments)
 Deut 25
Shebuoth (oaths)
 Lev 5
Ediyyoth (testimony)
Abodah zera' (idolatry)
Pirqe Aboth (Father's
 Sayings)
Horayoth (Decisions)
 Lev 4

Seder QODASHIM ("Holy Things")

Zebahim (Sacrifices)
Menohoth (Meat offering)
 Lev 2, 6, 14
Hullin (Slaughtering)
Bekoroth (First born)
 Exod 13; Lev 27
Arakin (Values)
 Lev 25
Temurah (Exchange)
 Lev 27
Keritoth (Ouster)
Me'ilah (Trespass)
 Lev 5; Num 5
Tamid (Daily sacrifice)
 Exod 29; Num 28
Middoth (measures)
Qinnim (Dove offering)
 Lev 1, 5, 12

Seder TOHOROTH ("Purifications")

Kelim (Vessels)
 Lev 11; Num 19
Ohaloth (Dead bodies)
 Num 19
Nega'im (Diseases)
 Lev 13, 14
Parah (Red Heifer)
 Num 19
Teharoth (Impurities)
Miqwoth (Ritual baths)
 Lev 14, 15; Num 31
Niddah (Female impurity)
 Lev 15
Makshirin (Defilements)
 Lev 11
Zabim (Discharges)
 Lev 15
Tebul Yom (Ritual bath)
 Lev 15, 22
Yadayim (Hands)
Uqsin (Stems)

To meaningfully compare Christianity with its Jewish counterpart we must compare the New Testament to the Mishnah. This encyclopedia of Jewish legal opinions was written around the year 200 CE, approximately the same time as the books of the New Testament. The Mishnah stands in the same relationship to the Hebrew scriptures for Jews that the New Testament does for Christians. Jews believe the Mishnah to be the completion and fulfillment of the Hebrew scriptures.

Rabbi Judah HaNasi (the Patriarch, or, the Prince) edited the Mishnah. Judah the Patriarch was the president of the Sanhedrin and the ethnarch (ruler of all the Jews), at the turn of the third century CE. Rabbi Judah the Patriarch organized the Mishnah as an encyclopedia of rabbinic legal opinions on important topics. In volume, the Mishnah is about the same size as the Hebrew scriptures.

Within a few generations of the publication of the Mishnah it was viewed as canonical, and all further developments in Jewish law and practice were based upon it.

Judah the Patriarch probably did not compose the Mishnah to lay down the law. It is not a book of laws, but a book of legal opinions, laid out in the pattern of a series of debates. For example: "Rabbi X says this, Rabbi Y says this, and the majority of the sages agree with Z." If the Mishnah is not a book of laws, what is it? Scholars have puzzled over this. Rabbinic Jews used the Mishnah as a lawbook by developing principles for deriving law from the opinions of the sages. Jacob Neusner, the outstanding modern scholar of the Mishnah, believes that the Mishnah is a philosophy, not in the Greek sense but expressed through legal reasoning. Others think that the Mishnah was a schooltext, or a summary of divine revelation as understood by the rabbis.

The Order of the Mishnah

The Mishnah explicates the laws of the Torah but it does not quote verses. The Mishnah does not follow the subject order of the Torah. This distinguishes "mishnah" as a process from "midrash," the verse by verse explication of scripture. The Mishnah does not even quote scripture. Why not? Probably because in the eyes of the rabbis it was scripture! The Mishnah orders Jewish law by subject. There are six books, further divided into sixty-three "tractates," or headings. Each tractate is divided into chapters; each chapter is made up of individual mishnayot (the plural of mishnah), each of which gives a variety of legal opinions on a specific topic. The six books are:

- Seeds (prayer, agricultural law, offerings)
- Holidays (sacred days as observed in the Temple)
- Women (laws of personal status in society, vows)
- Damages (function of the Sanhedrin, civil and criminal law—what we would consider legal matters in our secular society)
- Holy Things (items dedicated as gifts to God, which were donated to the Temple)
- Purities (mikvah, the three levels of ritual impurity and how to remove them)

Things to Note about the Mishnah

Note how much of the Mishnah deals with sacrifice and related matters, though the Temple had been destroyed 130 years before it was written! Did the rabbis expect the rebuilding of the Temple? The Mishnah displays no evidence of an activist political agenda. More likely, the Mishnah teaches how to live "as if" the Temple was still in existence. From the point of view of the Mishnah, the essential covenental relationship between God and Israel was unaffected by the destruction of the Temple. The communion of the Jews with their God continues as before.

The laws of the Mishnah deal with minutiae. One ignorant of rabbinic method or prejudiced against Judaism would find in the Mishnah grounds to indict Judaism as "legalism." A deeper understanding of rabbinic method reveals that the rabbis dealt with minutiae because they were interested in the "gray area," the outer boundaries of divine law. The obvious cases are taken for granted. Once the boundaries are established, everything else falls within or without. The rabbis sought a harmonious worldview in which every existent phenomenon of human life had its known and proper place in the divine order.

Another thing to note is the absence of biblical reference. The reason for this, as stated above, is that in the eyes of the rabbis the Mishnah is part and parcel of the Bible. The rabbis believed that when God gave the written Torah to Moses on top of Mount Sinai, God also gave Moses an oral explanation of the laws and rules for living by the Torah. This "oral Torah" was handed down from Moses to Joshua, from teacher to disciple, until it was written down in the Mishnah. The Torah and the Mishnah form a seamless whole, the written and oral Torah.

Another thing to note is that while the Mishnah is ordered mostly by subject, some subjects arise out of order because they are expressed in similar phrases. This order by form instead of content is typical of oral literature, which uses mnemonics (memory tricks) to store masses of information. For instance, there might be a mnemonic like, "there are ten items which come in groups of three." If the current discussion requires the third item in the list, all ten will come out, because oral information is recalled as it is memorized. For centuries the sages handed down their laws and traditions orally. They prohibited the writing of the oral law. When the rabbis finally wrote down their traditions in the Mishnah the material retained its oral nature. The Mishnah is not composed in complete sentences but in the kind of broken phrases, with much information not stated, that is typical of thought patterns. The literary term for this is that the Mishnah is elliptical (it contains many *ellipses*—unstated assumptions).

Another aspect of the oral nature of the Mishnah is that it has no beginning, middle or end. Every individual entry presumes a knowledge of the whole. This makes the Mishnah impossible to "read" as we read books today. The Mishnah can only be studied, under a teacher who already has mastered the entire text.

Any sage mentioned by name in the Mishnah is called by Jewish tradition a *tanna* ("tradent"—hander on of traditions). The earliest *tannaim* (pl.) quoted by name are from the time of the Hasmonean kings, the latest from the time of Rabbi Judah the Patriarch. Traditional Jews claim that the laws in the Mishnah go back to Moses. As far as historians can determine the earliest layer of the Mishnah contains Pharisaic laws from the time of Kings John Hyrcanus and Alexander Yannai. When we separate the historical layers in the Mishnah we find that most of its contents date from the period after the destruction of the Temple.

Jacob Neusner notes that the Mishnah does not present a strong view of the Messiah. This is in marked contrast to rabbinic writings published from the fourth century on, which demonstrate a Jewish response to the Christian agenda. To Neusner, this trait of the Mishnah shows that Jews were not especially concerned about Christians or Christianity until the Roman Empire became officially Christian and began trying to force Jews to convert. It was this event, and not Jesus himself nor the spread of the church, which made Christianity into an issue for Jews. E.P. Sanders and others have argued against Neusner's view that Jews had a messianic agenda in the second century, but legal literature by its very nature would not demonstrate this aspect of rabbinic belief. The *aggadic* (nonlegal) literature of Judaism, which shares with Christianity an eschatological agenda, just happened by chance to have a later publication date. Another objection to Neusner's view is that the rabbinic liturgy, which is close to the New Testament in its time of formulation, is oriented to future redemption. Despite the objections, Neusner must be right at least insofar as the Mishnah displays no particular defensiveness toward competing Christian claims. We can see that Jews did not feel a need to defend themselves against Christian critiques of Judaism until Christians acquired the earthly political power to materially affect Jewish existence. This occurred only in the fourth century when the Roman emperors became Christian.

New Testament as a Source of Jewish History

Parts of the New Testament display hostility toward Judaism. Some sections are especially hostile to the Pharisees, others toward the high priest and the Jerusalem aristocracy, others toward Jewish rituals. This tone of hostility was surely absent from Jesus' teachings, though Jesus criticized many specific practices and beliefs of various groups among his people. We may attribute the hostility in the gospel accounts to the fact that in the time of the gospel writers Jewish leaders were trying to suppress sectarian groups, including the Christians. The New Testament writers defended their sect against the opposition of the Pharisees and other Jewish leaders.

When using the New Testament as a source for the life of Jesus, we must note that it was written by people who did not know Jesus personally. There must have been many people who had known Jesus. Paul, writing twenty years after the crucifixion, could have interviewed such people, but he apparently had no interest. Jesus' earliest followers, who knew him personally, left no record for history. We do not know why, but it obviously did not seem important to them to write down their recollections. Perhaps the impetus to write came to early Christians only when those individuals who knew Jesus personally were passing from the scene. The gospel writers themselves were not especially interested in the details of the life of Jesus. Biography was for them a way of expressing the themes of Christian faith. The gospels and the book of Acts, and even more so the Epistles, are documents of faith, not historical writing and certainly not biography in the modern sense.

Recognizing that we are dealing with faith literature that reflects a lot of incomprehensible first century issues, we can still glean a lot of information about first century Judaism from the New Testament. The incidental background to the stories is most revealing, since it has no polemical or theological objective. We see Jesus reading and discussing scripture, preaching and teaching, observing the Passover. We see the work of the farmers and fishermen, country squires and Roman soldiers who speak to Jesus and appear in his parables. We see the folk belief in demons and miracles and healing. We see the various human types of first century Judea and Galilee.

Jacob Neusner claims that we can learn a lot about the actual Pharisees from the New Testament descriptions of them. All we have to do is cross out the judgmental adjectives and read what is left. The portrait is of a sect that is mostly concerned with issues of sectarian identity: tithes, marital purity, Sabbath law, and ritual purity. This portrait is consistent with the Pharisaic laws found in the Mishnah.

The Mishnah and the New Testament as Historical Sources

There are a few problems with using the Mishnah and the New Testament as sources of history. Underlying each text is not a desire to know "what really happened," but a religious myth. By "myth" we mean not a fairy tale, but a story that explains the meaning of history. For Christians, it is the story of the divine Christ; for Jews the story of the continuous revelation of Torah from God to Moses to the rabbis.

Another problem for historical interpretation is that the New Testament and the Mishnah were both written after the *Hurban*, the destruction of the Temple. Explaining God's purpose in destroying his "home on earth" is a major preoccupation within the Mishnah and New Testament. This was a matter of no concern in the time of Jesus.

Another problem with using the New Testament and Mishnah as history is their retrospective view of the Pharisees. The Pharisees were much more important when these documents were being written than they were in the time of Jesus and the Temple. The Pharisees were in charge of Judaism when the gospels were written. The rabbis who wrote the Mishnah looked back upon the Pharisees as their noble predecessors. The rabbis attributed to the Pharisees great power and influence. In the time of Jesus, on the other hand, the Pharisees were only one sect, struggling for position, respected by many and reviled by their rivals, lacking real power. The Mishnah and New Testament do not deal with the Pharisees as they really were in Jesus time.

When we factor out these problems, we may use the Mishnah and New Testament as historical sources.

Josephus

Josephus is the only true historian of our period. He wrote two books of Jewish history, *The Jewish War* just after the year 70 and, some twenty years later, *The Antiquities of the Jews*. We also have his *Contra Apion*, a defense of Judaism against an anti-Jewish Hellenistic writer and his *Life*, an autobiography.

Josephus came from a priestly aristocratic family. He claims that as a young man he studied in every school of Judaism and also with a scholarly hermit. In a few years of study he mastered the teachings of every sect. (Josephus was always boastful of his accomplishments.) At the outbreak of the Great Rebellion the Jewish leaders of Jerusalem sent Josephus to direct the defense of the Galilee. After the fall of the Galilee, Josephus went over to the Romans. He became Vespasian's advisor on Jewish affairs. When the Jewish war ended Josephus went to Rome. He received a pension from his patron, Vespasian. Josephus spent his time in Rome writing. He intended his books for a Gentile audience. This is one reason he wrote history, which was a Greek and not a Jewish genre of literature. Since his Greek was poor he wrote in Aramaic and paid a Greek translator to assist him. His writings were preserved by the church, and came to be considered classics of ancient Greek literature. Jews did not read the original, but in the Middle Ages a Hebrew summary called the *Yossipon* became widely popular with Jews.

Historians can only write objective history if they know the prejudices and objectives of their sources, but Josephus is difficult to figure out. Was he writing to justify the Jewish rebellion to the Romans or the Roman response to the Jews? Or, maybe he was trying to convince both sides that he himself had acted rightly during the Jewish war. Josephus always tried to make himself look good.

Another difficulty for us is that Josephus wrote only political history—the story of famed men and women, political intrigues, and wars. The religious leaders in whom today's Jews and Christians are most interested, such as Jesus and Hillel, were not of any interest to Josephus. Still, his detailed chronicle of events is all that allows us to know the sequence of second temple Jewish history. Without Josephus, the subject of second temple history would not exist.

There is much modern debate over the *Testimonium Flavianum*, the paragraph in Josephus that mentions Jesus (*Antiquities* 18:63–64). This is the only contemporaneous mention of Jesus outside the New Testament. Historians agree that the text as it stands is a statement of Christian faith that could not possibly have been written by the Jew, Josephus. It may have been interpolated by Eusebius, the fourth century church father who was the first to mention the passage. The passage reads:

Now, there was about this time Jesus, a wise man, if it be lawful to call him a man, for he was a doer of wonderful works—a teacher of such men as receive the truth with pleasure. He drew over to him many of the Jews, and many of the Gentiles. He was the Christ; and when Pilate, at the suggestion of the principal men amongst us, had condemned him to the cross, those that loved him at the first did not forsake him, for he appeared alive again the third day, as the divine prophets had foretold these and ten thousand other wonderful things concerning him; and the tribe of Christians, so named for him, are not extinct to this day.

Some modern scholars have attempted to save the *Testimonium Flavianum* from complete rejection by emending the text. They eliminate certain words and phrases to leave an objective statement that could reasonably have been written by Josephus. The difficulty is that, despite slim support from ancient translations, the emendations have little justification other than the desire to preserve Jesus' name in Josephus' book.

The emended text probably serves no necessary purpose. In the late nineteenth century some very skeptical historians proposed that Jesus of Nazareth never existed. He was a myth, based on the Egyptian sun god and other pagan myths. No one takes these arguments seriously anymore. There is virtually universal agreement that there was such a person as Jesus. What then do we prove by rewriting ancient books to provide an external attestation of Jesus?

Philo of Alexandria

Philo, a contemporary of Jesus, was a wise and learned Jew who lived in Alexandria, Egypt. He was the very epitome of the ideal Greek-speaking Jew. Philo was the political leader of the Jewish community and its greatest scholar. Typical of Hellenistic Jews, Philo felt no need to learn Hebrew. The Septuagint was his Bible. In his many books Philo interpreted the Bible as an allegory teaching philosophical truths. To Philo, Greek philosophy was true wisdom, and Jewish tradition was its greatest source. Though he was a radical in interpreting the meaning of scripture, Philo's pious practices were exacting. In praising the excellence of Jewish law Philo says that even sophisticated Greek-speaking Jews were very particular about Sabbath observance, ritual purity, and keeping kosher. The Alexandrian Jewish laws were sometimes distinctive, such as splashing with water instead of immersion for ritual purity. Generally, though, Diaspora Jewish practice was similar to that of Judean Jews. Sadly for Philo, the wealth, status and renown of his family made them susceptible to assimilation. Philo's nephew, Tiberius Julius Alexander, renounced Judaism. He became prefect of Judea, and later governor of Egypt. He was one of the Roman generals who ruthlessly suppressed the Jewish Great Rebellion. This man showed no fraternal feeling at all for his ancestral people.

Apocrypha

The rabbinic Sanhedrin, the council of rabbis at Yavneh, closed the Bible around the year 100. The Sanhedrin voted on certain questionable books, admitting Ecclesiastes and Song of Songs into the Bible. Some books that were examples of pious Jewish teaching were excluded for technical reasons. They may have disagreed with rabbinic laws or they may have been composed after the revolt of the Maccabees. Christians preserved a collection of these books as part of their Old Testament. This collection is called the Apocrypha. The Apocrypha includes the book of Tobit, a story about the rewards of piety. The book of Judith tells of a brave and pious heroine who saves the Jews from the Assyrians. The Wisdom of Jesus Ben Sira, also called Ecclesiasticus, contains the wise proverbs and teachings of a priest who lived during the Seleucid rule of Judah. The first and second books of Maccabees tell the story of the Hasmonean revolt. The first is a political history, the court history of the Hasmoneans. The second is a religious history, concentrating on martyr stories and doctrinal matters. These are just some of the books of the Apocrypha.

Pseudepigrapha

The Pseudepigrapha did not become a "collection" like the Apocrypha until the nineteenth century, when scholars began collecting ancient Jewish and Christian sectarian books. The collection of the Pseudepigrapha has grown as scholars have continued their detective work in obscure libraries. The latest collection in English translation was published in 1983, edited by James Charlesworth (*The Old Testament Pseudepigrapha*, 2 vols., Double day).

Included in the Pseudepigrapha are Jubilees and I Enoch, two important apocalyptic works that seem to have been widely known in ancient Judaism. The Testament of the Twelve Patriarchs is an expression of Jewish piety, reworked in places by later Christian editors. The Letter of Aristeas tells the legend of the Septuagint. There are many prayers and hymns, reworkings of biblical stories to better suit second temple era piety, and apocalyptic texts, usually attributed to biblical characters.

The Literary Quality and
Religious Concerns of the Pseudepigrapha

Despite the variety in the Pseudepigrapha, the literature as a whole shares certain traits. One we have already mentioned is false attribution to biblical authors. Another is that much of the material is apocalyptic—that is, it gives glimpses "behind the curtain" into the heavenly world. The writing is obscure, full of symbolic representations that are difficult to decipher. This obscurity may result in part from the sharing of secret symbols by sectarian initiates, in part from the oppressiveness of the Roman Empire. Those with radical views had to hide their message from censors. The Pseudepigrapha tends to be "eschatological"—that is, concerned with the coming end-time. There is an expectation of a coming cosmic cataclysm, to be followed by a new world order in which justice will triumph. There is an Elect, an in-group, who will be saved from the coming disaster to rule in triumph in the new world. This in-group is identified, of course, with the sect that is responsible for the literature. God will initiate the new order according to a plan which has existed since the beginning of creation, but boosted by the piety of the Elect. Passive waiting for God is combined with sweeping revolutionary ideals. Though their literature seems strange to us today, apocalyptic sectarians were not mentally unstable "wackos." Historians who know the concrete situation of the apocalyptic sects are able to interpret their strange symbols in relation to real and immediate earthly concerns. Apocalyptism can be rationally understood as a way of maintaining hope and finding meaning in a situation of powerlessness and unbearable oppression. In apocalyptism power is now understood as righteous living among the Elect. Success in overthrowing the oppressive regime is thus assured.

The apocalyptic literature is optimistic about the future age, but extremely pessimistic about the present. There is an overwhelming sense of sinfulness and a limited sense of repentance. The evil wrought by humankind has made the cosmic cataclysm inevitable.

Typical of the "prophetic" style of apocalyptic writing is that the ancient "narrator" begins by accurately predicting "future" events (which are, of course, well in the past from the time perspective of the author) and then continuing the predictions into the author's own time, ending with future predictions of the cosmic destruction and new order. Scholars date these texts by noting at what point in history the "predictions" become fuzzy and inaccurate.

The overwhelming concern of apocalyptic literature is this: God is about to display his justice and mercy on the stage of human history. How can we prepare ourselves for this event?

Historians cannot tell whether many apocalyptic texts in the Pseudepigrapha were composed by Jews, or by Christians, or written by Jews and rewritten by Christians. This shows that apocalyptically oriented Jews and Christians shared a common vision.

Pseudepigrapha and Sects

The volume and variety of the Pseudepigrapha may be evidence that ancient Judaism was not neatly divided into three sects, as Josephus suggests. There may have been as many sects as there are sectarian books. Ancient books were not preserved unless they had a group or institution to preserve them. Thus, each individual sectarian text may give evidence of the otherwise anonymous sect that composed and published it. Charlesworth believes that ancient Judaism was so sectarian that there was no mainstream, only many currents. E.P. Sanders, on the other hand, believes that ancient people, like modern people, may have kept libraries and read many types of religious literature. This would suggest that there was greater Jewish unity in practice than suggested by the great variety of texts.

Jewish and Christian historical scholars differ over the legitimacy of using the Pseudepigrapha and Apocrypha as historical sources for first century Judaism. Christian scholars are readier than their Jewish counterparts to rely on these sources. The argument of the Christian scholars is that these sectarian writings are the only Jewish writings contemporary with Jesus, while rabbinic writings come much later. The argument of the Jewish scholars is that the rabbinic writings, though published later, contain the first century material which represents the central teachings of Judaism. The views expressed in the Pseudepigrapha and Apocrypha are those of the peripheral groups which were not representative.

Jesus and the Apocalyptic Literature

How does the message of Jesus relate to the message in the apocalyptic writings of first century Judaism? Historians have long recognized that the principal message of Jesus lay in his call: "Repent, for the Kingdom of God is at hand!" Does this place Jesus as a preacher and teacher among the apocalyptics? Albert Schweitzer argued persuasively that Jesus' message was typical of Jewish apocalyptism. The "new age" that Jesus said was imminent was that which Jews were looking forward to—the overthrow of Rome and all wicked rulers, the political independence and glorification of Israel. Other scholars have argued that Jesus was proclaiming the "spiritual" or "otherworldly" new age. Some modern Christian historians call this spiritualized messianism the "breaking through of the kingdom." This writer can find no historical evidence that corresponds to the idea of the "breaking through"; it appears to me to be modern theology posing as historical analysis.

First century Jews would not have been satisfied with the promise of a heavenly new age without any change in their material, political status on earth. There is no reason to believe that the Jewish crowds who listened to Jesus, some of whom became his devoted followers, expected anything other than God's decisive action in human events. As objective historians have long realized, the Christian belief that Jesus' messianic action lies in the world of spirit, providing heavenly salvation, evolved as a reaction to Jesus' delay in returning to earth. The earliest Christians expected the *parousia*, the triumphant return, at the earliest moment, accompanied by traditional Jewish expectations. Having gone their separate way, the Christians developed over time a set of expectations different from those of the Jews. The "Christ" of Christianity became distinct from the "Messiah" of Judaism in purpose and function, though Christians continued to use the Hebrew term "Messiah" for the Christ.

Historians Using the Apocalyptic Literature for Anti-Jewish Polemic

We have seen that since the birth of Christianity and rabbinic Judaism, Christians have honored this ancient Jewish literary heritage more than Jews. Jews suppressed the "sectarian" literature; Christians or groups of Christians preserved large parts of it. Through the ages Christians studied this literature and identified it with their beliefs. Jews forgot that it existed until the nineteenth Century when Jewish scholars joined in the modern historical study of religion. In the modern age some prejudiced historians have used the apocalyptic literature to justify the doctrine of supercessionism. This is the belief that Christianity came to surpass an inferior and divinely rejected Judaism.

The great historical scholar Emil Schurer held that the true line of divine inspiration flowed from the biblical prophets into the apocalyptic literature and hence into Christianity. By rejecting apocalyptic, said Schurer, the ancient rabbis proved that they had lost the line of inspired religion, sinking into "mere legalism." Jews responded defensively that the apocalyptic literature does not reveal a spirit equal to that of rabbinic law and exegesis. One argument in their support was that the authors of this literature did not dare to write in their own names. They felt a need to buttress the authority of their works by ascribing authorship to biblical prophets.

In our times the finest scholars have come to see this vitriolic debate over the spiritual heritage of the Pseudepigrapha as obscurantist and unhelpful. Charlesworth has said that a deep study of these texts does not prove the "truth" of Christianity over Judaism, nor vice versa. The texts in themselves are neither more Christian nor more Jewish. What they do demonstrate is the great diversity of beliefs within first century Judaism. There was a great sea of doctrines and beliefs. Both early Judaism and early Christianity drew often and drank deeply from this sea.

A curious twist to the old arguments about apocalyptism is provided by Shusaku Endo, the Japanese author of the popular book, *A Life of Jesus*. Endo does not like apocalyptism. He finds it judgmental in the extreme, whereas he sees Jesus as friendly, warm and forgiving. Endo goes so far in his view that he distances Jesus from John the Baptist, that fiery apocalyptic preacher. The gospels praise John as the forerunner of Jesus, but Endo presents him as the antithesis to Jesus.

Endo is right about apocalyptic teaching. It is judgmental and tends toward self-righteousness. After all, it is composed by and for those who are convinced they belong to the Elect. But then, Endo inverts Schurer's polemic by asserting that apocalyptism is typically Jewish in its judgmentalism. Endo intends no harm or insult to Jews and Judaism, but in his judgment of apocalyptic literature he unwittingly falls into a stereotyped view of ancient Judaism.

The Dead Sea Scrolls

In 1947 a young Arab shepherd was idly throwing stones into a cave when he heard a jar break. He investigated and discovered an ancient scroll. This item passed into the hands of an Arab antiquities dealer who sold it to an Israeli archeologist. More Dead Sea Scrolls were discovered. Most of the more complete scrolls found their way into Israeli hands. They are stored and displayed in the Shrine of the Book at the Israel Museum in Jerusalem. Many fragmentary scrolls ended up in the Rockefeller Museum in East Jerusalem. These were under Jordanian rule until 1967. Then the museum came under Israeli sovereignty as a result of the Six Day War. Some of these fragments are only now being published, some fifty years after their discovery.

The discovery of the Dead Sea Scrolls electrified the Jewish and Christian world. To Jews, here was dramatic evidence of the ancient Jewish connection to the land of Israel, coming right at the time of Israel's War of Independence. To Christians, here were documents that came from the time of Jesus. Some early indications were that these scrolls were composed by an early Christian community, and might even discuss Jesus. This early expectation proved to be unfounded. Neither Jesus nor Christianity are mentioned in the documents.

The Dead Sea Scrolls are the library of a Jewish sect, very probably one that lived in the wilderness on the shores of the Dead Sea, at the ruins of Qumran. The scrolls probably belong to the Essenes, though there are other theories.

Sensational claims about the Dead Sea Scrolls continue to proliferate. The wildest ideas become the basis for best-selling books. The Dead Sea Scrolls do not "prove" Christianity, nor do they prove that any one branch of Christianity is more right than others. Neither do the Scrolls "prove" Judaism. They merely shed more light on the diverse ideas which were part of the fertile soil in which early Judaism and early Christianity grew.

There is no evidence that the Dead Sea Scrolls community was a secretive group of masterminds with a plan to control society. There is certainly no evidence to suggest that Jesus studied with this group, nor that he was a member of a secret society, nor that he was, in his public mission, a front man for this organization. These conspiracy theories about Jesus and the Essenes were first raised in Germany in the nineteenth century. They may have related to racist proto-Nazi ideas, or to the fantasies of some German academic intellectuals that they represented the masterminds of their own day who should use their positions at the university to control and direct society. Conspiracy theorists are unconstrained by the abundance of counter-evidence for their ideas. The delay in publishing some scrolls material was due to jealousies and turf battles between academic scholars. It had nothing to do with attempts to hide religiously explosive materials.

Setting aside all sensationalism, the Dead Sea Scrolls are still important for our understanding of Christian origins. Essenism does display certain traits in common with early Christianity.

The Dead Sea Scrolls include books of a variety of types. All the canonical books of the Hebrew scriptures are represented, except for the book of Esther. The Essenes may have been scandalized by this ribald tale, or the book may not yet have entered the canon. Then there are sectarian books known to us from other sources, such as the book of Jubilees and I Enoch. The Dead Sea Scrolls community apparently lived by the sectarian solar calendar promoted in these two books, as opposed to the lunar-solar calendar of rabbinic Judaism.

Finally, there are books peculiar to this sect alone. These show its organization, beliefs and way of life. The *Manual of Discipline* gives the strict rules of the order, its rites of initiation, its priestly hierarchy, and the punishments for insubordination. This book may clear up for us one puzzle from the New Testament. In the "antitheses" of the Sermon on the Mount, Jesus contrasts biblical laws with ethical teachings that go beyond the demands of the law. The last antithesis departs from the pattern of biblical quotation. Here Jesus says: "It has been said unto you love your friend and hate your enemy, but I say unto you to love your enemy..." (Matt 5:43–44). Nowhere in scripture does it say to hate your enemy. Just the opposite! But, the *Manual of Discipline* teaches that one must hate those who reject the ethical laws of the Torah. Jesus may have been referring to this Essene teaching in the final antithesis. (Does this suggest that, to Jesus, the Essene sectarian literature was just as scriptural as the Bible?)

The *War of the Sons of Light and the Sons of Darkness* describes the expected eschatological battle when the Elect ones will lead the armies of righteousness, aided by God, to victory over the more numerous armies of evil. The *Temple Scroll* gives an idealized view of the Temple and Jerusalem, with many new laws and rules added to those which governed the actual Temple. The whole city of Jerusalem was to be free of sources of ritual impurity, with no women in the city, and no outhouses either!

The *Habbakuk Commentary* goes verse by verse through the prophetic book of Habbakuk, commenting on each verse. The book of Habbakuk describes the conflict between Israel and Babylon. To the Dead Sea Scrolls community the book was really a prediction of the conflicts between their own group and the Temple priests. The commentary describes an ongoing conflict between the Teacher of Righteousness and the Wicked Priest. The Teacher is either an individual, the founder of the group, or a title for the leader. The Wicked Priest is either a specific high priest at the time the sect was founded— perhaps Yannai or Hyrcanus—or else a term for whoever held the office of high priest.

The Habbakuk Commentary shows how Jews read the prophets in their own time—not as books dealing with long-ago events, but as predictions of contemporary religious issues and conflicts. This is how the idea arose that prophets are essentially predicters of the distant future. This was not the original understanding of prophecy.

The Habbakuk Commentary helps us understand a situation in the book of Acts. The apostle Philip took a ride in a carriage with a minister of the Queen of Ethiopia, a man who had come to Jerusalem to study Judaism. Philip offered to explain to the man the scroll of the prophet Isaiah which he held in his hand. Philip explained each verse with a Christian interpretation, and the Ethiopian man became a Christian (Acts 8). The Christians were like other Jewish groups in applying the scriptures to their own situation. The Christian church retained the Jewish scriptures in its own scriptures, under the title Old Testament, because it served this purpose.

Traditional Jews and Christians accepted the first century idea that the prophets were predicting the future. Modern historians recognize that the biblical prophets were talking about their own times. The traditional Jewish and Christian interpretations of the Hebrew Bible belong to the heritage of first century Judaism. They are not inherent in the Bible itself.

One fragment of a Dead Sea Scroll has attracted much attention. Some Christian scholars have claimed that the fragment mentions a "pierced" Messiah—a dying rather than triumphant Messiah, as in Christian doctrine. Lawrence Schiffman has argued that the text actually mentions a "piercing Messiah." The text is so fragmentary that not much can be made of it. Some scholars make much of this document because they are anxious to prove that the doctrine of the Christ existed in Judaism before the coming of Jesus. The evidence is just the opposite. The Jews expected a triumphant Messiah. The belief that the Messiah would acquire victory through suffering and dying arose among Christians only after the crucifixion, as stated in the synoptic gospels themselves. The doctrine of the Messiah who wins victory through his own death is not found in the Dead Sea Scrolls nor any other first century Jewish document.

The Literary Genre of the New Testament

If Jesus had lived in the twentieth century and we wanted to read about his life we would know where to go in the bookstore or library. We would go to the non-fiction section and look under the heading,

"Biography." Many people of today read the gospels as if they were modern biographies. This way of reading the gospels can only lead to a misunderstanding of their message. We can only understand these ancient writings once we realize that ancient literary genres were not the same as ours.

The ancients did not distinguish as we do between "fiction" and "non-fiction." In modern literature history and biography are "non-fiction." This means that everything reported is supposed to correspond to actual events. When told that a given event or speech of Jesus reported in the gospels may not have occurred, a modernist may get indignant and say, "Are you accusing the evangelists of lying?"

Of course not! But, the evangelists wrote according to the genre of their time. Greek biographies were composed to make a point, not to record events. The biographer was expected to have the literary skill to place stirring and appropriate speeches in the mouths of the chief characters at significant moments.

The gospels combine a variety of Jewish and Greek literary genres of the first century. They are part Hellenistic biography, part midrash (scriptural exegesis), part Jewish legal text, part apocalypse. We can read the gospels as their authors intended only when we learn to recognize the various types of literature within them. The best way to know the literary genre of the New Testament is to study other examples of this literature from the library of first century Judaism.

9

The Trial of Jesus

Who Killed Jesus?

Our historical study of first century Judaism can help us understand the trial of Jesus. Who desired his death, and why? This question is important to Jewish-Christian relations. Jews are sensitive to the accusation that they are collectively responsible for the death of Jesus. This accusation is a prime source of anti-Semitism. Since the mass murder of six million Jews in the Holocaust some Christian churches have retracted this charge, recognizing that religious prejudice against the Jews provided the soil in which the secular Nazi ideology bore fruit. The Catholic Church, in its *Nostra Aetate* document on the Jews in 1963, noted that no one should be condemned for Jesus' death. Christians believe that it was Jesus' mission and desire to die on the cross. Historical study can help us to achieve a more dispassionate perspective on the passion story.

There are two possible historical reconstructions of the trial of Jesus. One way adopts the "pious Jewish assumption" that rabbinic legal literature—the Mishnah—accurately depicts the Jewish legal system in the time of the Temple. The Mishnah itself lays claim to an accurate memory of actual Temple practices. The second possible reconstruction adopts the "historian's assumption" that the Mishnah represents a late second century rabbinic fantasy of Temple jurisprudence. The Mishnah shows how the rabbis would have run the Temple had they been in charge. Historians say that we must reconstruct Jesus' trial from all available evidence of first century Judaism, much of which contradicts the Mishnah.

Jesus' Trial as Recorded in the Synoptic Gospels

Before we proceed, let us review the outline of Jesus' arrest and trial, as presented consistently in the three synoptic gospels. Jesus was arrested on the first night of Passover. The arresting officers were of the Temple guard, or possibly Roman troops. Jesus was brought before the Sanhedrin, a Jewish high court, where he was tried that very night. The gospels say that the high priest, Joseph Caiphas, presided over the trial. The Jewish court was anxious to convict Jesus, possibly because they feared he would stir up the crowd and cause a riot which would lead to killing of many Jews by the Romans. They are also accused of envy. The court found Jesus guilty of blasphemy and condemned him to death. Since they had no power to carry out the sentence they turned Jesus over to Pontius Pilate, the Roman governor of Judea. Pilate may have sent Jesus to his king, Herod Antipater (the ruler of Galilee, who was in Jerusalem for the Passover holiday), for a hearing. If so, Herod returned him to Pilate. Pilate found the man innocent, but condemned him to death upon the insistence of the Jewish leaders. According to the gospel of Matthew the entire Jewish people stood outside the court, crying, "Crucify him, and his blood be upon us and our descendants." (Matt 27:23–25) Pontius Pilate washed his hands to demonstrate his innocence and then ordered the crucifixion of Jesus. Jesus was scourged, then crucified. The sign over his head announcing his "crime" stated "King of the Jews."

Analysis of the Trial Using Mishnaic Law

From what the Mishnah tells us about Jewish law there are some problems with the trial story as it stands. The gospels say that the Sanhedrin found Jesus guilty of blasphemy. Yet none of Jesus' words or deeds are blasphemous according to Jewish law. It was not blasphemy to claim to be the Messiah, or to claim that one could knock down and rebuild the Temple by God's hand. If anything, these were claims of Jewish piety! The only crime of "blasphemy" according to the Mishnah is misuse of the holy divine name, YHWH (Mishnah Sanhedrin 7:5). Jesus was never accused of this, so he could not have been found guilty of blasphemy.

Jesus could not have been tried on a capital offense in the manner told in the gospel. According to the Mishnah there were many judicial rules designed to protect defendants accused of a capital crime (Sanhedrin 4:1). The trial had to be held before a full court. Conviction required a majority of at least two, but if all the judges voted to convict, the defendant was acquitted. Both the trial and the sentencing hearing had to be held during the daylight hours. The court could not convict on the day of the trial. They had to hear evidence one day and vote on the next day.

Jewish courts did not meet on festival or Sabbath days according to the Mishnah. Since a capital case required a two-day trial, no capital trial was initiated on the eve of a festival. This contradicts both the synoptics' timetable and John's.

We must conclude from this evidence that Jesus was not tried by a legally established Jewish court. He must have been tried by a kangaroo court called together by the high priest Caiphas, a notorious lackey of the Romans. Caiphas must have been acting on orders from the Romans, who wanted Jesus dead because they feared he would foment a rebellion.

It might be argued that Jesus was a peaceful preacher who taught that God's kingdom was of the spirit. He did not preach armed revolution. This may be so, but this was a fine point lost on the Romans. To Rome, all crowds were dangerous. All leaders who attracted a following were potential revolutionaries. Any claim of messiahship was anti-Roman. The Romans had reason enough to fear Jesus and to want him dead.

Pontius Pilate arranged Jesus' conviction by the kangaroo court of the high priest. Then he convicted Jesus of being a revolutionary and sentenced him to crucifixion, the punishment reserved for political crimes. This conviction is reflected accurately in the sign over Jesus' cross, "King of the Jews." In Pilate's eyes, Jesus was planning to replace Roman rule over the Jews with his own rule.

From the above evidence we would have to conclude that the Romans were responsible for Jesus' death. In the decades after the crucifixion, as the young Christian church shifted its missionary activities from the Jews to the Roman Gentiles, the church shifted blame away from potential Christians, the Romans, and toward the Jews who had rejected Christianity. In shifting blame, the gospels represent this missionary concern of their own period rather than the historical realities of Jesus' time.

The Historian's Reconstruction of the Trial of Jesus

The Mishnah says that the Sanhedrin was a court of seventy-one learned sages, under the leadership of the Pharisees. The Sanhedrin met in the Temple complex, in a room called the Chamber of Hewn Stones. This court was the highest Jewish authority. They supervised the high priest in all his activities and told him how to conduct the Temple worship. The Sanhedrin operated according to the highest principles of jurisprudence, appointing to membership only the most worthy, scrupulous and honest scholars who were completely dedicated to justice.

Many historians doubt that a Sanhedrin like that described in the Mishnah ever existed in the Temple. This Sanhedrin, say the historians, is an idealized projection into the past of the rabbinic Sanhedrin in the post-70 era. Before that time the Pharisees did not control any of the institutions of government, except briefly under the reign of Queen Salome (long before the time of Jesus). Historians believe that the high priest was the highest authority in Jewish self-government. He had to be responsive to his patron, the Roman governor or Herodian king, but the high priest did not have to answer to any body of Jewish supervisors.

The term "Sanhedrin" is a vague term, meaning simply "a council." This term could have been applied to different Jewish institutions in different eras. Historians propose that the Sanhedrin that met in the Temple was not a court or a legislature, nor were its members chosen for wisdom and learning. The Temple Sanhedrin was a cabinet of advisors selected by the high priest to help him make important decisions. Membership was given to powerful aristocrats. Some of them were Pharisees, but this was merely coincidental. *No one sat on the Sanhedrin because he was a Pharisee, or a member of any other party or sect.* Jews love the idea of an ancient legislature of sages, but it is probably closer to the truth that Judea, like all ancient nations, was ruled by a few personally powerful persons of noble birth. Most of those on the Sanhedrin were probably priests, since the hereditary priesthood supplied most of the nobility of the Jews.

The high priest's Sanhedrin, as a private council, did not have to follow any judicial standards. It could meet when it wanted and do as it wished. The sequence of events in the Synoptic Gospels may then be essentially correct. The High Priest called together his council in emergency session on the night of Passover, had Jesus brought to him, and sentenced him. We cannot be certain of the true charge. None of Jesus' followers were present at Jesus' trials, so the Gospels' reconstruction is only a guess.

Had the High Priest wanted to execute Jesus he probably could have. He would only have needed Roman permission to carry out a death sentence on his own authority. Josephus records numerous cases of high priests and Jewish kings exercising their capital power. As the Romans themselves executed Jesus, it must have been because Pontius Pilate wanted to exercise Roman authority in this case.

We know from Josephus that Pontius Pilate slaughtered numerous innocent Jews. It is unlikely in the extreme that he would have had any scruples about executing Jesus, whether he thought Jesus innocent or guilty. He most likely gave no thought to crucifying one who was, in his eyes, just another Jewish rebel, a man who had become dangerous.

The conclusion of the historians: Jesus was killed by some Romans and some Jews, a conspiracy between the homegrown and imperial rulers of the country, in order to keep the peace during the Passover holiday.

Why Was Jesus Killed?

What was the charge against Jesus? We surmise that Caiphas and Pilate believed that Jesus either intended an insurrection, or else he would be the cause of one. Proclaiming the kingdom of God was anti-Roman, whether the proclaimer expected the kingdom to come by armed rebellion or by divine intervention. After all, John the Baptist was universally admired, yet he was killed just because he was attracting crowds. Apocalyptic teachings in one sense encourage political passivity; the Elect must serve God faithfully and await the unfolding of the divine plan. Yet in another sense apocalyptic teaching is radical and explosive, since it raises hopes and expectations for social change to a fever pitch. The Romans were aware of this. Jesus threatened their peace. Around the time of Jesus the Romans cut down a person named Theudas and his four hundred followers, though they had done nothing more noxious than go out into the desert to await divine deliverance.

We can see from the above that no specific word or deed of Jesus was needed for the high priest and the Romans to feel threatened by him. Yet, there may have been a specific cause. It is conjecture, but not unlikely, that the arrest and trial of Jesus was related to Jesus' action in driving the money-changers and pigeon sellers out of the Temple.

This act of Jesus is hard for moderns to comprehend. The money-changers were providing a necessary service. People came to the Temple from all over. They needed local currency to pay their Temple dues, as required by Jewish piety. Jesus' action can be better understood in terms of the Hellenistic attitude to those who made money with money. The philosopher Aristotle had asked, "What is money?" His answer: "Money is nothing." Those who make money with money were making something from nothing. This, said Aristotle, is unethical. We moderns think of money as a commodity to be invested for profit. Ancients thought differently. The money-changers, though necessary, may have seemed an affront to economic justice, right there in the porticos of God's holy Temple.

There is something missing from the "cleansing of the Temple" story in the gospels. The money-changers and pigeon-sellers had a legal right to have their stalls in the Temple. They had probably even paid rent for the space. The Temple had a large guard to protect public order and the huge Temple treasury. At festival seasons the Temple was also surrounded by Roman soldiers who were constantly on the lookout for trouble. The Jews had learned to tolerate the Roman military presence as long as the soldiers were respectful. Jesus could not have driven out the money-changers with whips unless he were protected by a group of followers that was large enough and sufficiently well armed to protect him from arrest.

Some scholars are aware of this historical difficulty in the text but are reluctant, for reasons of their own, to attribute any militancy to Jesus. They have suggested that Jesus held the Temple guards at bay by virtue of his "aura of authority." It would be nice to know how this was accomplished!

Pontius Pilate, Guilty or Innocent?

The gospel of Matthew tells us that Pilate, here depicted as a man of conscience, washed his hands in innocence before convicting Jesus at the insistence of the Jews. This is not possible. Hand-washing as a sign of innocence was a Jewish custom, not practiced by Romans.

The circumstance of hand-washing is described in the Torah (Deut 21) and amplified in the Mishnah (Sotah 9:6). It deals with the case of a murder victim whose body is found in the open countryside. The authorities measure distances to determine the nearest city. The elders of that city must come out to the spot, perform a sacrifice, and then wash their hands while stating, "Our hands have not shed this blood, neither have our eyes seen it." The priests respond and, says the Torah, "the blood shall be forgiven them."

Pontius Pilate did not wash his hands in innocence. This is a story intended to absolve the Roman government of guilt for the death of Jesus.

The Crowd Scenes—The Jews' Feelings about Jesus

There are two crowd scenes and one "no-crowd" scene in the passion account. The first crowd scene is during Jesus' triumphant

ROMAN PREFECTS OF JUDEA 6 C.E. TO 67 C.E.

Coponius	6–9 C.E.
M. Ambibulus	9–12
Annius Rufus	12–15
Valerius Gratus	15–26
Pontius Pilatus	26–36
Marcellus	36–37
Cuspius Fadus	41–?
Tiberius Alexander	?–48
Ventidius Cumanus	48–52
Antonius Felix	52–60
Porcius Festus	60–62
Albinus	62–64
Gessius Florus	64–67

entry into Jerusalem. Here, the entire Jewish population turn out to welcome Jesus with wild acclaim. All are his followers. The next crowd scene is at Jesus' trial, in front of Pontius Pilate's palace. In this scene the "whole Jewish people" have lined up to demand Jesus' death on the cross. The third scene is of Jesus' crucifixion, later that day. Suddenly the crowd is conspicuous by its absence. Jesus is left completely alone on the cross. There are neither supporters nor detractors present.

Most writers on the role of "the Jews" in the crucifixion have ignored the inconsistency in the crowd scenes. One who has not is Shusaku Endo in his *A Life of Jesus*. To Endo the problem for Christians, from the first to the present day, is inconsistency. The crowd is fickle. One minute they follow Jesus, another they reject him, another they ignore him. Endo calls for a consistent, true devotion to Jesus. This is a lovely homily from a novelist who is a devout Christian, but does not really explain the crowd scenes.

The crowds in the gospel story are not historic. They serve as a Greek chorus. The chorus in Greek literature narrates the story and underlines the moral. Following the literary conventions of the day, the gospel writers use the crowd to establish their message. It is most unfortunate that actual Jews have suffered on account of this literary device.

Jesus lived within a totally Jewish world. All of his supporters were Jews. So were all of his opponents, and so were all of those who knew nothing of him but lived in near proximity to him. No statement about "all the Jews" in relation to Jesus can be a true statement.

It is not possible that all the Jews cried out to Pilate "his blood be upon us and our children," as charged in the gospel of Matthew. It is unlikely in the extreme that any Jew would say such a thing. For "blood to be upon" someone means, in Jewish idiom, to be guilty of murder. (See Gen 4:10, Gen 9:5-6, Gen 37:26, Deut 21:8, et al.) According to Matthew, the Jews are not merely accepting responsibility for Jesus' death, which would be surprising enough, but the people are saying, "We are guilty of murder and we want to be held accountable for murder, not only us but all of our children, forever." It is obvious that no one wishes to be held guilty of murder. And worse, who would willingly bring a curse and condemnation down upon the heads of their own innocent children?

We may not be able to reconstruct the causes of Matthew's accusation against the Jews, but let us remember that Matthew is the gospel writer who most desires to keep Christianity within the fold of the Jewish religion. He is a loyal Jew and he depicts Jesus as a loyal Jew. Matthew could not possibly have intended the suffering that his attributed saying has caused to his own people. Matthew's passion story may have originated as sacred theater. The Christian audience cries for Jesus' blood to be upon their heads. The audience experiences sin, condemnation and the grace of God's forgiveness as they recreate the passion of Christ.

The Passion Story and the Bible

Much of the passion story is a *midrash*, an interpretation of scripture. The events may be factual in outline, but the way they are retold is intended to call to mind certain scriptural passages which, according to the evangelists, were fulfilled in Jesus' passion. The passion story was composed with two Bible passages especially in mind—Isaiah 53 (the "suffering servant" passage) and Psalm 22. Jesus was crucified beside other political prisoners. The gospel identifies them as "criminals" to fulfill the verse in Isaiah 53:12, "he was numbered among the sinners." The story of the Roman soldiers who cast lots for Jesus' cloak is based on Psalm 22:19.

Many have been mystified by the report of Jesus' final words on the cross: "My God, my God, why have you forsaken me?" (Psalm 22:1). Luke and John report different words. Possibly they are scandalized by Jesus' seeming expression of despair. But it is possible that Jesus was not expressing despair at all. He was quoting the first verse of Psalm 22. (Whether he truly did so or whether the gospel places the words in his mouth is not material to the message.) A Jew in Jesus' time would know this Psalm. The first line is sufficient to call to memory the entire psalm, which begins with despair and concludes in triumphant self-assurance and divine praise. The point of the quote is that Jesus, dying on the cross, is confident that God has saved him. His death is a victory.

10

Sects

The Importance of Understanding Sects

Judaism in the time of Jesus was extraordinarily diverse. There were many variations of Jewish law and doctrine. Different Jewish groups attempted to establish the ideal sacred community. There were many versions of the future hope of Israel. In his own wanderings in the Jewish homeland Jesus dealt with members of a variety of sects. He discussed the law with Pharisees—sometimes in pleasant agreement, sometimes in sharp disagreement. He debated the doctrine of bodily resurrection with Sadducees. He submitted to immersion by John the Baptist, who was probably associated with the Essenes. We can understand the Jewish world of Jesus only if we understand the role of sects in first century Judea.

This study is also important to our understanding of the historic evolution of Judaism. Rabbinic mythology creates the impression that rabbinic Judaism flowed directly from God's revelation to Moses. Historically speaking, rabbinic Judaism grew out of a situation of diversity and conflict whose effects can still be perceived in the rabbinic literature. For example, rabbinic midrash on the relationship of Moses and Aaron as rabbi and priest can be fully appreciated only in the light of the conflict between scholars and priests in first century Judean society. Some historians argue that the Pharisees do represent a consistent mainstream in Judaism that the rabbis inherited. Other historians would argue that rabbinic leadership was not consolidated until after the destruction of the Temple, and even then only by degrees. The scholar Shaye J.D. Cohen claims that rabbinic rule was not universal among Jews until many centuries after the era that we are studying, perhaps as late as the seventh century. We cannot be sure which view is most correct, but it is clear that in the time of Jesus the Pharisees were not so much in control of Judean society as Talmudic legends would suggest.

133

Another issue in the "diverse Judaism" debate is the extent that Christianity is rooted in Judaism. Christianity is distinguished in many ways from Pharisaic-rabbinic Judaism. Did Christianity break decisively from mainstream rabbinic Judaism? Or, did Christianity take up and develop other strands which were already prevalent among groups of non-Pharisaic Jews? Christian originality and continuity can only be understood in the broad context of Jewish sectarianism in the time of Jesus.

Our analysis of the Pharisees is significant for Jewish-Christian relations. Jews are sensitive to the way Christians portray the Pharisees. We may well wonder why Jews should care. There are no Pharisees today whose feelings might be hurt. Rabbinic literature itself contains many of the same criticisms of the Pharisees found in the New Testament.[11]

There are two reasons why Jews are sensitive when Christians speak about the Pharisees. One is that the revered rabbis of old claimed the Pharisees as their predecessors. Hillel, the greatest of the sages, was a Pharisee. Jews feel that criticism leveled at the Pharisees insults revered Jewish religious leaders.

The more important reason for Jewish sensitivity is that modern historical scholars have used their analysis of the Pharisees as a means to level criticism at Judaism as a whole. Anti-Semites condemned the Pharisees for superficiality, legalism, hypocrisy, and so forth. Defenders of Judaism portrayed the Pharisees in glowing terms. This charged atmosphere has remained almost to the present day. Only in the most recent Jesus research have Christian and Jewish historians been free to objectively evaluate the Pharisees. The Pharisees were an organization of mortal humans. They had strengths and weaknesses. Among them were noble individuals and, undoubtedly, some who misunderstood the Pharisaic enterprise or abused it for personal honor. Has any religious movement in history been different?

Who Are the Sects?

The era of sects in Judaism is 165 BCE to 70 CE. The sects originate in the rebellion of the Maccabees. They fade away after the destruction of the Temple. We recall two reasons for the rise and decline of the sects. One is the lack of a legitimate Jewish leader. Many Jews thought of the high priests as illegitimate usurpers. Another reason was the need to adjust Judaism to a Hellenistic environment. The sects faded away as the rabbis, under the Nasi (the Patriarch, head of the rabbinic Sanhedrin), established hegemony over Jewish affairs.

Our sources of information on the Pharisees are Josephus, the New Testament, rabbinic literature, Philo of Alexandria, and some statements in Greco-Roman travelogues. Scholars build their extensive debate over the identity of the sects upon a surprisingly small quantity of ancient texts. Josephus gives the clearest exposition on the sects. All interpretations are built on his framework (*War*, Bk.1 Ch.5, Bk.2 Ch.8; *Antiquities* Bk.13 Chs.5,10, Bk.18 Ch.1, et al).

> At this time there were three sects among the Jews, who had different opinions concerning Jewish actions. The one was called the sect of the Pharisees, another the sect of the Sadducees, and the other the sect of the Essenes. Now for the Pharisees, they say that some actions, but not all, are the work of Fate, and some of them are in our own power, and that they are liable to fate, but are not caused by fate. But the sect of the Essenes affirm that fate governs all things, and that nothing befalls men but what is according to determination. And for the Sadducees, they take away all fate, and say there is no such thing, and that the events of human affairs are not at its disposal, but they suppose that all our actions are in our own power...
>
> (Josephus *War* 13:5)

> Now the Pharisees live simply and despise delicacies in diet, and they follow the conduct of reason, and what that prescribes as good to them they do....They also pay respect to such as are in years, nor are they so bold as to contradict them....They also believe that souls have an immortal vigor in them, and that under the earth there will be rewards or punishments according as they have lived virtuously or viciously in this life...they are able to greatly persuade the body of the people; and whatsoever they do about divine worship, prayers and sacrifices, they perform them according to their direction, insomuch that the cities gave great attestations to them on account of their entire virtuous conduct, both in the actions of their lives and their discourses also.
>
> (Josephus *Antiquities*, 18:1)

Josephus uses the term "heresies," which in first century Greek means "sects." He calls the sects three "philosophies" of Judaism. This was for the sake of his Gentile audience. Romans knew of different philosophical schools—the Cynics, the Stoics, the Epicureans, and so forth. Josephus encourages his Gentile readers to think of Jews in this positive light—as a nation of philosophers, divided into different schools.

Josephus says that the Jewish sects are three, plus one. The three are the Sadducees, the Pharisees and the Essenes. The "Fourth Philosophy" is the Zealots, who are like the Pharisees except that they serve "no ruler but God." Josephus claims that in his youth he studied with all three groups, mastering the wisdom of each, then settled on joining the Pharisees.[12]

The New Testament seems to corroborate in general terms the picture generated by Josephus. Essenes are not mentioned in the New Testament, but there are many probable references to them. The portrait of the Sadducees, while sparse, is consistent with Josephus. The Pharisees appear often, usually in conjunction with people called scribes. Matthew respects Pharisees but is highly critical of them, while Luke generally praises them.

Rabbinic literature mentions Pharisees and Sadducees often, but only in the context of differing interpretations of law. Few individuals are positively identified as a member of either group. We assume Hillel was a Pharisee for many good reasons, but the sources only call him "Hillel the Elder." "Elder" is a vague honorific, not a title.

The rabbinic literature mentions other conflict groups which may be related to the Pharisee-Sadducee conflict. These are:

Pharisees	Sadducees
Haverim (Associates)	Am Ha'Aretz (People of the Land)
Bet Hillel (House or School of Hillel)	Bet Shammai (House or School of Shammai)

Rabbinic literature never mentions any of the above groups except in relation to its opposite. This might indicate that "Pharisee" was not a primary mode of self-identification. A Pharisee thought of himself as a Pharisee only in relation to Sadducees. Other than that he was a Jew, period. It seems that Pharisees, Haverim and Hillelites are all the same group. At least they shared common concerns, and probably common members. The conflict groups on the right are distinct from one another. It would seem from this that Pharisees engaged in various conflicts. They identified themselves differently in relation to each one. There is a limit to how much of this we can explain.

Hillel and Shammai, and their Schools

We are confident in designating Hillel as a Pharisee. Everything we know about Pharisees matches everything we know about him. But who was Hillel's friendly opponent, Shammai? At the beginning of the modern era scholars presumed that Hillel was the leader of the Pharisees, while Shammai was the leader of the Sadducees (e.g., Graetz, *History of the Jews*). The current thinking is that Hillel and Shammai were the leaders of two schools of thought within the Pharisaic sect. Hillel created the "liberal" wing which interpreted the law with leniency. They considered the effect of their rulings on the life of the poor. Shammai founded the more aristocratic "conservative" wing. Shammai and his followers interpreted the law strictly, stayed closer to the literal meaning of the Torah, and represented the interests of the more well-to-do.

The two "Houses" or "Schools" of Hillel and Shammai interpreted the Oral Torah in the method of their respective founders. The Mishnah records only a few disagreements between Hillel and Shammai, but many between the two schools. It appears that the conflict between the two schools grew over the course of time. The schools seem to have lasted from the time of their founders (c.30 BCE) until the time of the Bar Kochba rebellion (132–35 CE). After this the Hillelites dominated.

We might compare the two wings of the Pharisees to Democrats and Republicans in relation to the U.S. Constitution. Democrats tend to be "loose constructionists," reading new rights into the Constitution. Republicans tend to be "strict constructionists," trying to determine and abide by the original intent of the writers of the Constitution.

The "liberal" and "conservative" wings find different champions in each era. In the first generation at Yavneh, Rabbi Joshua is the liberal and Rabbi Eliezer ben Hyrcanus is the conservative. In the next generation Rabbi Akiva is the liberal, Rabbi Ishmael the conservative. Rabbi Akiva thrived in the early second century. He died a martyr in the Bar Kochba rebellion of 132–35. Rabbi Akiva assured the final victory of the liberal wing. His legal manuscript became the basis for the Mishnah, and more Talmudic laws are quoted in his name than any other rabbi.

If we accept that Hillel and Shammai led two wings of the Pharisees, and not two different sects, it follows that their debates were purely internal sectarian affairs. The legal debates of Hillel and Shammai affected only the practices of the members of the Pharisees, not the life of the Jewish nation as a whole. Only many years later, when rabbinic Judaism became the main stream, did the rulings of the schools of Hillel and Shammai become law for all Jews. The influence of Hillel, the most revered of the early sages, was more retrospective than contemporaneous.

There are many different historical theories about the identity of each Jewish sect. Because the subject is so complicated we shall have to simplify. The descriptions of the sects given below combine Josephus' descriptions with a mixture of likely hypotheses from modern scholarship.

Sadducees

The Sadducees were priestly and aristocratic. They came from the highest classes of society. They favored the Romans and cooperated with them in ruling the country. They were not popular with the masses.

Their "Torah," the oral tradition of the Sadducees, was very conservative. The Pharisees accused them of being "innovators"—quite a strong denunciation in ancient times—but the historical truth is probably just the opposite. The Sadducees probably maintained ancient priestly traditions that went back to the pre-Hasmonean priesthood. The Sadducees denied the divine origins of the oral Torah of the Pharisees. They did not believe in angels nor in bodily resurrection nor in conversion, newer doctrines which had been introduced by the Pharisees.

The Sadducees believed that death is final. Many positive statements about Pharisees in the New Testament relate to the shared Christian and Pharisaic belief in resurrection, in opposition to the Sadducees. At Paul's trial before the Sanhedrin he pleads for sympathy from the Pharisees because, as he says, he is being tried only for preaching the doctrine of resurrection (Acts 23:6–9). Jesus debated resurrection with the Sadducees (Mk 12:18–27, parallels in Matt. and Luke).

Josephus speaks of each sect's teaching on the subject of "Fate." Josephus says that the Sadducees do not believe in fate at all, the Essenes believe in fate completely, and the Pharisees take a middle position. This report makes sense only if we presume that by "fate," a term understood to his Greek speaking audience, Josephus really meant "divine providence," a Jewish idea which is quite different from fate. Fate means inevitability, while providence means that God intervenes to reward good and punish evil. Understood this way, Josephus means to say that the Sadducees did not believe in providence. They believed that God is utterly transcendent, above all human concerns. God takes no interest in human deeds. God neither rewards nor punishes.

The Sadducees had power because they controlled the Temple. Their numbers were drawn from the chief priests. The High Priests were generally Sadducees.

Our sources share a negative view of Sadducees. Perhaps if we had some of their own writings we would have a more sympathetic view of them based on their own self-understanding.

Essenes

Essenes may have been, not a single sect, but a variety of organized groups with similar ideals. Among possible Essene groups are John the Baptist and his followers, the Theraputae known from Greek sources, the Dead Sea Scrolls community at Qumran, and a group in Damascus known from the Dead Sea Scrolls.

The Essenes had very strict laws of Jewish observance. They were especially fastidious about ritual purity and Sabbath rest.

Many Essenes lived a celibate life in the wilderness, away from the corrupting influence of the settled areas and cities. Other Essenes lived in the cities and married, though only for procreation.

The Essene communities were strictly hierarchical. Their social structure imitated that of the Temple priesthood. They thought of themselves as the true Temple priesthood in exile. The chief priests led the group and were seated at the head in communal meals, followed by the ordinary priests, then the laity. There was voluntary poverty, and all property was shared. Food was measured out to each member of the group in strict equality. Every member of the commune worked hard and joined in group worship ceremonies and sacred communal meals.

After a novitiate period of one or two years a candidate was accepted into the group with great and solemn oaths. One rose in group status through study and obedience. Major decisions were made by the consensus of a great council, minor decisions by the priestly leaders. Disobedience was punished with decreases in food rations. Severe disciplinary problems were handled with temporary or permanent expulsion from the group. Those expelled came close to starvation, for their oaths prevented them from eating any food but that of the sect. Sometimes those expelled were taken back in compassion when they were on the very point of death.

The Essenes opposed the Temple priesthood, which they considered corrupt beyond redemption. The Essenes had their own sacred calendar, a solar calendar, which placed all of the Temple's observances on the "wrong" day, from the Essene point of view. The Essenes were also very anti-Roman. They expected to be the vanguard troops in a divinely initiated war against the Forces of Darkness. They believed God would send two messiahs, one royal and one priestly, with the priestly messiah being the main one. They also believed in a "final prophet." The Essenes believed that after the final battle between good and evil they would be revealed as the true Chosen Ones of God. The Essenes taught love of neighbor but hatred against the evildoers who opposed the sect and its teachings. Their apocalyptic expectations may have caused the Essenes to join the Great Rebellion against the Romans in 66–70. The Essenes were wiped out in this war, never to surface again.

The Essenes believed in complete divine providence. God had determined the entire plan of history from the very beginning. The conclusion of history was inevitable. In the Essene view humankind was sharply divided between the forces of Light and Darkness. They did not much acknowledge inner psychological struggle, nor the possibility of repentance. Everyone would suffer or enjoy the common fate of their group, blessing for the chosen few and condemnation for the rest.

Despite the strictness of their laws and what seems to us to be their extremism, many people admired the Essenes for their piety. Ancient Jews were impressed by the "back to the wilderness" movements that had periodically arisen in Jewish history. It seemed like a return to the time of the forty years of wandering under Moses. This was the betrothal period in the love affair between God and Israel.

Zealots

It has been shown (Martin Hengel, et al.) that the name "Zealot," properly speaking, belongs to a group that formed only during the Great Rebellion. Its duration was not much more than a year, until the end of the battle for Jerusalem. Until recently, historians used the term Zealots to describe all the rebel groups, centered in Galilee, that formed from 6 C.E. until the war with Rome. More careful analysis has shown that there was no continuity from one Jewish peasant rebellion to the next. The peasant rebels of Galilee had no connection to the Sicarii, the urban rebels of Jerusalem. Historians were misled by Josephus, who describes the Zealots as a "Fourth Philosophy" of Judaism. Josephus says that the Zealots were like the Pharisees except for their slogan "no ruler but God." They refused to live under Roman rule. Josephus probably styled the Jewish rebels as an independent party in order to remove the stigma of rebelliousness from the Jews and place it onto a single faction. The various rebel groups did not really constitute a separate sect of Judaism.

Pharisees

We have saved the Pharisees for last, for they are the most important party. They paved the way for rabbinic Judaism. Their agreements and conflicts with Jesus are a major concern of the New Testament writers. Some contemporary scholars doubt that the Pharisees were significant in Jesus' time. The attention they receive in the texts tells us that the Pharisees really were important in the time of Jesus.

Josephus says that the Pharisees were distinguished as scholars of the laws and traditions of Judaism. They were the most popular party with the masses. Most likely the masses respected them as a repository of Jewish wisdom, law and tradition. Nevertheless, it is unlikely that the masses observed the particulars of Pharisaic sectarian rules. Josephus, the New Testament and the rabbinic literature agree that the Pharisees were held in high popular esteem, but Talmudic tales and the New Testament make it clear that there was also class conflict between the Pharisees and the masses. The Pharisees saw the common folk as ignoramuses, while the common folk resented the haughtiness of some Pharisees. Rabbi Akiva, who rose from the masses, was fond of telling his fellow sages of his former hatred for learned scholars (Talmud Pesahim 49b). Our acknowledgement of this social conflict need not draw us into caricatures of the haughty "hypocritical" Pharisees. It is quite possible for the people to respect and admire their leaders yet also resent them. It is likewise possible for leaders to love the folk and be concerned for their welfare, even while looking down on them as social inferiors.

Josephus praises the Pharisees for their virtuous and simple life. In his *Jewish Antiquities* he claims to be a Pharisee, though this claim is absent from his *Jewish War*. This is probably because in the twenty years that intervened between the two books the Pharisees, under Yohanan ben Zakkai and Gamaliel II, had become the effective rulers of the Jewish people. Once they rose to power Josephus was anxious to be associated with them.

The Pharisees took a middle position on divine providence, says Josephus. This is consistent with rabbinic sayings, such as the words of Rabbi Akiva: "All is foreseen in heaven except for the fear of heaven." That is, everything is predetermined by God except for human obedience to the Torah. That is up to individual choice, and God will reward or punish accordingly. This middle position makes possible the emphasis on repentance and divine forgiveness which was the shared legacy of the Pharisees and Jesus.

The Pharisees appreciated the *Pax Romanae*, the Roman Peace, which prohibited any nation in the empire from warring against any other. Thus, they were not entirely anti-Roman. Neusner suggests that Hillel guided the Pharisees out of power during the time of Herod and turned them into a purely religious sect. They returned to politics only after the destruction of the Temple. Others suggest that the Pharisees always desired power but had no opportunity to rise to power under Herod and the procurators. Keeping their distance from the Roman authorities without fomenting sedition put the Pharisees in a good position to take over Jewish leadership once the Great Rebellion was over.

The Pharisees disagreed with the Sadducees in their belief in angels and in the resurrection of the dead. The "traditions of the Pharisees" known to Josephus are probably the early stage of what the later Rabbis called the "oral Torah." These are the legal traditions preserved in the Mishnah and the Talmud. Jewish tradition attributes to the Pharisaic leader, Hillel, "Seven Rules" of logical analysis for interpreting scripture. These rules represent the early stages of the rabbinic mode of liberally interpreting Torah law to meet new situations.

The Pharisees had a program for Judaism which included every aspect of Jewish life. They had a particular concern for their sectarian issues, the special rules of their order which marked them as a sect among their fellow Jews. Unlike the Essenes, the Pharisees lived among the people, working at their occupations, living in the towns, and attending the synagogues. They distinguished themselves only by their sectarian rules. These concerned ritual purity, care in tithing agricultural produce, eating only kosher food, keeping the Sabbath according to their traditions, and marrying only women who fit their rules of pure descent. We note that these sectarian rules are, roughly speaking, the very issues for which the New Testament writers criticize the Pharisees. We should expect one sect of Jews to criticize another for their unique rules. Jesus and the evangelists seem to have no argument with the Pharisee's broader program of scholarship and obedient devotion to God.

The sectarian concerns of the Pharisees are similar to those of the Haverim—the Associates. Haverim were Jews who ate only food that had been properly tithed. They only ate with one another, since they did not trust most Jews to tithe fully and properly. Their term for outsiders was *Am Ha'aretz*. In later Judaism this term came to mean an unlearned person. In the first century it meant "a boorish person, one lacking in manners." It is likely that the Haverim were also Pharisees, since their religious concerns seem similar. We note that in the New Testament the Pharisees contend with Jesus over his dining with sinners. Publicans and prostitutes surely did not follow the laws of tithing and ritual purity.

The book of Matthew contains a speech attributed to Jesus which is highly critical of the Pharisees (Matt 23). The constant refrain of this speech is, "Woe to you scribes and Pharisees, hypocrites!" This speech is not likely to have originated with Jesus. We have no other instance of Jesus speaking such vituperative language. It is more likely that Matthew is defending the Jewish-Christian church against the attempts of the Pharisees to suppress the new Christian sect. Matthew places his counter-charges against the Pharisees in the mouth of Jesus.

The charge that the Pharisees were hypocritical and legalistic has been convincingly disproved by Christian and Jewish scholars. The charge of superficiality and legalism, contrasted to Jesus' inwardness and spirituality, reflects the prejudices of the nineteenth century scholars of the German Enlightenment. They attributed to Jesus their own view of the essence of religion. They took the Enlightenment view that true religion is a matter of individual conscience unrelated to material social concerns. They relegated to the Jewish Pharisees everything they hated about religion (everything they hated, that is, about the established Christian churches of Europe in their own time).

The recent consensus of the best scholars is that of all the various types of Judaism existing in Jesus' time, Jesus was closest in spirit and teaching to the Pharisees. We may hope that better historical judgment will soon supplant old prejudices.

This is not to say that all Pharisees were perfect. Jesus was surely correct in criticizing those snobs who used knowledge and religious authority for public preening and social climbing instead of true divine service. We should not imagine, though, that Pharisees exhibited these human traits in any greater degree than other people, especially in light of the universal respect in which they were held. Even their worst opponents honored them for their virtues and conceded their popularity.

The Pharisees were hardly limited by their sectarian interests. They had a vision for all Israel, a vision so powerful that it generated the religion of rabbinic Judaism which has survived through good times and bad. Even to the present day Jews take inspiration from Pharisaic teachings, live by their interpretations of Torah, and find the answers to their spiritual questions in the doctrines of the Pharisees. Jacob Neusner has summed up the higher vision of the Pharisees in these words: "The Priesthood of all Israel." The Pharisees took literally the words of Exodus 19:5-6, "You shall be to Me a kingdom of priests, a holy nation." The Pharisees tried to realize this vision by living as if they were priests. Like priests, they ate every meal in ritual purity. Like priests, they studied Torah. The Pharisees wanted the whole world to be God's temple. They especially strived to make their humble family dinner table into the altar of God. Tithing and purity laws were merely the outward symbol of this great spiritual vision. As priests were to the Jewish people, so all Israel was to be to the peoples of the world.

What Kind of Groups Were the Sects?

Once we have said everything we know about the sects, there is still a lot we do not know. How many members did they have? How much power did they hold? What identified a member of a sect from other Jews? Was a sectarian identity a primary identity, or was one a member of a sect only at sectarian functions?

Let us look at a contemporary example that illustrates our problem. A Unites States Senator is a Democrat or a Republican in many capacities, but every senator, regardless of party, represents all of his or her constituents. Every Senator is first and foremost an American, upholding the Constitution. That Senator may be proud to be a Rotarian, but he or she only identifies as a Rotarian at Rotary meetings. Otherwise, it doesn't come up much. The Senator may be a lawyer by profession, or own a business. The Senator may be a proud graduate of Harvard, or perhaps Yale. The Senator may belong to a religious denomination and go to a church of the denomination, but he or she will not bring this up with the electorate unless they are of a similar mind in matters religious.

Was being a Pharisee more like being a Senator, or like being a Democrat, or like being a Rotarian, or like having a profession, or like being an alumnus of a certain school, or like belonging to a particular church? Which analogy is most appropriate?

One proposal of the earlier historians is that the sects were political parties. The Pharisees and Sadducees battled for control of the Sanhedrin, which served as a sort of Jewish Parliament. In this view every Jew was a registered member or supporter of a particular sect.

Today's scholars have decisively rejected this view. We now realize that the sects were small groups of social elites. The vast majority of Jews practiced their customary religion with no concern for sectarian rules. Each sect promoted its own platform for the ideal organization of the Jewish people as servants of God, but the sects did not conduct parliamentary debates.

Another theory is that the sects were like philosophical schools, a renowned phenomenon in Hellenistic culture. In the Roman world wise philosophers ran academies, where the children of the upper classes went to study in one school or another for a period during their adolescence. Each academy followed one of the major trends of Greco-Roman philosophy—Stoicism, and so forth. The sects may have been a Jewish version of this phenomenon. Josephus does call them "philosophies," though of course he is writing for Greeks who would not understand Jewish sects in their own terms. It has long been noted that Pharisaic social ethics have much in common with Stoicism, and some Roman Stoics seem to have considered rabbis to be "the competition" for the patronage of wealthy Romans.

Another theory is that sects were sects only in terms of their relationship to the Temple. Every sect had its own idea of how the sacrifices and priestly hierarchy should be run. Except for this, Jews were just Jews. According to this view sects had an extremely limited role in Jewish life and their conflicts should not be exaggerated.

A prevalent view today, cogently argued by Anthony Salderini, is that the sects resembled the clubs or associations that were formed by ambitious people in the Roman world in order to acquire the patronage of the powerful. These associations helped their members move up in the social order. They promoted the shared social agenda of the members. The association, acting in harmony, had a greater likelihood of success than individuals acting on their own. The religious rules of the order served a social function, helping to create the required sense of group identity and mutual obligation. If the association could find sufficient patronage among the truly powerful then their program could become the platform of government, and they could be appointed as the government officials to run the program.

Class Structure and Sects

According to Salderini's view, the position of the sects in relation to the class structure of first century Judea would be something like this:

RULERS: These were the Roman governor and army, the Herodians, the remainder of the Hasmonean nobility, the high priest and the aristocratic priestly families. The rulers owned land, controlled the economy, and had military forces at their disposal. The *Sadducees* were to be found among this group.

RETAINERS: These are people who can be of use to those in power. They have no power themselves, but hope to rise in society by acquiring the personal patronage of the powerful. Their skills, especially their literacy, make them useful. Those in the retainer class were ambitious and learned. They were fearful of falling into the masses, which could happen in they found no patron. Retainers served as scribes, civil servants, bureaucrats, and judges. The *Pharisees* are to be found among the retainer class.

POWERLESS AND CONTENT: These included landed peasants and urban artisans. They lived at the subsistence level and paid high taxes, but were content as long as they could support their families and live their traditional life. The peasants were extremely conservative by nature. They did not like change. They would react with fury against any challenge to their traditional Jewish way of life, but otherwise they had no social goals.

POWERLESS AND DISCONTENT: This group included displaced peasants and the urban proletariat (plebeians). Population pressures were intense in the Roman Empire. Peasants were marginalized and thrown off the land as populations increased and as the powerful built up large estates worked by slaves. Urban unemployment was a major problem in the Roman Empire. In Rome itself, the unemployed were kept content with "bread and circuses," free food and entertainment. Displaced peasants became brigands. Poor urban people turned to crime. In troubled times these groups could organize and become revolutionary. The *Zealots* and *Sicarii* are to be found in this class.

OUT OF POWER: These are groups of individuals from the retainer class who have ceased struggling for patronage and power. They are joined by disgusted or displaced social elites. These groups move to the edges of society, where they try to establish utopian societies more to their liking. They are no longer competing within the system, but establishing an alternative system. The *Essenes* belong to this group.

Conclusion: Some Points to Remember about the Pharisees

The Pharisees were important in the time of Jesus but not all-powerful. They were struggling against other groups for access to power.

We must be cautious about portraying the Pharisees as either superheros or as snobbish hypocrites. These extreme views result from Jewish-Christian polemics, not from dispassionate historical analysis. The Pharisees had a great religious vision, but Jesus and the sages rightly criticized those Pharisees who preferred social advantage to divine service.

The Pharisees do not represent Judaism as a whole in the time of Jesus. They were one sect of leaders among many. None of the sects controlled Jewish practice, which was largely determined by ancient tradition. Jews served God as their ancestors did, not as Pharisees or Sadducees decreed. Sectarian legal debates substantially affected only the practices of members of the sect.

The power attributed to the Pharisees by our sources is more retrospective than actual. The Pharisees were more influential in the second century period of canonical writing than they were in the early first century period of Jesus' lifetime.

The Pharisees saved Judaism after the destruction of the Temple with their comprehensive reinterpretation of Judaism. The Pharisees taught that the Torah was the means to salvation through observance of the divine commandments. They taught the Jews that they had an available means of salvation even without the Temple sacrifices. The Pharisees insisted that the destruction of the Temple did not represent a divine rejection of Israel. Life would go on as before.

The Pharisees saw the source of human suffering in the failure of humankind to obey God's laws. Renewed piety and obedience to the Torah would cause a merciful God to send the Messiah. The Pharisees encouraged religious activism rather than political activism. This was a wise decision when Rome was all-powerful.

The Pharisees were flexible in interpreting the Torah. They made it relevant to the new age. The Pharisees used their interpretive powers to updated Torah law first for Hellenistic society, then for post-Temple Judaism. The Hillelite School of Pharisaism which became the basis for rabbinic Judaism represented the greatest flexibility, liberalism, and concern for the poor.

11

Hillel

Hillel the Elder was the leader of the Pharisees around the years 50–10 BCE, during the reign of Herod the Great. Rabbinic tradition looks back upon Hillel and his intellectual opponent Shammai as the founders of rabbinic Judaism. The later rabbis called Hillel and Shammai *Avot Ha'Olam*, the "Fathers of the Universe." According to rabbinic tradition Moses was the agent who brought the written Torah from Heaven, but Hillel completed the Torah by giving it its proper interpretation. If we look at Judaism and Christianity as two first century offspring of biblical Judaism then we may say that as Jesus is the central figure of the Christian branch, so Hillel is the central figure of the Jewish branch. Should we seek one outstanding contemporary Jew for comparison with the figure of Jesus, Hillel would be that person.

The Legend of Hillel's Life

Stories about the life of Hillel are found in the Talmud. These stories as we have them date to many centuries after the life of Hillel, but they have roots in earlier Jewish tradition. Scholars debate whether the traditions about Hillel really go back to his own time, with the more orthodox scholars favoring an early date. There can be no final answer, since we have no earlier stories about Hillel for comparison to our fifth century sources.

Hillel was a poor man from Babylonia who came to Jerusalem to learn Torah in the academy of Shemaiah and Avtalion, the leading sages of their era. Hillel worked as a woodcutter (one of the lowliest professions in antiquity). Each day he earned half a dinar. With half of this he supported his family, and with half he paid the daily tuition to the doorkeeper of the academy. One cold wintry day Hillel could find no customers. Lacking tuition money, he climbed up onto the roof of the academy and listened at the open skylight. So intent was he on the lesson that he did not notice when snow began to fall. Hillel froze stiff under the snow. The next morning was the Sabbath, and Shemaiah and Avtalion came early to open the study house for worship. They noticed something blocking the light, so they climbed up on the roof. There they found Hillel under the snow. They brought him down and lit a fire to warm him. "For one such as this," they said, "it is permissible to desecrate the Sabbath." From that day on Hillel received free tuition. All his life, even after he became a leader in Israel, Hillel continued to earn his living as a humble woodcutter. Shammai, for his part, worked as a charcoal burner. They would not use the Torah as a road to wealth or glory.

Hillel Is Made the Nasi

After the death of Shemaiah and Avtalion a legal question arose. How did one properly observe the Passover sacrifice when the festival fell on a Sabbath? It had been a long time since this had last occurred, and none of the members of the Sanhedrin knew the law. They inquired, and only the humble student Hillel knew the answer. Immediately they raised Hillel up to the office of Nasi, President of the Sanhedrin, effective ruler of the Jewish people.

According to one version of the story, Hillel was able to answer the question because only he remembered the tradition that Shemaiah and Avtalion had taught. Hillel alone had listened and remembered all of the oral traditions of the Torah.

In another version of the story Hillel uses clever exegesis (interpretation) of the Torah to solve the legal issue. He argued by analogy from the daily sacrifice to logically prove that the Pesah sacrifice takes precedence over the Sabbath.

The existence of these two versions of the story is significant. Rabbinic law derives from two sources—the chain of tradition, and scriptural interpretation according to authorized rules. Hillel is depicted as the great master of both of these methods.

Hillel sat on his new throne and taught laws all day long, while the scholars listened in awe. As the hours went by his heart grew haughty, so God caused him to forget. A question arose which he could not answer, concerning how to carry the slaughtering knife on the Sabbath. Hillel replied that the Jewish people themselves would supply the answer. Sure enough, the people came for the Passover sacrifice the next day with their knives tucked in the wool of the sheep or tied to the horns of the goats, as the oldest men in the villages had taught. God now returned Hillel's wisdom to him, and he never again moved from his humility.

Hillel's Famous Character

Hillel was renowned for his gentleness and kindness, his love for all people. Once a certain fellow bet his friend four hundred silver zuzim that he could make Hillel lose his temper. He came to Hillel's house on Friday afternoon, when Hillel was always in the bathtub, and knocked on the door. He asked Hillel a silly question, but Hillel gave a serious answer, speaking with kindness. The man came back and knocked again, and yet again, but Hillel answered him calmly. "I have many questions," said the man at last. Hillel wrapped his towel more tightly around him and sat down on the stoop next to the man. "Go ahead and ask, my son," said Hillel. At that the man shouted at Hillel for causing him to lose his bet. "It is better that you should lose 400 zuzim," said Hillel, "than that Hillel should lose his temper."

Hillel and the Prozbul

As Nasi, Hillel showed his flexibility and humane concern in his liberal interpretation of halakha, Jewish law. He was always concerned for the plight of the poor. The Torah commands the cancellation of all debts on the Sabbatical year, the Seventh Year. The purpose was to aid the poor by eliminating their debts, but Hillel saw that the effect of the law was not in the interest of the poor. The wealthy would not give them loans when the Sabbatical year drew near. As a result the poor were worse off than before. Hillel invented the legal fiction of the *prozbul*, a promissory note which transferred the debt from the lender to the court for the period of the Sabbatical year. Since the Sabbatical year cancelled only private debts but not public debts, the debt remained in force. At the conclusion of the Sabbatical year the court returned the debt to the original lender. Now the wealthy opened their hands to the poor, who were grateful to Hillel for responding to their plight.

Hillel and Shammai Debate the Law

Hillel became the founder of a school of Jewish law and biblical interpretation—the School of Hillel. Shammai was leader of the opposition party—the School of Shammai. Shammai served in the Sanhedrin as Av Bet Din—"Father of the Court," the title of the vice-president. Hillel and Shammai took different positions on nearly every legal issue. In almost every case Hillel took the lenient position, Shammai the strict position. After their deaths their two schools continued in their separate paths. Disputes multiplied. The Mishnah and Talmud record the disputes between Hillel and Shammai and their respective schools.

The School of Hillel outnumbered the Shammaites in the Sanhedrin in every case, according to the Talmud, except once during the Roman siege of Jerusalem when the Sanhedrin met in emergency session and the Shammaites made up a majority of those in attendance. With the exception of the laws voted on that day, Jewish law follows Hillel.

Looking back at Hillel and Shammai, the Talmudic rabbis said *Eilu v'eilu divre Elohim hayyim*, "the words of both of them are the word of the living God." Nevertheless, said the rabbis, the law follows Hillel because he was humble and kind.

Hillel and the Messiah

The Talmud claims that all the presidents of the Sanhedrin from the first century until its demise in the fourth century were descendants of Hillel, except for Yohanan ben Zakkai, who was Hillel's youngest disciple. Hillel was said to be descended from King David on his mother's side. In the language of early Judaism this was a way of saying that Hillel was not the Messiah, but he was nearly so. Had his Davidic descent been in the paternal line he would have been the legitimate King of Israel, the Messiah.

The sages said that Hillel was worthy of receiving the inspiration of the Holy Spirit—that is, of speaking with direct divine authority— but because the generation was not worthy, the Holy Spirit was withheld from him. This was a way of saying that Hillel was equal to the prophets, even though he was not a prophet.

Hillel and the Golden Rule

Once a certain Gentile decided to mock Judaism. He came to Shammai and said to him, "I will convert if you can teach me all of Judaism while standing on one foot." Shammai pushed the man away with a cubit-stick he had in his hand.

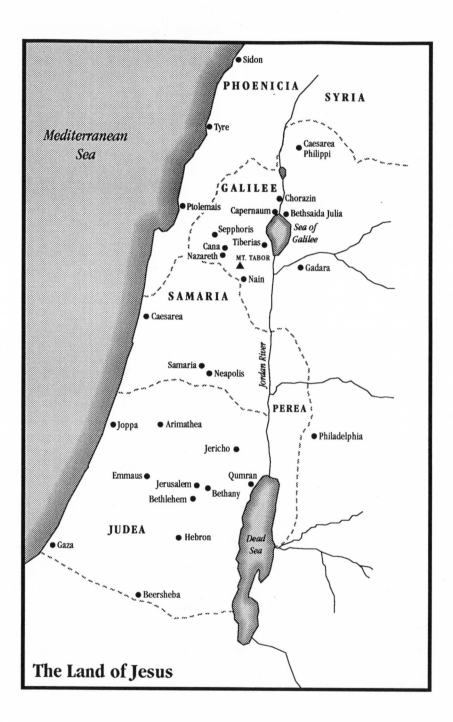

The Land of Jesus

Then the man came to Hillel. "I will convert" he repeated "if you can teach me Judaism on one foot."

Hillel said to the man, "What is hateful to you do not do to anyone else. (Rephrasing the verse from Lev. 19:18 "Love your neighbor as yourself.") All the rest is commentary. Go and learn it!"

The man was so impressed with Hillel's response that he converted on the spot. He went and studied and became a wise Jew. "Hillel's kindness saved my life," he told people, "while Shammai in his strictness nearly lost me my soul."

Historical Analysis of the Legends about Hillel

It is unlikely that Hillel really went from poor immigrant to leader of all the Jews in a single day. It was extremely rare in antiquity for a person to rise to a higher social class, much less for a commoner to become a ruler. Similar tales of a meteoric rise to leadership are common in Hellenistic literature. The Greeks also told tales of great leaders who made their living in humble professions. We cannot say that the legend of Hillel's rise to fame is not true, but it certainly fits into the pattern of Hellenistic myth. The legend created a fact for later Jews in that the rabbis prohibited themselves from making a living by their knowledge of the Torah. The rabbinate was not made a paid profession until the Middle Ages, and even then only by a legal fiction. A rabbi is not paid for his work, but for the work he would have been doing had he not been busy being the rabbi.

We do know of a second century rabbi who rose from obscure poverty to greatness. Akiva ben Joseph (d.ca. 135 CE) was a poor and ignorant shepherd. When he became a student in midlife his genius showed itself and he became the most influential rabbi in the Sanhedrin, the *de facto* leader of Judaism in his time. Rabbi Akiva's rags to riches story rings truer than Hillel's. It took a lot of time and struggle. Akiva was helped by his wealthy and aristocratic wife. Later he acquired wealth in his own name; sources differ on how this happened. Even then Akiva is reported to have complained that he did not receive his full due on account of his humble origins. When Gamaliel II was briefly overthrown Rabbi Akiva was bypassed for the office of Nasi—because, he complained, he lacked aristocratic birth. All of these mitigating factors which make Akiva's story believable are absent from the Hillel story.

Many modern historians doubt that Hillel and Shammai were the leaders of the Sanhedrin. Historians consider it more likely that Hillel and Shammai were leaders only within the sect of the Pharisees. When the rabbis became the leaders of all Judaism, they honored their founders, Hillel and Shammai, by attributing to them an office and a broad authority that they did not really possess. If Hillel really was the Nasi and greatest Jewish leader in his time then it is a mystery why Josephus never mentions him. The only characters from the rabbinic legend of Hillel who appear in Josephus' histories are Shemaiah and Avtalion, whom Josephus calls Samais and Pollion. Some pious Jewish historians have posited that Pollion is Greek for "Hillel," but this is clearly not so. Hillel was obscure in his time except among the Pharisees. This explains why Hillel and Shammai are remembered in rabbinic tradition only by the title of Zaken—"Elder." Had Hillel truly been Nasi he would have been remembered as Hillel HaNasi rather than Hillel HaZaken.

The historian Jacob Neusner has suggested that Hillel's historical significance lay in his transformation of the Pharisees from a political interest group into a spiritual fellowship. This transformation helped the Pharisees to survive Herod's purges and the Roman destruction until they were able to return to power after the destruction of the Temple. At this time they imposed their spiritual program on all Jews and made it the standard for Judaism. Other historians, notably Salderini, disagree with Neusner. Salderini argues that the Pharisees always strove for power, but it was not always available to them.

Jacob Neusner worked to distinguish the various historical layers in the Mishnah. He says that in the earliest layers the teachings of Shammai predominate. The later layers show Hillelite editing. Neusner argues from this that the Shammaites predominated in the Pharisaic party until after the Bar Kochba rebellion of 132–35. Then the Hillelites, following their martyred teacher and leader Rabbi Akiva, took control of the Sanhedrin. It was Rabbi Akiva's potent influence that made Hillel, in retrospect, the father of rabbinic Judaism. When Rabbi Judah the Patriarch organized the Mishnah, he based it upon the earlier Mishnah text of Rabbi Akiva which followed the teachings of the School of Hillel.

The story of Hillel's display of wisdom, as we have stated, is significant as a validation of the Pharisaic-Rabbinic mode of reading scripture. Pharisees derived their authority in society from their knowledge of the laws of the Torah. These laws had two sources–the oral traditions of the Pharisees, handed down from teacher to student in the academy, and the clever interpretation of scripture following laws of logical exposition.

The Talmud calls the most basic rules of scripture interpretation, "The Seven Rules of Hillel." These include the argument from minor to major (*a fortiori, kal vahomer*) and the argument by analogy (*hekesh*). In the argument from minor to major one argues that if the law is X in such a case, then even more so must it be X in this other case. In the argument by analogy one argues that if the law is X in this verse where a certain word is used, then the law must be the same in this other verse where the same word is used.

In later layers of tradition we find the "Thirteen Rules of Rabbi Ishmael," then the "Thirty-two rules of Rabbi Yosi the Galilean." There is a constant expansion of the use of linguistic analysis to interpret scripture. Rabbinic tradition traces the origin of the method to Hillel.

Jewish historians debate whether Hillel's principles of exegesis were an original Jewish invention or whether the Pharisees learned these from the Greeks, who used similar logic to interpret the works of Homer. Traditional piety insists on Hillel's originality. It is possible that these rules were invented more than once, but there is a remarkable resemblance between Pharisaic and Hellenistic modes of literary interpretation. It is likely that the Pharisees learned exegetical techniques from their Greek neighbors.

The legends of Hillel's character, his love and kindness, his concern for the poor, and his ethical maxims, clearly parallel the Christian traditions about Jesus' character and his teachings. While Hillel is not deified, nor even granted the authority of a prophet or messiah, he certainly plays a role in rabbinic religion in some ways as great as the role of Jesus of Nazareth in Christian religion.

The Comparison of Hillel and Jesus

Through most of Christian history there was little consciousness of the Jewish origins of Jesus. Christians presumed that all the words attributed to Jesus in the gospels were original sayings, uninfluenced by Jesus' environment. For example, since Jesus said: "Love your neighbor as yourself," it was often presumed that Jesus had invented this saying. Before him no one had ever preached love of neighbor. (Despite the fact that it is explicit in the gospel that Jesus was quoting Jewish scripture. See Matt 22:34–40 and Lk 10:25–28). From the idea that all of Jesus' teachings were new it would follow that Jews did not preach nor practice love of neighbor, and such was the all too common conclusion.

When Christians began to research the life of Jesus in the nineteenth century, they discovered that Jesus was in many ways a man of his time and place. It became obvious that Jesus' words must be understood in comparison to rabbinical literature—the Mishnah and Talmud and Midrash. These texts revealed the beliefs and practices of Jews in the time of Jesus.

The search for the historical Jesus took place in the climate of rising European anti-Semitism. Some anti-Semitic scholars ignored or denied any Jewish influence on Jesus. (Rudolph Bultmann, who found the historical Jesus to be rather too Jewish for his taste, concluded that Jesus himself had virtually no influence on primitive Christianity.) Some proto-Nazi scholars even claimed that Jesus was an Aryan merely visiting in Jewish territory. Other anti-Semitic scholars acknowledged the Jewish background of Jesus' life and teaching, but insisted there was a distinct break between Jesus and the Jews. (Emil Schurer was one such historian.)

A school of Jesus scholars more friendly to Jews insisted that Jesus was well grounded in the Jewish world of his time. His teachings were an extension of Pharisaic Jewish teachings as found in the rabbinic literature. The leaders of this school of thought included Albert Schweitzer in Germany, George Foot Moore in America, and Travers Herford in England. After comparing the teachings of Jesus with the rabbinic texts, these scholars concluded that Jesus was a Hillelite Pharisee with apocalyptic leanings. The many parallels between sayings of Jesus and sayings of Hillel suggested that Jesus was a follower of Hillel, perhaps even a young disciple. According to these scholars, when Jesus taught that "Love your neighbor!" is the essence of religion he was quoting his teacher Hillel. The belief that Jesus belonged to the School of Hillel became widely accepted amongst those who championed the Jewish identity of Jesus.

This felicitous conclusion did not bring an end to the anti-Jewish polemics of the other side. The intellectual scholars who carried on the search for the historical Jesus had learned from the philosophy of the Enlightenment that the most important function of religion was to generate an ethical human being, a good citizen. The anti-Jewish scholars now set out to demonstrate that the ethics of Jesus were superior to the ethics of Hillel.

In the Middle Ages Jews were forced to debate the interpretation of the Old Testament with Christian scholars. The debate was over Truth—who had the true understanding of God's word. Now that academic scholars were subjecting the Old and New Testaments to historical analysis there was no truth-claim to debate. The new object was to demonstrate that New Testament teachings were ethically superior to rabbinic teachings.

In the words of the historian E.P. Sanders:

...in the eighteenth and nineteenth centuries many Christians began to lose confidence in the creeds. They defined Christianity humanistically, not by the creeds, but by religious and ethical virtues. They then needed a contrasting religion, one that denied what Christians believed in. A Christianity that is defined by love of neighbor, belief in God's grace, and good works that do not earn merit, but rather flow naturally from a person's basic religious orientation, needs a Jewish opponent, a religion that denies these views. Christian scholars found their opponent in rabbinic literature and concluded that the Pharisees opposed love, mercy and grace; they were legalistic, regarding good deeds...as items in an account book...Jewish heirs of the Pharisees, quite naturally, replied that Pharisaism was the champion of love, mercy and grace.
(*Judaism: Practice and Belief 63BCE-66CE*, p.400)

The debate centered around Jesus' rephrasing of Hillel's statement of the Golden Rule. Hillel had used the negative formulation: "Do not do to another what is hateful to you." Jesus had used the positive formulation: "Do unto others as you would have others do unto you." The anti-Jewish argument was that Jesus' formulation far exceeded Hillel's in its ethical demand. Hillel merely forbade evil works, while Jesus taught altruistic self-sacrifice for the sake of others. Their conclusion: Hillel taught love, but Jesus brought the teaching of love to its highest level. Thus they believed they had demonstrated the superiority of Christianity to its antecedent, Judaism.

The classic Jewish response to this argument was formulated by Ahad Ha'am, the leading intellectual of the Zionist movement at the turn of the twentieth century, in an essay entitled "Judaism and Christianity." Curiously, Ahad Ha'am began his defense of Judaism by accepting the truth of the Christian claim. Ahad Ha'am conceded that Jesus' formulation of the Golden Rule was more altruistic than Hillel's. But Ahad Ha'am reversed the judgement on the two formulations. He claimed that Jesus' altruism was impractical, an impossible reversal of human nature. Since it could not be put into practice, it could not lead to the improvement of society. Hillel's formulation, claimed Ahad Ha'am, was based on the firm principle of "absolute justice," which placed the "self" on an equal footing with the "other." Ahad Ha'am claimed that Jesus' ethics generate self-sacrifice, but Hillel's ethics generate the saving of life—a preferable outcome by the standards of late nineteenth century philosophy.

Judaism prefers abstract principles, such as "absolute justice." The moral laws of the Gospels ask the "natural" man to reverse his natural attitude toward himself and others, to reverse his natural self-centeredness and to put the "other" in his own place. The morality of the gospels is Egotism turned around...Judaism gets rid of egotism completely. Its morality is based on something objective, absolute justice, which gives moral value to the individual as such, without regarding whether it is oneself or another person...The sense of justice must be independent of individual relations. All people, including one's own self, must be equal. All people, including the self, are under obligation to develop their lives and their abilities as much as they can, and to help their neighbor as much as is possible. But just as I have no right to ruin the life of another for my own sake, so I may not ruin my own life for another's sake. Both of us are people, and both our lives have the same value before the throne of justice.

I know no better illustration of this point of view than the following well-known *baraita*. Suppose two men journeying through the desert. (One has in his possession enough water only for himself, the other has no water. Ben Petura says: He shares the water, as it is written "That thy fellow may live with thee" (Lev.) But Rabbi Akiva said: The Scripture means that he drinks the water himself, and lives.)

We do not know who Ben Petura was, but we know Akiva, and we may be sure that his is the authentic voice of Judaism. Ben Petura, the altruist, does not value human life for its own sake. For him it is better that two lives should perish, where death demands no more than one, so long as the altruistic sentiment prevails. But Jewish morality looks at the question objectively. Every action that leads to loss of life is evil, even if it springs from the most pure feelings of love and caring. In the case before us, where it is possible to save one of the two lives, it is a moral duty to overcome the feeling of care for another, and to save who can be saved. But which person? Justice answers, "let he who can save himself." Every person's life is entrusted to his own keeping, and to preserve your own life is a duty which comes before that of preserving another's.

But, when a man came to Raba, and asked him what he should do when one in authority threatened to kill him unless he would kill another man (Raba told him he must not kill to save himself, for "we do not know whose blood is redder.") And Rashi explains thus: "The question comes up only because you know that no religious law is binding in the face of danger to life, so you may think that in this case also you may overrule the prohibition of murder to save your own life. But this evil is not like others. You do not know whose life is more precious, yours or another's."

Most Jews and Christians of today are unfamiliar with this old debate. The great significance of Ahad Ha'am's essay is that it had a permanent effect on the self-concept of modern Jews. To this day many Jews, when listing what they believe to be the merit of Judaism, will proclaim that "one of the best things about Judaism is that it has practical ethics." Jews take for granted that the ethics of Judaism are summarized in Hillel's maxim: "If I am not for myself, who will be for me If I am for myself alone, what am I? And if not now, when?" (Avot 1:14) Understood in the light of Ahad Ha'am's critique, this maxim balances self-interest against selflessness.

When Jews of today proclaim practical ethics as the essence of Judaism they are generally unaware that until the late nineteenth century polemic Jews did not single out Hillel's maxim, nor did they analyze the ethics of Judaism for practicability.

The Comparison of Hillel and Jesus Today

From the light of today's scholarship the old debate over the ethics of Jesus and Hillel seems mean-spirited and unnecessary. Most philosophers of religion today do not agree that the goal of religion is limited to creating good citizens. We have a broader view of the role of faith and religion in human life.

The Golden Rule really says pretty much the same thing regardless of its formulation—Jesus' positive form, Hillel's negative form, or that of the Hebrew scriptures in Leviticus 19:18 (You shall love your neighbor as yourself!). Broader ethnographic studies have demonstrated that the Golden Rule is found in virtually every society. It is a universal principle, not an invention of Hillel or Jesus. Every society attributes the Golden Rule to its greatest sage. In China it is attributed to Confucius. Sometimes the Golden Rule is found in the positive formulation, sometimes in the negative, without any apparent awareness of a distinction in its ethical demand on the individual. The man who came to Hillel on one foot was not impressed because Hillel told him the Golden Rule. He must have heard that old proverb before. He was impressed because he had come to mock but Hillel treated him kindly and took him seriously.

It may be that the negative formulation is "typically Jewish" in that systems of law, like Judaism, tend to state what is forbidden rather than what is permitted. The positive formulation may be "typically Christian" in that Christianity is a philosophical system given to broad statements of principle. It is equally possible that the different formulations are a matter of mere chance, without significance. There is no way of knowing if the Talmud and New Testament writers recorded the exact words of Hillel and Jesus, or only the essence of their statement. The different negative and positive formulations attributed to Hillel and Jesus may reflect nothing more significant than the word choice of the editors who put the tradition into writing.

Scholars of today, no matter how friendly to Judaism, would not agree with former scholars that Jesus was a disciple of Hillel. True, Hillel lived a generation prior to Jesus, but the stories and laws attributed to him were not written down until a century or more after the composition of the gospels. It is astounding that Christian scholars in the early twentieth century, who were so skeptical in interpreting words and events recorded in the New Testament, would unquestioningly accept the testimony of the Talmud (fifth century) concerning Hillel, who thrived four hundred years earlier than the publication of the Talmud. They made themselves credulous in their eagerness to defend the Jews from anti-Semitism.

Scholars of today are careful to note that when we compare Hillel's teachings to those of Jesus, we are comparing third–fifth century Jewish texts against first and second century Christian texts. Hillel lived first, but the Christian traditions were set down earlier. Priority in time may belong to the Jesus sayings, not to the related Hillel sayings. We have no way of knowing.

Instead of trying to guess "who came first, Hillel or Jesus?" it makes more sense to speak of the parallel Christian and Jewish traditions concerning, respectively, Jesus and Hillel. Priority is not then a concern. We shift our attention from unhelpful comparisons to the underlying commonality of the two traditions. When we compare the teachings attributed to Jesus and those attributed to Hillel we find two great religious traditions similarly concerned with love of our fellow man and woman, devoted service to God, and the establishment of social justice. The Jesus and Hillel traditions both reflect a noble religious agenda.

Some Sayings Attributed to Hillel

Hillel said: Be of the disciples of Aaron, loving peace and pursuing peace, loving your fellow creatures, and drawing them near to the Torah. (Avot 1:12)

He used to say: A name made great is a name destroyed; he who does not increase his knowledge decreases it; and one who does not study deserves to die; and one who makes worldly use of the crown (of Torah) shall pass away. (1:13)

He used to say: If I am not for myself, who will be for me? But if I am for myself alone, what am I? And if not now, when? (1:14)

Hillel said: Do not separate yourself from the community; do not trust yourself until your day of death; do not judge another until you have stood in his place; do not say anything which is not understood at once in the hope that it will be understood in the end; do not say "When I have leisure I will study," it may happen that you will have no leisure. (2:5)

He used to say: A boorish person does not fear sin; the ignorant cannot be pious; one who is overly shy cannot learn and one who is overly strict cannot teach; not everyone who excels in business is wise. In a place where no one is a mensch, strive to be a mensch. (2:6)

Once he saw a skull floating on the water. He said to it: because you drowned others they have drowned you, and in the end those who drowned you shall themselves be drowned. (2:7)

He used to say: the more flesh the more worms; the more property the more anxiety; the more wives the more witchcraft; the more maidservants the more sexual indiscretion; the more manservants the more theft. The more Torah the more life; the more schooling the more wisdom; the more counsel the more understanding; the more justice the more peace. One who acquires a good name has acquired it for himself; one who has acquired Torah has acquired eternal life in the world to come. (2:8)

At the Simhat Bet Hashoevah, Hillel would go down and say: If I am here everyone is here, but if I am not here, who is here? (Talmud Sukkot)

And why do they record the opinions of Shammai and Hillel when they do not prevail? To teach the generations that come after that none should persist in his opinion, for lo, the "Fathers of the Universe" did not persist in their opinion. (Avot 1:4)

12

Gospel Titles and Types in First Century Judea

One instructive way to understand Jesus in his historical setting is to list the various titles that the gospels attribute to him. We can then see what those titles meant in first century Judean society. This method was pioneered by Geza Vermes, a Jewish scholar from Oxford University in England, and has since been pursued by others. Who was Jesus to his earliest followers, to those who came to hear and see him, and to his opponents? Let us see if we can tell.

Philosopher

There are some similarities between Jewish religious leaders and contemporary Greek philosophers in the first century. The Stoics are often compared to the Pharisees. They had a certain similarity in outlook on life, and were sometimes rivals for the patronage of aristocratic Romans who were looking for spiritual enlightenment.

The Cynic philosophers freed themselves of all human needs and wants. They achieved true "freedom" in a world of tyranny by desiring and possessing nothing that could be taken away from them. They wandered from place to place with wallet and staff (compare Matt 10:8–10). John D. Crossan has suggested that Jesus was a sort of Jewish Cynic philosopher. While the parallels are interesting, they should not be taken too seriously. Jesus was deeply ensconced in the Jewish world, and Nazareth in Galilee was hardly a crossroads of cosmopolitan ideas. Jesus never even visited Sepphoris, Tiberius or Scythopolis, the major cities of the Galilee where Greek influence would be felt. He seems to have scrupulously avoided these places. He certainly could not have

been a formal student nor proponent of a Greek philosophical outlook. Judea was a province of the Roman Empire but the Jews stood as
something of a people apart. In ancient times international culture was
limited everywhere by the force of local custom. We must understand
Jesus more in the light of his particular situation as a Jew in a Jewish
land, and not as a Mediterranean peasant in a Greco-Roman world.
How different from other peoples were the people of the land of Israel?
Different enough to create the Bible! Different enough to give birth to
Judaism and Christianity! Different enough to produce Jesus of
Nazareth! To look at Jesus through too distant a lens is deceiving, like
describing New York City based on a photo taken from the space
shuttle. The influence of Greek philosophy was felt everywhere in the
Roman Empire, but Jesus was hardly a philosopher at heart.

Rabbi, Sage, Wise Man

Learned Jewish teachers arose in the Second Temple era as
interpreters of scripture and repositories of traditional law and lore.
The Pharisees were one such group. In the New Testament Pharisees
often appear alongside "scribes," a group whose exact definition eludes
us. Possibly "scribe" was a professional class, many of whose members
were Pharisees. The term "sages" (Hahamim) covers all the various
groups of wise scholars and teachers of the law. The sages were, in one
sense, the Jewish version of the "philosopher" of the Hellenistic world,
though sages exist in many cultures. The Jewish sages were not rooted
in philosophical ideas but in a Jewish worldview which saw divine law
as the guiding principle of life.

Some time after the year 70 the title "rabbi" was applied to Jewish
scholars of the law, and this title has been in use ever since. In
antiquity a "rabbi" was not a pastor, but a scholar of Jewish legal
traditions who had received ordination from another rabbi. The rabbis
had their own particular methods of teaching and leading. Their
authority came from knowledge that had been handed down orally
from teacher to teacher. Rabbis demonstrated this authority by quoting
the law in the name of the teacher from whom they heard it. Rabbis
also were masters of logical analysis of scripture. They proved and
demonstrated their rulings with scriptural verses, applied via
recognized modes of interpretation. A rabbi's exegetical ingenuity was
limited by tradition. He could not validate just any ruling with a proof
text from scripture. Rabbinic rulings had to be in line with current
practice and the opinions of the sages in general.

Jesus' disciples seem to have addressed him as "teacher" or "master"—probably "rabbi" in Aramaic. Granted that the formal title "rabbi" did not exist yet in Jesus' day, it probably existed informally as a title of respect to a learned sage. Was Jesus, indeed, a rabbi in the formal sense?

Probably not. Jesus is seldom presented as an interpreter of scripture, and never as a preserver and teacher of ancient traditions. In those instances in the gospels where Jesus is presented as debating Scriptural verses in a rabbinic way (e.g., the forms of oaths, healing on the Sabbath, etc.) there is good reason to believe that these texts are not original to Jesus but were attributed to him by the later church. They reflect the nascent church's conflict with rabbinic leaders, presenting a defense of church practice in rabbinic Jewish terms. These texts seem to say "Jesus was not a rabbi, but if he was a rabbi, this is how he would have argued his point." The evangelists wish to demonstrate that, if he wanted to, Jesus could be the greatest among the rabbis. Such is the tale, told in Luke, of young Jesus amazing the elders in the synagogue. Luke, in particular, is eager to show that Jesus has standing among the Pharisees, while Matthew takes the view that Jesus stood in sharp conflict with them.

When Jesus speaks to the crowds, the gospel report is that they come away amazed. And see what amazes them! (Matt 7:28–29) Not the content of the Sermon on the Mount, which is typically Jewish ethical teaching, but the fact that Jesus spoke "with authority." That is, he did not quote sources nor interpret scripture. He spoke in his own name. The perspective of the gospel writer is that Jesus is the divine Christ, even if this is not yet known to his audience. Jesus' own words have the authority of God. Jesus' teachings need no support from tradition. The gospels affirm then that Jesus was not a rabbi.

It is possible that Jesus did on occasion debate the meaning of scriptural laws with Pharisees and other scholars, but that was not central to his calling. There is no evidence that Jesus had studied formally in any advanced school for scholars, nor did he receive any formal ordination.

Some have said that Jesus spoke rabbinically in his use of parable. The rabbis did teach in parables, but our records of rabbinic parable show them to be of a different type than Jesus'. Rabbinic parable was nearly always a parable of a king, with the acts of God compared against those of human rulers. Jesus has some parables of this type, but most of his parables are earthy, drawn from everyday examples of immediacy to his listeners. Jesus even draws lessons from the cleverness of evildoers, suggesting that the good be no less clever in their service to God (for example, the parable of the steward in Matt. 6). Jesus' parables have a power and freshness which, in this devoted Jew's opinion, formalized rabbinic parable cannot match. Not until the Hasidic story of later centuries do we find in Jewish teaching parables of comparable style or power. A reading of Martin Buber's classic *Tales of the Hasidic Masters* should not mislead us into thinking that first century rabbis told parables like those of Jesus. How ironic that in an age when so many are seeking to identify the new or original aspects of Jesus' teachings, many Christian scholars have classified one of the most creative and original aspects of Jesus' teaching as "typically rabbinic!"

Jesus was like rabbis of the time in calling disciples and training them to carry on his work. A candidate for rabbinic ordination in Jesus' time did not just find himself a schoolteacher to transmit lessons. The candidate became a disciple. He waited hand and foot on his master (thus the title "rabbi," "my master," which is the address of the disciple to his teacher). The "Torah," the "instruction" of the master, consisted not only of his lectures, but his whole style of living. The disciple learned by the way his teacher ate, sat, rested, and comported himself with others. Similarly, Jesus' disciples not only heeded his words, but they tried to imitate his example.

Brigands, Sicarii, Zealots, Peasant Protesters

We have already noted the various kinds of outlaw and protest groups that existed in first century Judea. The Galilean peasantry, in particular, was a source of often violent protest against Roman rule. Was Jesus the leader of a protest group, preaching the overthrow of the aristocracy and the Roman tyrants? Was Jesus opposed to the hierarchical social order of his day?

Let us review the various types of protesters known to us from our sources.

There were ordinary brigands. These were displaced or disgruntled peasants who turned to a life of crime, working in bands to hold up travelers on the roads. Josephus brands all Jewish rebels against Rome as common brigands. He is making a political point; he is defending Jews from the charge of being anti-Roman by suggesting that only a small criminal element was responsible for the Jewish rebellion of 66–70. Although Josephus' report is prejudiced, there were many true brigands. They did constitute a sort of social protest group, in the same sense that Robin Hood came to symbolize the injustices committed by the barons against the poor peasants of Medieval England.

There were nonviolent peasant protesters who offered to lay down their lives rather than transgress God's law. Two primary examples of nonviolent protest are that which took place during the prefecture of Pontius Pilate concerning the Roman military standards, which were sheathed thereafter in Jerusalem, and that during the reign of Caligula concerning his demand for emperor worship.

Some peasant protesters established a political agenda. We first hear of a politically organized violent protest group under John the Galilean in 6 CE, in response to the Roman census. The rallying cry of this group was "no lord but God." Violent peasant protests arose periodically. There was no sustained organization, but one Zealot leader during the Great Rebellion was a descendant of John. Violent revolutionary groups included the Zealots, the Sicarii, and others. The Sicarii who held out against the Romans on Masada until 73 CE were the last such group to survive. All organized violent protesters were wiped out by the Romans.

There were also apocalyptic uprisings led by prophetic types. These apocalyptic prophets called for followers to join in a divine war against Rome. They called the people to faith, not to arms, expecting God to fight for them through miracles. Among these prophetic revolutionaries was Theudas, who led four hundred people into the desert, and a mysterious person called the Egyptian. The Egyptian gathered a large following onto the Mount of Olives, predicting the collapse of the walls of Jerusalem by divine fiat. The Romans attacked such groups as they formed. Theudas and his followers were massacred. The Egyptian escaped during the Roman massacre of his followers; he was not heard from again. As Jerusalem was falling to the Romans in the summer of 70, another such prophetic revolutionary appeared, calling his followers to rally in the Temple, where God would perform a miracle for them and defeat the Roman army which was even at that moment running wild through the streets of Jerusalem. This unnamed leader and the hundreds who followed him were burned alive in the Temple when the Romans set it afire.

Was Jesus a Zealot-type revolutionary, encouraging armed rebellion against Rome? Or, was Jesus a revolutionary prophet, rallying the faithful to him with the prediction that God would soon bring about the overthrow of Roman rule? Jesus has been portrayed by some modern interpreters in both of these ways. Others have insisted with the greatest vehemence that Jesus was a peaceable prophet, a spiritual teacher who taught that God's kingdom was in another world, unaffected by Roman rule and unconcerned with it. Those who take this point of view say that Jesus is not to be blamed if some Jews, and the

Romans, misunderstood Jesus' spiritual message in their anxiety about anti-Roman revolution. Some interpreters have suggested that Jesus' own disciples were divided on this point. Some welcomed the kingdom of the spirit while others awaited the word to revolt. There is a view that Judas Iscariot was leader of the Zealot faction, whose "betrayal" of Jesus was really a misguided attempt to force the master to initiate the divinely ordained overthrow of Rome.

If Jesus did preach violence against Rome, it is understandable that the authors of the New Testament would downplay this aspect of Jesus' teaching. They were writing in Greek for a Roman audience. They would not wish to be accused of sedition against Rome.

Some would see Jesus not as a political revolutionary against Rome but as a social revolutionary hoping to overthrow unjust social structures and initiate a classless, genderless, egalitarian society. Modern social critics and radical scholars have woven the message of the gospels into the social concerns of Marxism, liberation theology and radical feminism. Jesus did stand with the poor and the outcasts, but it is no more likely that Jesus was a twentieth century style social protester than it is that he was a nineteenth century style Enlightenment philosopher. Social protest readings of the gospels belong in the realm of theological studies, not historical study. It is difficult for a modern person to place oneself into the first century social context, to understand the meaning of Jesus' dining with tax-collectors, his dalliance with sinners, his complex relations with women followers and supporters. Jesus' socially radical behavior seems to relate to his expectation of God's sudden intervention in the course of human history. If the historical Jesus meant to establish a radically egalitarian society then it is strange that his words were so profoundly misunderstood by all Christians until contemporary radical social critics made them explicit for us.

Many modern scholars try to distinguish revolutionary protesters from peaceful spiritual teachers. Such a distinction would be lost in the world of first century Judaism. There was a continuum from utopian prophets to apocalyptic preachers to messianic claimants to militant revolutionaries. All envisioned the same ultimate end—unmediated divine rule over Israel. The attitude of the Romans seems to have been "kill 'em all and let God sort 'em out!"

Prophet, Eschatological Prophet

In first century Judaism, as in modern times, the term "prophet" is used in two ways, formal and informal. Formally, a prophet is one who receives a message directly from God and speaks that message to the people. The words of a prophet in the formal sense are scripture. Informally, we use the word "prophet" to describe one who is wise, one who predicts the future or sets a direction for the future, one who gives a moral imperative to the nation. In this informal sense we may say that Martin Luther King, Jr., was an American prophet. We mean that he was a great moral leader for our nation, not that we are going to include his speeches within the covers of our Bible.

Similarly, individuals in the time of Jesus are described as prophets. This is said in the informal sense, not in the formal sense. It was accepted Jewish belief that formal prophecy had ended centuries earlier, around the time of Ezra the Scribe. The biblical books of the prophets were closed forever. "Prophets" were believed to be abundant, but only in the informal sense. Josephus fancied himself a prophet because of his great learning and because he had foreseen the outcome of significant events such as Vespasian's rise to Roman emperor and the outcome of the Jewish rebellion. John the Baptist was widely acknowledged to be a prophet because he was a great moral leader and a holy person. Various apocalyptic preachers were styled as "prophets." Still, even those who fervently desired a return of biblical prophecy acknowledged that the prophets of their own time were not the same as the prophets of the Bible. There was a longing for "true" prophets. For example, when Simon the Hasmonean was confirmed as prince and high priest he made a bow to piety (and acknowledged his illegitimacy for the throne) by making his appointment a temporary measure "until a true prophet should arise." Again, the Talmud judges against the many apocalyptic prophets who arose after the destruction of the Temple in the saying that, "after the destruction, prophecy was given over to madmen."

In the synoptic gospels the disciples constantly discuss whether Jesus is a prophet. Ultimately the church itself rejects the application of this title to Jesus. It is not useful in the ultimate understanding of Jesus as Christ. Despite this the gospels faithfully record the memory of the early speculation about Jesus as prophet.

We must carefully distinguish between Jewish belief in prophets, and Jewish expectations of what scholars call the "eschatological prophet." By this we mean the prophet who would appear at the end-time to announce the coming of the new world order. The eschatological prophet was Elijah, returned to earth. This belief was based on the promise in the book of Malachi (see discussion in chapter Two) that God would send Elijah "before the coming of the Day of the Lord." By the first century this eschatological prophet took his place alongside the Messiah or Messiahs in many apocalyptic-eschatological belief systems. The final prophet was understood to be either Elijah returned, or else "one like Moses"—a second Moses. Synoptic speculation about the possible prophetic identity of Jesus probably refers to Jesus as eschatological prophet, rather than as a biblical prophet of yore. Ultimately, Christian eschatologists assigned this role to John the Baptist.

Some historians have speculated that Jews perceived Jesus as a charismatic prophet in the style of Elijah and Elisha, as opposed to the classical literary prophets. They suggest that literary prophecy belongs to Judea, while charismatic prophecy belongs to Galilee, the home territory of both Elijah and Jesus. This argument is without merit. The relationship of charismatic prophecy to classical prophecy is one of time, not place. Charismatic prophecy died out in the eighth or seventh century BCE, more than half a millennium before the time of Jesus. Classical literary prophecy replaced it. There is no record of any charismatic prophet in Galilee or elsewhere during this period of seven or more centuries. To suggest a continuous Elijah tradition in Galilee is an argument from silence, to say the least. We may well ask, what could cause anyone to make such a claim? Clearly, some people want to see a continuous line of prophecy from the Hebrew scriptures to the New Testament. We have studied enough history at this point to convince ourselves that any such claim is without foundation.

In the early twentieth century some Jews, when writing on the historical Jesus, claimed that Jews of today see Jesus as a great prophet. While meant to sound respectful, this statement is devoid of content. Which of Jesus' teachings do Jews consider prophetic? Most Jews of today who think about a Jewish definition of Jesus would probably prefer a more honest statement that Jesus was a teacher or, following Martin Buber, "our great brother."

The rabbinic view of prophecy, as eventually developed in the Talmudic literature, is that it had died out once and for all. The sages said that Hillel would have been worthy of receiving prophecy, but the age was not worthy. There is a *bat kol*, a heavenly voice (literally, an "echo") that speaks the divine message from time to time. However, this "bat kol" is without authority.

Messiah, or Christ

Shortly after the crucifixion of Jesus, a decade or two at most, the Christian church settled on the title "Christ" for Jesus. This is a Greek translation of the Hebrew term *mashiakh*, usually anglicized as *messiah*. Messiah means "anointed one," a person who has had oil (perfume) poured over the head. Anointing was the ceremony in ancient Israel for appointing a king or a high priest. The prophet Samuel anointed Saul (I Sam 10:1), and later David (I Sam 16:11–13). To speak of "the messiah" or "God's messiah" is a poetic term for "the proper king of the Jewish nation." Similar is the English term "the crowned heads of Europe," which refers to ordinary kings. European monarchs are crowned rather than anointed, hence the different but related terms. The dynasty of King David survived for five centuries in First Temple times (ca. 1000 BCE–500 BCE). As far as Jews were concerned only a king from the dynasty of David son of Jesse was of the true royal line. The Hasmoneans were usurpers, all the more so Herod.

For many centuries the Jews had done without a royal messiah. This seemed to suit them just fine. The Jews for the most part preferred to have a high priest as their head, a system of government which Josephus proudly called "theocracy"—the rule of God. Jews did not object to being subject to a large empire—in truth, this seemed to solve the problems that had always attended the monarchy, since few kings lived up to the prophetic ideal. The Jews tolerated the Hasmoneans and Herod.

In the first century, for reasons not clear to us, a desire arose among the Jews for a return to sovereignty under their own legitimate rulers. The texts of the period show the development of this doctrine of the messiah. The various sects held differing views. The messianic idea as fully developed in rabbinic literature meshes a lot of ideas, some of which had not yet developed in the time of Jesus and others which existed independently among various Jewish sects. Despite the variations, there are some constants in first century Jewish messianic doctrine.

The Messiah was a king of the royal line of David. He was therefore a flesh and blood human being, divinely appointed like all true Jewish kings but not divine nor angelic in any way. Even when accompanied by supernatural miracles, as in some versions of the messianic legend, he is still a human person. Some Talmudic legends speak of the Messiah being "held in reserve" in heaven or on earth, yet he is still a mortal human being.

The primary function of the Messiah is to defeat the oppressive enemies of Israel, returning the Jews to sovereignty. The Messiah is victorious in battle. No matter how understood, messianism was inherently a rebellion against Roman rule. The antithesis of the kingdom of God is the kingdom of Evil, which is Rome.

After defeating the forces of evil the victorious Messiah establishes justice on earth. He does this by ruling according to the laws laid down in the Torah. The "Law" governs much more than details of ritual observance; it establishes the basis for a just society in which peace reigns. The Messiah does not supersede the law; he faithfully abides by it.

The community who wrote the Dead Sea Scrolls believed in two Messiahs, one priestly and one royal. The priestly Messiah is the more important of the two. Some historians have taken this as an indication that Jews could have a doctrine of multiple messiahs (perhaps including one more like the Christian Christ), but this is not a justifiable conclusion. The high priest, like the King, was always a messiah, an anointed one. There is nothing new here. It is natural for the Dead Sea Scrolls community, organized as a priestly hierarchy, to care more for the priesthood than for royalty. There is room in Jewish messianic doctrine for a final prophet to announce the end-time (see above), a victorious royal Messiah, and perhaps a messianic high priest to preside in the perfected Temple. There are no other messiahs in Jewish lore.

In later Judaism there was a dual messiah concept. First comes Messiah ben Joseph (the Messiah from the tribe of Joseph, from the Northern Kingdom of Israel). He fights the battle against evil and is tragically killed at the moment of victory. Then comes Messiah ben David (descended from David, from the Southern Kingdom of Judah) to rule justly over the perfected earth. In some versions Messiah ben Joseph is born and killed again and again, in every generation. This doctrine does not arise until many centuries after the time of Jesus. It is probably influenced by Christian doctrine, or perhaps it is an attempt to rescue messianic doctrine from the disaster of the Bar Kochba rebellion. The Messiah ben Joseph is so late that it cannot be a source for the Christian concept of the Christ.

The Christian concept of the Christ differs from the Jewish messianic doctrine in a number of important ways:

- The Christian Messiah fulfills his function by dying rather than by winning military victory.
- The Christian Messiah rules over the heavenly or "spiritual" realm. There is no change in the social and political situation on earth.
- The Christian Messiah is divine, God become human.
- The primary function of the Christian Messiah is salvation from sin and its consequences. In Judaism salvation is achieved through Torah and repentance; the Messiah has no role in this. The Jewish Messiah does not save from sin, but from earthly oppressors.

The doctrine of the Christ *does not exist anywhere in first century Judaism.* Historians universally agree that the Christian belief in the dying Messiah, who achieves spiritual victory through earthly defeat, arises as the young church's response to the crucifixion of Jesus and the delay of the "parousia" (Jesus' triumphant return to earth). The doctrine of the Christ as conceived in Christianity does not exist before the first Easter. It does not play a role in Jesus' teachings. The few passages in the synoptic gospels in which Jesus acknowledges that he is the Christ are considered by virtually all historians to be late passages. They are tacked onto the end of earlier literary discourses about "who is Jesus?" (See Mark 8:27–29, Matt 16:13–17, and most instructively Luke 9:18–22 in which the reference to "Christ" in v. 21 is completely ignored in v. 22 which reverts to "Son of Man" terminology.) The Johannine Christ knows from the very beginning of his mission that he is the Christ. John's gospel begins with the eternal Christ and moves from there to Jesus. The self-confessing Christ of John is recognized by most historians to be more doctrinal than historical.

Some Christian scholars are anxious to prove that there really was a doctrine of the Christ in pre-Easter Judaism. There is no good evidence to support their claim.

Christian faith does not rest upon the pre-existence of a doctrine of the Christ. On the contrary, we might more fruitfully see the doctrine of the Christ as the most original contribution of Christianity to world religious thought. If there was no prior doctrine of the Christ then the firm faith in the Christ demonstrated by Paul and the evangelists may pleasingly be understood by Christian believers as a demonstration of the reality of the risen Christ. Jesus' scattered and disheartened followers soon came to believe that Jesus had fulfilled his mission after all. Yet against all evidence, some historians feel a need to demonstrate continuity between the messianic doctrines of ancient Judaism and the nascent Christian religion.

The belief that the doctrine of the Christ predates Easter fulfills a pleasing childlike view of Jesus' preaching career, in which the Galilean crowds who surround Jesus are enthusiastic Christians, while Jesus' enemies "failed to perceive that the time of their visitation was upon them." In many television versions of the life of Jesus this idea is placed into the mouth of an "objective" Roman centurion or ruler. Looking on at Jesus and his followers, the Roman says to his fellow, "Could this be the Savior that the Jews have been expecting for so long now?" As if the Jews had a doctrine of the Christ and were just waiting for his appearance to fulfill their expectation! The historical fact is that Jesus' followers, as well as his opponents, were not Christians but Jews. Their doctrines were Jewish, their messianic expectations were Jewish, and they welcomed Jesus as a Jewish leader. If you can imagine yourself back in time as one of Jesus' impassioned followers and supporters, listening to him speak the Sermon on the Mount, then you must temporarily set aside your belief in the Christ and imagine yourself a Jew.

Josephus notes that after the Jewish rebellion the Romans went around killing "descendants of David." Some scholars quote this passage as proof that first century genealogies going back to King David, such as the genealogy of Jesus in Matthew, could be historically valid. This is not so. We hear nothing of Davidic descendants for centuries. The Hasmoneans, and then Herod, made a point of killing all potential rivals to the throne, and yet no descendants of David are mentioned in connection to them. The meaning of the passage in Josephus is that the Romans were killing every Jew who claimed to be the Messiah.

Son of Man

It appears that the earliest title the young church used for Jesus was not Christ, but "Son of Man." If we can understand the meaning of this term in first century Judaism, we shall probably be able to go back in time to the struggles of the earliest Christians to define for themselves the meaning of Jesus' life and death.

"Son of Man" in Hebrew is "ben Adam," literally a "descendant of Adam." In Hebrew usage the term is a poetic idiom for "human being." It is best translated as "mortal one." In Aramaic, the language spoken by Jesus, the equivalent term *bar nash* has a broader range of meanings. The term "bar nash" can, like the Hebrew, mean "a mortal, a human being." As such it was often used as a euphemism for "I, me, myself," in order to avoid the appearance of egotism in speech. Similar is the English language custom of saying "One does..." instead of "I do..."

"Bar nash" can also refer to a mythical divine or angelic being mentioned in the book of Daniel (7:9–14). In this passage Daniel sees a heavenly vision. The passage reads in part:

> Thrones were set in place, and the Ancient of Days took His seat. His garment was white like snow, and the hair of his head was like lamb's wool...As I looked on in the night vision, one like a human being (k' bar nash) came with the clouds of heaven. He reached the Ancient of Days and was

> presented to Him. Dominion, glory and kingship were
> given to him. All people and every nation must serve him.
> His dominion is an everlasting dominion that shall not pass
> away....

The passage is mysterious and difficult to understand. The Ancient of
Days is clearly God, depicted as a kindly old man with a long white
beard sitting on a throne. The "one like a son of man" perhaps
represents Israel. Earlier in the vision various animals, representing the
wicked empires, have come and gone. The symbol of Israel has a
human form, an obvious and profound distinction. Daniel is assured
that Israel's time to rule, when it comes, shall exceed all others' in
glory. Israel's sovereign kingdom shall not decline and fall like these
wicked empires.

Is the "one like a son of man" an angel? Could he be the guardian
angel or heavenly "prince" of Israel? Or, is he a special divine creation?
Is he a glorious human messenger? The text of Daniel leaves us to
speculate.

There is some evidence that apocalyptic Jews before the time of
Jesus did speculate on the meaning of this figure from Daniel and his
role in the coming end-time.

The first book of Enoch is obscure now, but it may have been
widely known among first century Jews. Fragments of the book are
found among the Dead Sea Scrolls. Known to us mainly from an ancient
Ethiopian translation, first Enoch is one of the great apocalypses of the
first century BCE (along with the book of Jubilees). The "son of man" is
mentioned in a few passages of the long (108 chapters) book of I
Enoch.[13] Here we read, in a vision similar to Daniel's, "This is the Son of
Man, to whom belongs righteousness, and with whom righteousness
dwells. And he will open all the hidden storerooms, for the Lord of
Spirits has chosen him, and he is destined to be victorious...(I Enoch
46:3). The role of this Son of Man is to be victorious over all the wicked
kingdoms, destroying them. I Enoch 48 describes the Son of Man as
eternally existent in heaven, reserved by God for his role at the end-
time. There is difference of opinion on the significance of the I Enoch
passages. It may show that there was among first century Jews much
speculation about the Son of Man, or it may be that I Enoch was so
obscure, its influence limited to fringe apocalyptic sects, that the
passage demonstrates little.

The one *k'bar nash*, "like a son of man," can have three possible
meanings:

1. a euphemism for the self, a simple reference to a human person.
2. the mysterious divine being mentioned in Daniel and I Enoch.
3. a title, capitalized as Son of Man, used by Christians in reference to Jesus.

Since ancient language has no lowercase letters, we cannot tell when in the New Testament *bar nash* means "son of man," a person, and when it means "Son of Man," a formal title applied to Jesus. To illustrate the problem let us look at a story in the gospel of Mark, chapter 2:23–28 (variations in Matt 12 and Luke 6).

Jesus is passing through a grainfield on the Sabbath. He allows his disciples, who are hungry, to pluck grains and eat them. The Pharisees criticize Jesus for this leniency in the application of Sabbath law. According to the gospel story Jesus gives two responses to the Pharisees. First, Jesus gives a complex proof text from a biblical story, intended to prove that the permission he granted was within the bounds of the biblical laws of Sabbath rest. Thus Jesus satisfies the Pharisees by using Pharisaic argument, proving a legal stance from the authority of scripture. But then Jesus concludes with a different argument entirely. He states: "The Sabbath was made for man, and not man for the Sabbath, so the `bar nash' is lord even of the Sabbath."

This argument can be read in two ways:

1. Jesus quotes to the Pharisees their own principle, that the Sabbath must serve human needs. The Pharisees used this principle only in response to danger to human life. Jesus extends the principle to apply to a situation of human discomfort, or perhaps he sees it as a situation in which the biblically ordained enjoyment of the Sabbath is endangered by an unnecessary stricture. Jesus concludes that since the Sabbath was given to man, the mortal human being (*bar nash*) is lord (master, the one in control) of the Sabbath. In other words, people may interpret the biblical command of Sabbath rest as they please!
2. Jesus quotes to the rabbis their principle, that God has given human beings the right to interpret the biblical commandments. Jesus then goes a step further. The Son of Man (Jesus, the divine one) has been made Lord (divine ruler) of the Sabbath. Read this way, the story means that the Father has granted to the Son complete dominion over the earth, including dominion over the divinely ordained commandments of the scriptures. As the Son of Man interprets the Law, "binding and loosing," so shall it be!

Which of the two meanings is intended, "1" or "2"? We cannot choose between them, nor need we. The ambiguity of the term *bar nash* is probably one thing that made it useful as a title for Jesus in the early days of Christianity, while Christians were still struggling with the question, "Who is Jesus?" The title Son of Man filled this ambiguous role perfectly until the church arrived at its permanent title for Jesus, the Christ.

Charismatic Preacher and Healer

The discussion of Jesus as Son of Man, eschatological prophet or savior is limited in the gospels to the inner circle of disciples. How did the masses to whom Jesus preached understand his message? Who did he seem to be to them? Since the masses did not have a doctrine of the Christ into which they could fit Jesus, what did they think he was? It does not seem that they mistook him for a militant rebel leader, and he did not speak to them like a rabbi. Yet the crowds obviously thought of Jesus in terms of some familiar type of figure, because that is the way people think, by classifying. In what class did they place Jesus?

Look at what Jesus actually did before the crowds! He preached a message of repentance and the coming of God's kingdom. He performed exorcisms, chasing out demons. He performed supernatural miraculous healings.

Jesus' public ministry has been a stumbling block to historians since the very beginning of the modern era. Most historians are scientific rationalists who do not believe in miracles nor in demonic possession. How then explain, especially if they are devout Christians, that their Lord spent most of his public career performing healings and exorcisms?

In the early modern period there were many awkward responses to this problem. Some suggested that the miracles occurred, but they were not really miracles. Jesus fed the multitude from a few loaves and fish, but there was no multiplication. The people were satisfied with a mere crumb because they so enjoyed Jesus' company. Jesus did walk on water, but he stepped on the rocks. People were not really possessed, just out of their minds, but Jesus set their minds at ease and brought them back to normality. Such interpretations do violence to the gospel texts. They make both the stories and their modern interpreters appear silly.

A better method used more recently is to suspend judgement on miracles and exorcisms. Instead we ask the question: "What was the function of the belief in miracles and of miracle stories in first century Judaism?" Clearly, Jews of that time believed that God was providential. God could do anything, and God was graciously pleased to reward the faithful. Miracles were a sign of God's grace and providence. The stories about Jesus as a healer, exorcist and miracle worker demonstrate the belief of Jesus' followers that he had a unique capacity to draw God's saving grace into the world.

During the 1960s, in the midst of the "New Search for the Historical Jesus," Joachim Jeremias made the claim that Jesus was the first and only Jew to address God as Father in the familiar form, "Abba." Jeremias' view was popularized in America during the late 1960s by his disciple, Norman Perrin. Jeremias claimed that Jews addressed God as "Father" or "Our Father in Heaven." They would not have dared be more familiar. Jesus addressed God as "Abba," "Daddy." This represented a new intimacy with God. With this address to God Jesus introduced a whole new religion into the world. (The implication is that Christians have a closeness to God that Jews never did have and never will.) This teaching was widely adopted for a time although it is insulting to Judaism and, for that matter, not especially complimentary to anyone of intelligence. Could a simple change of address, from Father to Daddy, have justified two millennia of efforts by Christians and Jews to distinguish their faith from one another? No wonder contemporary scholars delight in demonstrating that Jeremias' concept, besides being silly, is also untrue. Jeremias acknowledges that he is ignorant of Jewish literature, but he sent his students searching through Jewish prayer literature for the use of the term "Abba." Had they looked instead at Talmudic legend, they would have found it.

Significantly, the address to God as "Abba" is found among one particular type of figure in ancient Judea, the charismatic miracle worker. There are four named examples in the rabbinic literature—Honi the Circlemaker, his grandsons Abba Hilkiah and Hanan ha-Nehbi, and Hanina ben Dosa (incorrectly called "rabbi" in the Talmud). Their stories are told in the Babylonian Talmud tractate Taanit (19a, 23a–b, 24b–25a), which deals with fasts for rain. It was the custom in Judea that if Sukkot passed and rain did not come the people would fast every Monday and Thursday until it began to rain. Rain was the primary material blessing that Jews sought, through prayer, from a caring God who listens and responds, rewards and punishes.

> One year it did not rain. All the fasts and prayers of the people did not avail. The people called on Honi to pray for rain. God answered every prayer of Honi's, said the Sages, because he was entirely free of sin. Honi made a circle and stood in it. He said, "God, I shall not move from this spot

until you have mercy on Your children." God sent the rain. It continued to rain until there was danger of flooding. The people came to Honi again. He told them it was prohibited to pray for it to not rain, but since they pleaded he offered a sacrifice and said: "God, your children cannot endure too much punishment nor too much blessing. Please take away the rain." The wind blew, it stopped raining, mushrooms sprouted, and the people ate them.

Simeon bar Shetah (he was the leading Pharisee, you may remember, in the time of Queen Salome Alexandra) sent word to Honi: "I would excommunicate you if you were not Honi. But what can I do? The One who is everywhere treats you `like a son who ingratiates himself with his father, who then grants his every wish.' No matter what the son requests, the father gives it to him."

We note that Simeon bar Shetah was in conflict with Honi, despite his grudging admiration for Honi's deed in bringing rain. This reminds us of the conflicts between Jesus and the authorities of his day, including the Pharisees and scribes. This suggests to us that Jesus' conflicts were not just a result of his personal activities. They are a reflection of the ongoing battle (which continues to this day in every society) between charismatic authority and traditional authority.

It is told of Abba Hilkiah, grandson of Honi the Circlemaker, that once the Sages came to him to pray for rain. Abba Hilkiah said to his wife: "I know why they have come. Let us privately go up on the roof and pray for rain, and then we shall not receive the credit." They did so. The cloud began to form first over the head of his wife. When they came down from the roof to greet the Sages, it was already raining. Abba Hilkiah said to them: "Blessed be the All-present, who has not made you dependent on Abba Hilkiah." (That is, it is God and not me who brings rain.) The Sages said to him: "We know it is by your merit that rain has fallen....Why did God respond first to your wife? He replied: "My wife gives the poor bread which benefits them immediately, while I give them money whose benefit is delayed."

We note that the Abba Hilkiah story differs from that of Honi in its emphasis on virtue (humility and charity) rather than on charisma. What brings God's mercy? Intense personal relationship, to be sure, but aided by superior character. This reminds us of Jesus' emphasis on private devotion as opposed to outward show in religious matters, and of his ethical maxims.

> Hanan ha-Nehbi was the son of Honi's daughter. The Sages would send the schoolchildren to him. They would take hold of the hem of his garment and say to him "Abba, abba, give us rain." He would then plead with the Holy One "Master of the Universe, do it for the sake of those who do not know the difference between the Abba who gives rain and the abba who does not!"
>
> Of Hanina ben Dosa it was said that he lived in great poverty, surviving on carobs, though the whole world was granted food only for his sake. Once Hanina's daughter accidentally filled the Sabbath oil lamp with vinegar. Hanina said to her, "My daughter, be not concerned. The One who causes oil to burn can cause anything to burn." The lamp burned throughout the Sabbath. (Other miracles are attributed to Hanina in the Talmud and in Ecclesiastes Rabba and Ruth Rabba).
>
> Once Hanina was walking along with a basket of salt on his head when it began to rain. He cried out: "Master of the Universe, the whole world is at ease but Hanina is in distress." The rain stopped. When he got home, he said: "Master of the Universe, the whole world is in distress, and Hanina is at ease." Immediately it began to rain once again.
>
> It was said of Hanina ben Dosa that when he prayed for the sick he would say then if they would live or die. The people asked him "Are you a prophet?" No, he said, but if the prayer comes easily to my tongue then I know that God will heal them. If not, I know my prayer is rejected. Once Rabban Gamaliel sent to him to pray for healing for his son who was sick. Hanina went to the upper room to pray for him. When he came down he said, "Go, for the child's fever has broken." Later they inquired and found that the child had become well at the exact moment Hanina had spoken. (Talmud Berakhot 34b). When Hanina healed the son of Rabban Yohanan ben Zakkai, his wife asked him, "Is this one then greater than you?" Yohanan replied to her, "No, but he is like a servant who attends the king (and can come and go as he wishes) while I am like a nobleman who attends the king (and can only come when summoned.)

There are other healing and miracle stories as well. We note that Hanina ben Dosa's activities were similar to those of Jesus. There is a similar story of Jesus healing a person from a distance (Matt. 8:5–10, Luke 7:1–10).

The following story is instructive. It may remind us of Jesus' teaching on sin and repentance.

> Our masters taught: In a certain place there was a snake that would injure people. They came and told Hanina ben Dosa about it. They showed him the snake's hole. He placed his ankle over it. The snake came out, bit him, and died. "You see, my children," said Hanina, "It is not the snake which kills; it is sin which kills." On that occasion they said: "Woe to the one who meets up with a snake. Woe to the snake who meets up with Rabbi Hanina ben Dosa." (Talmud Berakhot 33a)

The parallels between Jesus and the charismatic miracle-workers of Talmudic legend are numerous:

- The miracle worker is perfect and sinless.
- He has an intimate father-son relationship with God, closer to God than other people, even great sages, are able to achieve
- He is able to perform healings, even from a distance.
- Traditional authority figures look on him with disapproval and even threaten him, yet they too are awed by his power. There is natural conflict between those whose authority is based on traditional power structures and those whose authority is personal and charismatic.
- The miracle worker has great standing with the common folk. This may arouse the envy of traditional leaders, who nevertheless find themselves at times dependent upon his powers.
- The miracle worker is, in some cases, an exemplar of virtue and wisdom. (Not always. Honi came to a bad end because of his haughtiness.)

It would seem from all this that we have located the person-type of Jesus in his public ministry as a miraculous healer, exorcist, preacher of virtue and repentance, champion of the poor and the rejected, and intimate of God. Jesus' audience would have taken him to be a charismatic healer.

There is a further parallel between Jesus and the others we have mentioned here. Honi, his grandchildren and Hanina are all rainmakers. Jesus comes as a bringer of salvation. These roles are not so distinct as they may appear to us. In the land of Israel rain is the primary symbol of salvation and redemption. Not only is rain salvation to material existence, but also to the spirit. The rabbis believed that the resurrection of the dead would be brought about by a special dew that God had reserved in heaven for the end-time. Thus Honi, his grandchildren, and Hanina ben Dosa are, like Jesus, also salvational figures.

Later Charismatic Figures in Judaism

It is interesting to compare Jesus and the miracle workers of rabbinic literature to similar figures who arise later in Jewish history. There are remarkable parallels between Jesus and the story of Rabbi Isaac Luria (thrived c. 1570) and Rabbi Israel ben Eliezer, the Baal Shem Tov (d. 1760). There is no direct line of charismatic leaders from the first century to the sixteenth or eighteenth, so there is no direct historical significance. But we do see how similar social phenomena can arise again and again under similar social conditions, so the comparison of Jesus to Isaac Luria and the Baal Shem Tov is of interest and may be instructive.

Rabbi Isaac Luria is called The ARI (means "lion," acronym for Ashkenazic Rabbi Isaac). The ARI was born and raised in Egypt. In his early 30's he came up to the town of Zefat in the Galilee, where Jewish mystics had gathered to mourn the exile of the Jews from Spain (1492) and seek the final redemption of the Jews from exile. The ARI immediately became the leader of all the great mystical adepts. He taught his doctrines to his circle of disciples, and led them in intensive prayer, meditation and rites of self-negation. He taught that living in this way, coupled with the proper inner attitude and devotion (kavannah) could bring the redemption, which at this moment was all but complete. It was said of the ARI that he could speak the languages of the birds and beasts, that he conversed with deceased saints of old, that he could read the signs of the future in the events of nature, and that he needed merely to look at a person to know his whole life, the state of his soul, and how to bring him to repentance. After a public career of about two years the ARI died of an illness. He left no writings, but his teachings were distilled and written down by his student Haim Vital (Just as Paul and the evangelists composed the New Testament!). The ARI's teachings spread rapidly and became the basis for an entire new understanding of Judaism, the Lurianic Kabbalah.

Israel ben Eliezer was called the Baal Shem Tov (literally "Master of the Good Name," idiomatically, "Miracle-worker.") His acronym is

"The BeShT." The Baal Shem Tov was born in southern Russia, in an area devastated by the Cossack rebellions against Poland and by the partition of Poland by Russia, Austria and Prussia. Jews had become impoverished. The traditional academies of learning had closed. The Jews, unlearned and suffering, could not relate to their learned rabbis. The social gap between haughty learned rabbis and the people was filled by wandering preachers (the "maggid") and miracle workers (the "baal shem"). The Baal Shem Tov arose and organized these folk religious leaders into a new spiritual movement of overwhelming force—Hasidism.

As a young man the BeShT kept his powers hidden. He worked as a schoolteacher's assistant, watching over the children while at night he secretly studied hidden lore. He married and became an innkeeper in a distant village in the Carpathian mountains. The BeShT knew his powers, but remained hidden until the time came to reveal himself. When he was 33 years old (note the parallel to Jesus!) the BeShT began his public career. He went from town to town—healing, performing miracles, preaching sermons of consolation full of earthy parables (the famous Hasidic tales), uplifting the spirits of the people. In a short time his following included most of the Jews of Galicia (southern Poland, including much of what is now the Ukraine).

The charismatic BeShT was opposed by the rabbis, whose authority was based in their knowledge of the Talmud and of Jewish law. The homeland of rabbinism was Lithuania. Lithuania had been spared the devastation of war, and its traditional Jewish society was still intact. (Compare to the conflict between Judea and Galilee in Jesus' time!) The Hasidim called the Lithuanian rabbinical Jews *Misnagdim* ("Protestants"). The leader of the Misnagdim was Rabbi Elijah, the Gaon ("Genius") of Vilna. After failing to halt the spread of Hasidism with multiple threats of excommunication, the Gaon softened and agreed to meet with the BeShT. Their private meeting lasted for four hours. No one ever learned what was said, but the result of the meeting was that the Hasidim remained within Judaism. Had their rebellion gone much further, or had the Misnagdim pushed them harder, Hasidism may have become a new religion separate from Judaism. It may well be that the Gaon of Vilna was aware of the parallels between Jesus' Christian movement and the Baal Shem Tov's Hasidism. He may have acted in order to avoid the type of rift that led to the split of Christianity from Judaism. This is speculation, but it is likely.

Like other charismatic leaders the Baal Shem Tov was neither an organizer nor a writer. He left behind him an idea and a group of followers. After his death his disciples organized into a movement under the leadership of Dov Baer, the Maggid of Mezeritch. Dov Baer was, we may say, the "Paul" of the Hasidic movement.

Nothing was written about the Baal Shem Tov until some decades after his death. Then, beginning with the book *Shivhei HaBeShT* ("In Praise of the Baal Shem Tov"), books were written describing his miracles, his parables and pithy statements and his relationship with his disciples. The parallels to the writing of the New Testament are noticeable.

Many of the BeShT's parables echo precisely the teachings of Jesus. Of course the BeShT could have learned these lessons from his Christian neighbors, but this is most unlikely. The Baal Shem Tov spoke only Yiddish, not Polish or other Gentile languages. In the atmosphere of his day no Jews studied or listened to any Christian teachings. The Baal Shem Tov's teachings were new from his lips, even when they resembled teachings of Jesus.

Since Isaac Luria and the Baal Shem Tov were both mystics who founded mystical movements (Lurianism and Hasidism), we are left to wonder if Jesus was also originally a mystic. Our sources do not portray Jesus in this way, but it is a fascinating possibility to ponder.

13

The Parting of the Ways

The gospels tell us that all of Jesus' followers fled after his arrest. They were scattered and disheartened. Amazingly the disciples reappear on the scene of history a short time later, confident in their faith and seeking new adherents to their faith. Some twenty years after the crucifixion, Paul of Tarsus launched the Gentile church. In the time of the Roman emperor, Nerva, this fast growing new religious movement came to be called the "Christians," after their founder who was called Christ. What renewed the confidence of Jesus' followers? What was the impetus for this fast growing religious movement? According to the New Testament it was the reappearance of the crucified Jesus to the disciples, resurrected either in body (Luke 24:13–49) or in spirit (Acts 9:3–9). The resurrection of Jesus is an article of Christian faith which is not subject to historical analysis. It stands outside the bounds of this book. As historians we can only marvel at the remarkable restoration of Christian fortunes after the initial disappointment at his arrest and execution. What Jesus' followers first experienced as failure, they came to understand as a great triumph which inspired them to seek followers for Christ throughout the world.

It would be nice if we knew more about the first decade or two of Christianity, but no texts from that time survive. Christianity first springs onto the scene in historical memory through the epistles of Paul, then through the four gospels. Already in these texts we can see that Christianity was rapidly pulling away from its Jewish roots, soon to become a separate religion entirely. In this chapter we shall trace this parting of the ways.

Might history have turned out differently? Could Christianity have been kept within the Jewish fold? Might all Jews have joined the Christian sect, making Judaism one and the same with Christianity? Could Judaism rather than Christianity have become the religion of the Roman Empire? Could Judaism and Christianity have evolved in friendship and mutual support rather than in rivalry? These questions are not answerable, but we can understand and improve upon our present situation by learning from the past.

Judaism from the Hurban to the Talmud

After the Hurban (the Jewish word for the destruction of the Temple) the Jewish leaders reorganized under the leadership of Yohanan ben Zakkai, a Pharisaic leader in the School of Hillel. Ben Zakkai organized a new Sanhedrin in the village of Yavneh. The Pharisees were the leading group in this new Sanhedrin of 71 Jewish leaders. They gave Judaism its new, post-Temple direction. Soon Pharisaic identity disappeared as old sectarian issues were no longer relevant to the new situation. The Torah scholars in the Sanhedrin came to be known as rabbis.

When Yohanan ben Zakkai passed away the leadership went back to a traditional aristocrat—Rabban Gamaliel II. He was the son of Simeon ben Gamaliel whom we know from Josephus. He was the grandson of Gamaliel I, who was kind to the apostle Paul. Gamaliel II and his colleagues established the practices and doctrines of rabbinic Judaism. Non-rabbinic groups, such as priestly factions, remained influential for a long time after the Hurban (possibly centuries), but rabbinism grew steadily to eventually become the Judaism of all Jews.

Under Rabban Gamaliel II Rabbi Ishmael, a priest, represented the conservative interpretation of Torah, Rabbi Akiva the liberal view. Rabbi Akiva's views were adopted by Rabbi Judah the Patriarch, author of the Mishnah. The liberal school of thought, representing flexibility in new situations and consideration for the needs of the poor, won in the end over the more conservative ways of interpreting Torah.

Rabbi Akiva and Rabbi Ishmael were both killed by the Romans during the Bar Kokhba rebellion, tortured to death along with many other rabbis, probably in the arena in Antioch. The Jews rebelled in the year 132 CE under the military leader Simon bar Kokhba on account of the anti-Jewish policies of the emperor Hadrian. The Jews objected particularly to his plan to build a new pagan city, Aelia Capitolina, over the ruins of Jerusalem. A revolutionary named Simon bar Kosiba changed his name to bar Kokhba (son of a star, referring to the messianic "star that shall come forth from Jacob" in the Torah [Nu 25:17]). Rabbi Akiva gave official sanction to the rebellion, declaring that Simon bar Kokhba was the Messiah. The Romans destroyed Bar Kokhba's forces. The fall of his final fortress of Betar was a great massacre. It was said that the eastern Mediterranean Sea ran red with Jewish blood. Later Jews called Simon "bar Kozba," the "son of a liar."[14]

After the Romans put down the Bar Kokhba rebellion they allowed the Jews to reestablish the rabbinic Sanhedrin. With Judea devastated by the destruction of two wars, the center of Jewish life now shifted to the Galilee. The Sanhedrin eventually settled in Tiberius, the city established by Herod on the shores of the Sea of Galilee. There Rabbi Judah wrote the Mishnah, and there the Sanhedrin thrived until about the year 400, when the line of rabbinic ordination was broken. The persecutions of the Christianized Byzantine (Eastern Roman) Empire forced the shutting down of the rabbinic academies of Caesarea and Tiberius, and of the Sanhedrin. The Jerusalem Talmud was hurriedly put together at this time to record the teachings of the academies.

The center of Jewish life shifted to Babylon. Jews had lived there in peace and prosperity since the first Exile, though we know little of their earlier life and practice. Rabbi Judah the Patriarch had sent two disciples to Babylon to found academies of rabbinic learning. The academies of Sura and Pumbeditha became the centers of Jewish life in Babylon. The Babylonian Talmud was edited around the years 500–600. The Babylonian Talmud, promoted by the heads of the academies, was gradually accepted by Jews throughout the world. The success of the Babylonian Talmud made Pharisaism, retroactively, the ancestor of all later Judaism.

The Earliest Christians and Judaism

The earliest Christians were loyal Jews. They would gather in the Temple porticos. They faithfully brought sacrifices to the Temple. They observed the food and purity laws of Judaism.[15] Paul of Tarsus broke from the Jerusalem-centered Jewish church when he permitted Gentiles to join the Christian movement without Jewish conversion, thus establishing the Gentile church. Paul permitted Gentile Christians to live by their own laws rather than Jewish law, except for the basic moral code of Judaism (including the prohibition of eating blood, an aspect of Jewish dietary law). Some church leaders objected to Paul's mission to the Gentiles, but soon the Gentile church was so well established that it overwhelmed and absorbed the Jewish Christians.

When the rabbis gained leadership in the Sanhedrin, they attempted to establish their authority over all Jews. One part of this work was to suppress all sectarian movements. There is no indication that the rabbis paid special note to the Christian movement, which was still quite small and powerless, but the Christians for their part naturally felt heavily oppressed by rabbinic opposition to their movement. The gospels were composed in this era. They reflect the conflict between the rabbis and the church, and the bitterness of the church leaders over their lack of acceptance by the Jewish authorities.

In this era Rabban Gamaliel II ordered another prayer added to the daily liturgy—*birkat minim*, the "blessing of the sectarians." The name is a euphemism; the prayer calls upon God to curse the sectarians. The function of this prayer was to drive the sectarians out of the synagogue, since they could hardly pray for God to bring curses down upon their own heads. Modern scholars debate whether this prayer was directed specifically against Christians. We cannot know for sure. The prayer condemns all sectarians without identifying them. We cannot know if the authors of the prayer were thinking of Christians at the time. We do know from Paul's own writings that he received a hostile reception in the synagogues of the Diaspora and was not allowed to preach. It was this rejection by his fellow Jews which led him to his mission to the Gentiles.

In reading the New Testament we must remember that many of the conflict stories do not reflect Jesus' own conflicts with Jewish authorities, but rather the conflict between the primitive church and the official Jewish leaders, who after the year 70 were the Pharisees. It has been unfortunate for the history of Jewish-Christian relations that the New Testament was composed in this atmosphere of mutual hostility. Historical understanding allows us to rise above first century politics in our own understanding of Jesus' message.

Paul, the Evangelists, and Judaism

Each one of the New Testament authors had his own distinct concept of the relationship of Christianity to Judaism. Much scholarly study has been devoted to this subject. We shall limit ourselves here to a brief sketch.

Paul is usually portrayed as the one who established a sharp and complete contrast between Christianity and Judaism. Paul contrasted the old failed dispensation of the Torah to the new salvational dispensation in Christ. There is much in Paul's writings to support this view. See, for instance, Galatians 3, in which Paul compares the "curse" of the Law to the salvation through faith in Christ.

Until recently most modern Jews have followed the Jewish scholar Joseph Klausner in considering Paul rather than Jesus to be the first Christian and the true founder of Christianity. This view is that Jesus was a loyal Jew, observing the Torah, but Paul established a religion about Jesus which negated the Torah. This perspective was developed with a view to "reclaiming Jesus for Judaism," thus hopefully raising the social stature of Jews in modern society. Recent scholarship has shown that this view is an oversimplified judgement. Christianity has its roots in Jesus in many ways. Paul formalized the break from Judaism by establishing the Gentile church, but his own views on Judaism were far from monolithic and were not always aimed toward a break. Though he condemns the Torah in some passages, in others he declares himself a loyal and devoted Jew. We must recall that while Paul allowed the Gentile Christians to disregard the Torah, he himself observed the Torah faithfully in all of its details as well as in spirit. He declared himself to be a true Jew, a "Pharisee and a member of the tribe of Benjamin." We do not know how to judge Paul's claim to be a Pharisee, and first century Jews did not really know their tribal ancestry, but Paul's point is clear. He wished his fellow Jews to consider him as a loyal and faithful Jew. Had he meant to fully repudiate the Torah he would not have made these claims for himself.

Without claiming to understand Paul, I believe that there are two factors in the life and times of Paul that must be taken into account in considering his relationship to Judaism. One is that Paul probably conceived of the transformed life of faith in terms of Torah law. He believed that faith in Christ was a more sure path to right living than the laws of the Torah, but how could one such as Paul conceive of that "right living" in any way other than that defined by the "way of the Torah?" Secondly, Paul believed that within the church Jews would remain Jews and Gentiles would remain Gentiles (Romans 11:17–18). The Gentiles would be a "wild branch" grafted onto the "olive tree," which remains rooted in the people Israel. The church did not evolve as Paul had imagined it. The church became entirely Gentile, which gave Paul's words a different ring than in their original context. Christians did not have Torah within them as Paul had due to his extensive Jewish education. In the course of time any Jew who became Christian lost his Jewish identity and became a Gentile himself.

The gospel of Matthew was composed after the epistles of Paul, and probably in opposition to Paul's dismissal of the law of the Torah. Matthew has Jesus say that, "Not one littlest letter nor crown (decoration on a letter) shall fall away" (Matt 5:17). Modern theologians have suggested that Jesus' statement that he came "not to abolish the Law but to fulfill it" does have the practical effect of abolishing the Law for Christians, but that is probably not Matthew's intent. Matthew speaks for Jewish Christians who believed that every Christian must first become a Jew and observe all the laws of Judaism.

Matthew's heated controversy with the Pharisees is an internal Jewish matter. Matthew believed that Christians must observe the Law, but the Law was in the hands of the Pharisees. The Pharisees were attempting to suppress the Christian sect. How could one obey the Pharisees in other matters but disobey them by remaining a Christian? Matthew's solution is: Respect the Pharisees as teachers and leaders, but they are hypocrites, while Christian Jews must observe the Torah with sincerity (Matt 23).

Matthew repeatedly depicts Jesus as offering his message and his salvation only to Jews. Jesus tells his disciples to preach only in Jewish villages, avoiding Samaritans and Gentiles (Matt 10:5–6). He heals Gentiles only with reluctance (Matt 15:21–28). The negative view of Gentiles in the book of Matthew has been unjustly attributed by some modern scholars to a "typical Jewish attitude" of the time. That is a wrongful charge on two counts. First, Matthew attributes this attitude to Jesus himself, not to the disciples or the Jewish community. Secondly, we see from historical analysis that Matthew was not expressing a general Jewish attitude to Gentiles but his own opposition to the establishment of the non-Jewish Gentile church. In comparison to Matthew, the preserved words of the Jewish sages reveal a variety of attitudes to Gentiles. Some Jews were contemptuous toward the non-Jewish world. Some Jews believed in maintaining cordial relations. Some Jews had a friendly and cordial attitude to Gentiles and even dined with them, eating "kosher style" and avoiding certain types of food that may have been tainted by idolatry.

The author of the gospel of Luke has a friendly attitude toward Judaism. He depicts Jesus and his family as devout Jews, fulfilling all aspects of Torah. Mary brings her sacrifices to the Temple after the birth of her son. Jesus amazes the scholars of Torah with his brilliant arguments while just a boy of twelve (is this his "bar mitzvah" ceremony?) Jesus maintains cordial relations with the Pharisees and is admired by many of them.

Luke's positive portrayal of Jesus' Jewish life does not necessarily derive from a positive evaluation of the role of Judaism in God's plan for humankind. Luke is a Gentile Christian who believes that the Christians have become the "true Israel," while the Jews have become the "rejected Israel." God's rejection of the Jews is represented by the destruction of the Temple, a "prediction" in the Jesus story but a recent reality at the time Luke composed his gospel.

Luke adopts the prophetic view of a "saving remnant" of faithful Jews who carry on the covenant when the people have abandoned it. To Luke, the saving remnant becomes smaller and smaller until, in the time of Jesus, it is represented only by Jesus himself and his disciples. After Easter, the saving remnant is the church, and the number of covenanted persons grows again within the church. This has been called the "hourglass view" of Jewish history. Luke's view of Jesus and Judaism has been interpreted by "supercessionists" to mean that Christianity arose not just as a new religion, but as a divinely ordained replacement for Judaism. In this book we have rejected supercessionism, suggesting instead that Judaism and Christianity each have a role in God's plan. We agree with the recent teaching of many Christian churches that "God does not renege on promises" (I Sam 15:29). God's covenant with the people Israel remains eternally valid alongside the Christian covenant.

Luke's positive portrayal of Jesus and his family as loyal Jews can be interpreted to support this dual-covenant theology.

There is a general consensus that the gospel of John is the most non-Jewish of all the gospels. John is a Gentile Christian for whom the Jewish origins of Jesus have lost all meaning. John portrays Jesus as a Christian among non-believing Jews. Some New Testament scholars have adopted just the opposite view, that John is the most Jewish of the evangelists, but one would have to look hard to find a Jewish reader of John who would agree with this view. It can be argued that the "Jews" in the gospel of John are "Judeans." Their opposite is not "Christians" but "Galileans." If so, John is portraying authentic Jewish regional rivalries rather than later Jewish-Christian conflicts. This is clearly true of some passages in John, but it seems unlikely in most cases.

Historical Causes of the Split between Judaism and Christianity

Despite Paul's establishment of the Gentile church, Christianity remained a sect within Judaism for quite some time. It took centuries for a complete break to take place. There was no sudden rift between Christians and Jews, but rather an ever-widening chasm that grew over the years. Some of the causes were doctrinal. Others were social and historical. We can identify some of the major causes of the split:

Paul's Mission to the Gentiles

As we have seen, Paul allowed Gentiles to become Christian while retaining their national identity as Greeks, Romans or whatever. Christianity became an extra-national identity, while Jews were Jewish by nationality as well as religion. Gentile Christians lived under their customary laws rather than Jewish law.

Birkat HaMinim

The "curse upon the sectarians" in the daily liturgy forced sectarian groups out of the synagogue. Christians could no longer pray amongst their fellow Jews. They needed to establish their own houses for worship and Christian preaching. These separate Christian gatherings became the churches.

Shift of Blame for the Crucifixion

As Christians abandoned the mission to their fellow Jews and proselytized among the Gentiles they shifted blame for the crucifixion of Jesus from the Romans to the Jews—not just some Jews, but the Jewish people as a whole. The Jews were branded as deicides—killers of God. This accusation became a deep source of hatred against the Jews.

The Great Rebellion

The Jewish Christians, centered in Jerusalem, did not join in the rebellion against Rome. They removed themselves as a group to Antioch. This probably created a social rift between Jews and Christians. The break in social relationships and resentments over the war may have been more significant in the Jewish-Christian split than all the religious issues of doctrine and practice. After the war the Romans branded the Jews as rebels. There was less admiration for Jews, more contempt. It no longer behooved Christians to associate their movement with the ancient Jewish tradition. From this point in time it made more sense for Christians to distance themselves from the Jewish people, especially in light of their mission to convert the Gentiles.

Theodicy

The word "theodicy" means justifying the acts of God. After the year 70 Jews needed to explain to themselves how God could have allowed the wicked Romans to destroy his own Temple. The Christians had an answer: God was punishing the Jews for rejecting Christ. Jews rejected and resented this answer. The Jews' own answer was: God has punished us for our sins, but if we live by the Torah and repent God will take us back in mercy and rebuild the Temple. Jews resented Christian taunts about the destruction of the Temple, while Christians were annoyed by what seemed in their eyes to be "spiritual blindness" among the Jews for failing to recognize the "true" cause of their sufferings.

Roman Recognition

Around the year 98 the Roman emperor, Nerva, decreed that Christians did not have to pay the *fiscus Judaeus*, the punitive annual tax upon the Jews. This amounted to legal recognition on the part of the empire that Christians were not a sect of Jews, but a separate religion. This was not entirely a benefit for Christians. Judaism was a licit religion, protected under the laws of the Roman state. Jews had a special dispensation from the Romans that went back to Julius Caesar—for example, the right to withdraw from pagan civic rites. Now that Christians were not recognized as Jews, theirs was an outlaw religion. Christians were persecuted for disobedience to the emperor because they would not worship the gods of the state.

The Bar Kokhba Revolt

When Simon bar Kokhba led his rebellion against the Roman Empire (132–135 CE) Rabbi Akiva gave him an official rabbinic imprimatur as the true Messiah. This may have been the last straw for Jewish Christians. They could tolerate the disapproval of Jewish leaders toward the Christian sect. The one thing they could not tolerate was the declaration of a rival Messiah. Many historians believe that this was the most significant event in the rift between Judaism and Christianity.

Friendly Relations and Syncretism

Our review of the conflicts between Jews and Christians may leave us with the impression that their relations were entirely negative in character. That is far from the truth. There is much evidence that on a daily basis Jews and Christians interacted freely and with great cordiality. Since many Christians, including Gentile Christians, observed Jewish religious customs it was not entirely clear where the line was drawn between Jewish identity and Christian identity. We can imagine that this line was extremely important to bishops and to rabbis. As we go further down the ladder of religious authority, people cared less about the distinctions. It is likely that for centuries many people went back and forth between church and synagogue with no particular sense of conflict or incongruity. They took what they liked from each, while not overtly breaking any Jewish biblical prohibitions. They observed the social/religious customs that were common to both groups, such as hand-washing and Sabbath observance.

The Christian Empire and Christian-Jewish Relations

In the early 300's the Roman emperor, Constantine, converted to Christianity. He legalized the religion, then began to promote it. Christianity was eventually declared the official religion of the empire.

Constantine moved the capital of the empire to the East, to the city of Constantinople on the Bosporus straits in Asia Minor (modern-day Istanbul in Turkey). He abandoned the Western empire to the onslaughts of the Germanic tribal invaders. The Christian Eastern Empire is called the Byzantine Empire.

Byzantine Persecutions

Now that Christianity was the religion of the empire, Constantine set about unifying the faith. His interest was not only religious but political, to use religion to unite his subjects. In a series of great meetings the Byzantine bishops established the Nicene Creed as official Christian doctrine. They set about suppressing heretical forms of Christianity. Among the heresies was Arianism. Arian Christians did not believe that Jesus was divine. Their form of Christianity was similar to Judaism and Arians were friendly to Jews. At the other extreme the church condemned Marcionism, a Gnostic form of Christianity which was hostile to Jews and Judaism. The Marcionists wanted to eliminate the Hebrew scriptures from Christianity, which would have completely separated Christianity from its Jewish roots. The form of Christianity that prevailed was moderate in its attitude to Jews, neither as antagonistic as Marcionism nor as friendly as Arianism.

The Jews would have been in big trouble had Judaism been declared a heresy, but fortunately Judaism was acknowledged as a separate religion, and the Jews were validated as the biblical people of God. Christian policy, which was to be fairly constant for the next 1,500 years, was to permit Judaism to survive but to surround Jews with degrading persecutions designed to nudge them toward conversion. The Byzantine emperors passed numerous anti-Jewish laws. They prohibited Christians from converting to Judaism. They prohibited the building of new synagogues. They freed Jewish-owned slaves who converted to Christianity. They prohibited Christians from working for Jews. Many of the anti-Jewish laws were not observed in practice except during brief times of persecution.

The Failure to Rebuild the Temple

In 362 Julian the Apostate, the last non-Christian emperor, acceded to the throne. Julian was a devout pagan. He tried to suppress

ROMAN EMPERORS FROM
AUGUSTUS TO CONSTANTINE

Augustus	27 B.C.E.-14 C.E.
Tiberius	14-37 C.E.
Caligula	37-41
Claudius	41-54
Nero	54-68
Galba	68-69
Vespasian	69-79
Titus	79-81
Domitian	81-96
Nerva	96-98
Trajan	98-117
Hadrian	117-138
Antonius Pius	138-161
Lucius Verus	161-169
Cammadus	176-192
Septimius Severus	193-197
Clodius Albinus	193-197
Pescennius Niger	193-194
Caracalla	198-217
Geta	209-212
Macrinus	217-218
Diadumenianus	218
Elagabalus	218-222
Severus Alexander	222-235
Maximinus	235-238
Philip the Arab	244-249
Decius	249-251
Trebonianus Gallus	251-253
Valerian	253-260
Gallienus	253-268
Aurelius	268-270
Aurelian	270-275
Probus	276-282
Diocletian	284-305
Maximianus	286-305
Constantius I	293-306
Galerius	293-311
Constantine I	306-337

Christianity and bring back the old religion. Julian promoted Judaism, possibly just to annoy Christians, or possibly because he believed that Jewish sacrifices were pleasing to the divinity. Julian granted the Jews permission to rebuild the Temple in Jerusalem.

The project had barely gotten underway when Julian was killed in a military campaign against the Persians. His successors were Christian, and the permission to rebuild the Temple was rescinded. The Jewish hope of restoration came to nought.

Jewish historians are mixed on the importance to Jewish history of the failure of Julian's plan to rebuild the Temple. Some historians believe that this was a major disaster for the Jews, possibly even more disastrous than the two rebellions against Rome. Some believe that after Julian's death Jews defected to Christianity en masse, driven by despair and profoundly affected by the Christian taunt that God was humiliating the Jews for rejecting Jesus. This era, claim some historians, was the low point in all of Jewish history.

Other historians view the evidence differently. They claim that most Jews were not interested in Julian's plans to begin with. It was he, and not the Jews themselves, who initiated the project. There is no evidence of massive Jewish support. Possibly by the fourth century Jews no longer really missed the Temple very much. Their religion was complete without it. Scholars who adopt this point of view believe that Judaism continued to thrive, that Judaism remained strong throughout the Diaspora, and that despite government persecutions the Jews remained aggressive in support of their faith and defiant of their opponents. They point to the fact that in the early seventh century, when the Persians invaded Jerusalem, the Jews had the heart to join the Persians in military conflict against their oppressors.

Suppression of the Judaizing Heresy

Around the year 380 CE the church father, John Chrysostom, was appointed Bishop of Antioch. When he came to the city, he was shocked to find his flock regularly attending the synagogue, enjoying the sermons there and socializing with Jews. The Christians treated rabbis as holy men, going to them for amulets, blessings and cures. John Chrysostom responded with his ten famous sermons *Adversus Judaeus*, "Against the Jews." He condemned the Jews in the strongest terms as servants of the Devil. He forbade social and economic contact of any kind with Jews, much less a sharing of religious ideas and practices.

John Chrysostom's strong polemics were typical of the rhetoric of the time. He himself maintained cordial relations with Jews, even while thundering his sermons from the pulpit. However exaggerated in style, these sermons became the basis for church policy. Judaism was utterly condemned as a debased, even Satanic religion. Contact with Jews was restricted. Attendance at Jewish rites was prohibited. Christians were prohibited by law from "Judaizing"—that is, from observing Jewish rites, laws and customs. Christians were prohibited from keeping kosher, celebrating Jewish holidays, or visiting synagogues.

The Ebionites, or Jewish Christians, had become increasingly marginalized. Now they disappeared altogether. To become a Christian was to reject Jewish identity and become a Gentile, with no exceptions.

The church made an effort at this time to eliminate any dependency upon Judaism. They established rules for the Christian sacred calendar so as not to be dependent on rabbis for the setting of dates. The rules for dating Easter were changed to make sure that Easter would never fall on the eve of Passover, lest anyone mistake the one observance for the other. Sunday rather than Saturday was the Christian day of rest.

Judeo-Christianity Today

From the late fourth century on the break between Judaism and Christianity was complete. From this point on we see two separate and distinct religions, each with its own exclusive path to salvation, sharing a common history but also differing from one another in many respects. There is no going back to the beginning, no undoing the final and perhaps inevitable break between Judaism and Christianity.

It is interesting to note that in the fourth century Christians felt threatened by "Judaizing" Christians, while in our times the Jews feel threatened by "Jewish-Christian" movements.

In the early centuries of the Common Era Christianity was still a young and new religion. Many people thought of Christians as "some kind of Jews." The Christians had to struggle hard to establish their own identity, lest they be swallowed up in the Jewish fold and lost.

Today, after two millennia of Jewish powerlessness, the relationship is reversed. Christian identity is not at stake, with more than a billion Christians living on earth. It is the Jews—few in number, powerless, often subject to persecution, who fear being swallowed. Whichever group is relatively small and powerless feels that attempts to minimize differences are really threats of destruction by the more established party. Jews of today, like fourth century Christians, wish to be acknowledged as believers in a separate and distinct religion that is complete in itself. Every religion has its own integrity. The ultimate goal is not merger but mutual respect.

Conclusion

Our story is now ended. Out of the biblical religion of the people of Judah two new religions have evolved—rabbinic Judaism, destined to be the religion of the Jewish people, and Christianity, destined to be the religion of more people than any other religion on earth.

We have studied the causes of this religious revolution to the extent that historians can discover them—the centralization and then elimination of sacrifice in Judaism, the cultural clash of Hellenism and Judaism, the crisis of Jewish leadership after the Maccabean revolt, the growth of new doctrines, the conflict of sects, the great conflict and open war between Rome and Jerusalem. We may also, if we wish, permit ourselves to perceive the hand of God working behind the scenes.

In our historical study we have traversed the eras of the Persian, Greek, Roman and Byzantine empires. We encounter the Jews as they return from exile in Babylon and confirm that the Torah will be the constitution of their new country. The people welcome the conquests of Alexander the Great, but eventually fall into conflict with their Greek overlords. After the revolt of the Maccabees, the Hasmoneans become high priests and kings in Judea. They establish a brief era of independence until the Romans take over. The Romans rule for decades through their client King Herod, then directly through governors. Judea lies in ruin after the failure of two Jewish rebellions against Rome. The Jews reconstitute themselves as a nation under the leadership of the rabbis. Meanwhile a small sect of Jews, the Christians, grows and extends into the Gentile world. In the fourth century Christianity becomes the religion of the Roman emperors, then of the empire.

We have studied the religious beliefs and rites of first century Jews—their holy days, their daily sacred service, their prayers and ceremonies, their concept of holiness and purity, the divine law by which they lived. We have learned about the various texts which are the source of our knowledge of early Judaism and early Christianity. We have seen that Christianity and rabbinic Judaism are both grounded in the varied Judaism of the first century, each religion in its own way.

We can perceive in our study how Jesus fits into the religious, political and cultural scene of his time. His teachings, his life story, his relationships, the things that were said of him by early Christians—all are best understood against the backdrop of Jesus' own times and place.

Out of our study, we pray, we shall come to know ourselves better, and appreciate one another all the more.

Notes

1. Jews prefer the terms BCE and CE to the terms of Christian faith BC (before Christ) and AD (Anno Domini, Year of our Lord). BCE means "Before Common Era." CE means "Common Era"—the era in which we live.

2. We will learn more about all of these sectarian and sacred writings in a later chapter.

3. This was the theory of Elias Bickerman, who attributed the survival of Judaism to the Jews' unique willingness to translate their scriptures into the Greek tongue.

4. The anonymous prophet of the Exile, Deutero-Isaiah, author of Isaiah 40 ff., is a major proponent of this idea.

5. No relationship to the Hasidic movement which arose in eighteenth century Poland under the Baal Shem Tov.

6. This story is repeated in the Talmud as the tale of a mother and her five sons. In the Talmudic version the arguments for bodily resurrection are not present, and the story is presented only as a tale of martyrdom.

7. See Braun, Jesus of Nazareth, Ch. 12 "Jesus' Authority," Phila., Fortress, 1979.

8. The earliest texts which discuss Torah as logos are from the 4th century, but clearly the idea had a much longer development. One cannot say which came first, the Jewish association of logos with Torah or the Christian association with Christ. No direct influence is necessary, since the concepts of Greek philosophy were prevalent and readily available to all.

9. In the First Temple the Ark of the Covenant stood in the Holy of Holies, surrounded by the two cherubim. In the Second Temple the Holy of Holies was completely unfurnished.

10. It is redundant to say "seder meal." The term "seder" includes the meal, the ritual, and the liturgy which accompanies it.

11. Talmud Sotah 20a–22b, Yerushalmi Sotah 3:4, 19a and 5:7, 20c.

12. How curious that in all the written record only two individuals ever claim to be Pharisees, Paul and Josephus! One was an apostate from Judaism, the other a traitor. This leaves us at a loss for how to evaluate their claims. No one knows what it meant to say of oneself "I am a Pharisee."

13. See I Enoch 46 and 48, pp. 34ff in The Old Testament pseudepigrapha, vol.1, ed. Charlesworth, Doubleday 1983.

14. It is interesting that letters in his hand and signed by him were found in the Judean desert, and are on display in the Israel Museum in Jerusalem. Imagine, the actual writing of a famous personage from a mere century after the time of Jesus!

15. This is a good indication that Jesus did not condemn food and purity rituals per se. He criticized those who performed these rites without proper intention.

Reader's Bibliography

The books below are recommended to the reader who wishes to learn more about Judaism in the time of Jesus from the original texts and from the top scholars in the field.

ORIGINAL SOURCES

Bible, *Harper Collins Study Bible*, New RSV, contains Hebrew Scriptures, Apocrypha and New Testament), 1993.

Mishnah, transl. Herbert Danby, Oxford Univ. Press, London, 1933.

Old Testament Pseudepigrapha, The, 2 vols., ed. James Charlesworth, Doubleday, NY, 1983.

Dead Sea Scriptures, The, ed. Theodor H. Gaster, Anchor Books, NY, 1976.

Dead Sea Scrolls in English, The, ed. Geza Vermes, Penguin, Baltimore, 1962. (This work appears in a number of editions, each one containing more materials than the last.)

Josephus, The Works of, transl. William Whiston, Hendrickson Publishers, Peabody MA, 1987.

Talmud, The Babylonian, multiple vols., London, Soncino Press, 1935–48.

Temple Scroll, The, transl. Johann Maier, JSOT, Sheffield England, 1985.

RECENT SECONDARY WORKS

Readability Index: * very readable; ** readable; *** difficult

Abernathy, David, *Understanding the Teaching of Jesus*, Seabury Press, NY, 1983. *

One of many textbooks which summarize the findings of the "New Search for the Historical Jesus." It is unfortunate that this and many college textbooks on the life of Jesus repeat theological prejudices about early Judaism being a religion of strict judgement, sexism, hypocrisy, inferior ethics, and dry ritualism—even while trying to avoid anti-Judaism.

Braun, Herbert, *Jesus of Nazareth: The Man and His Time*, Fortress Press, Phila., 1979. *
Another college textbook on Jesus, taking an extremely rationalist point of view toward Jesus' life and teachings.

Charlesworth, James H., *Jesus Within Judaism*, Doubleday, NY, 1988. **
Great Christian scholar of Pseudepigrapha gives an appreciative account of the Jewish religion and society which was the world of Jesus and his early followers.

_____, *Jesus' Jewishness*, Crossroad, 1991. *
Nine essays by leading Jewish and Christian scholars on the Jewish background to Jesus' life and work and the Jewish self-understanding of the early church.

Cohen, Shaye J.D., *From the Maccabees to the Mishnah*, Westminster Press, NY, 1987. *
Excellent historical survey of the period in which early Judaism and early Christianity blossomed.

Connick, C. Milo, *Jesus: The Man, the Mission and the Message*, Prentice-Hall, Englewood Cliffs, NJ, 1974. **
Another college textbook.

Crossan, John Dominic, *The Historical Jesus*, Harper, 1991. **
In 500 pages, Crossan summarizes everything!—all of the search for the historical Jesus and the new search, all the research done by everyone on the more recent Jesus scholarship. He is objective and more than fair to Judaism and Christianity. He perhaps pays too much attention to the Greco-Roman setting of Jesus' life and not quite enough to the peculiarities of Judea, and his list of "authentic" Jesus sayings is as suspect as everyone else's, but there is not much to quibble with here. Hunker down and read!

Davies, W.D., *The Setting of the Sermon on the Mount*, Scholars Press, Atlanta, 1989. **
The Jewish background to Jesus' ethical teachings.

_____, *Christian Origins and Judaism*, Westminster, Phila., 1962.**

_____, *Paul and Rabbinic Judaism*, Fortress Press, Phila., 1980. ***
Rediscovering the self-proclaimed "Pharisee of Pharisees" in the writings of Paul, for those who want to enter into the exceedingly complex question of Paul's views and his effect on the relationship of Judaism and Christianity.

Dodd, C.H., *The Founder of Christianity*, Macmillan, NY, 1970. *
    Begins as a book on history and gradually shifts to become a work
    of theology. Demonstrates how modern Christian belief can be
    informed by the study of history, with a result that is respectful to
    Judaism and full of Christian spirit.
Endo, Shusaku, *A Life of Jesus*, Paulist Press, 1973. *
    A novelistic life of Jesus by a Japanese writer. Very popular book.
    Endo is an amateur of limited scholarship. He is anxious to avoid
    anti-Semitism but he falls into it anyway, perhaps because as a
    Japanese he lacks the cultural cues. Avoids deicide accusation, but
    characterizes Judaism as arid legalism and strict judgmentalism.
    Today's Christians like Endo's view of Jesus as, above all, a
    personal friend.
Hadas-Lebel, Mirielle, *Flavius Josephus*, transl. Richard Miller, Mac-
    millan, NY, 1993. *
    Written in colloquial English, delightful to read, traces Josephus'
    life and reveals the world in which he lived.
Hengel, Martin, *The Zealots*, T&T Clark, Edinburgh, 1989. ***
    Very scholarly and thorough. You can read his conclusions in
    more readable form in the works of Horsley (see below) and
    Crossan (see above).
Horsley, Richard A., w/ Hanson, John S., *Bandits, Prophets and Messiahs:
    Popular Movements at the Time of Jesus*, Harper and Row, 1985. *
    Objective history mingled with a bit of left-wing liberation
    theology on first century Judaism as class-conflict.
Kee, Howard Clark, *Jesus in History: An Approach to the Study of the
    Gospels*, 2nd edition, HBJ, NY, 1977. **
    College textbook. Emphasis on sources of the New Testament and
    the development of Christian traditions about Jesus.
Kraft, Robert A. and Nickelsburg, George W.E., eds., *Early Judaism and
    its Modern Interpreters*, Scholars Press, Atlanta, 1986.
    A brief review of the issues with a summary of secondary texts.
    Essentially a bibliography, useful for scholarly reference.
Lee, Bernard J., *The Galilean Jewishness of Jesus*, Paulist Press, Mahwah
    NJ, 1988. **
    A theological exploration which seeks the Christian meaning of
    Jesus' Jewish identity.
Neusner, Jacob, *From Politics to Piety*, Ktav, NY, 1979. **
    A definitive account of the history of the Pharisees, based on all
    textual evidence, including the New Testament.
Parkes, James, *The Conflict of the Church and the Synagogue*, Atheneum,
    NY *

Great Christian proponent of interfaith dialogue explores the ancient parting of the ways between Judaism and Christianity and traces the development of Christian anti-Judaism.

Salderini, Anthony J., *Pharisees, Scribes and Sadducees in Palestinian Society*, Michael Glazier, Wilmington, DE, 1988. ***

Source for the very popular (non-Marxist) class conflict theory of the Pharisees. Difficult reading. The book gets more readable as it gradually shifts from sociological theory to historical analysis of the texts.

_____, *Jesus and Passover*, Paulist Press, Mahwah, 1984. *

The great scholar writes here for the general audience, bringing to life the experience of Passover in Jesus' time and the meaning of Passover symbolism to Christians.

Sanders, E.P., *Jesus and Judaism*, Fortress Press, Phila., 1985. **

Superb scholarship, chapters cover a variety of topics of interest. Many of the issues will be covered in Sander's latest views in his 1992 work (see below).

_____, *Jewish Law from Jesus to the Mishnah*, Trinity Press Int'l, Phila., 1990. ***

Five studies. A work of the highest importance, though it is not reading matter for the faint-hearted. Sanders is to be commended for studying Jesus' relationship to Jewish law on a case by case basis, rather than generalizing. He brings necessary corrections to Neusner's work, though with something of a grudge. He gives some interesting insights on the identity of the Pharisees in relationship to "normative" Jewish practices of the time.

_____, *Judaism: Practice and Belief 63BCE–66 CE*, Trinity Press Int'l, Phila., 1992. **

Comprehensive, appreciative yet objective. A fine work, which summarizes all of recent scholarship. If you are only going to read one scholarly book and you are willing to work hard, this is the book!

Schiffman, Lawrence H., *From Text to Tradition: A History of Second Temple and Rabbinic Judaism*, Ktav, NY, 1991. *

Excellent historical survey of the events and movements that lead to early Judaism and early Christianity, with emphasis on the roots of rabbinic Judaism and its central text, the Talmud.

Schurer-Vermes, *The History of the Jewish People in the Age of Jesus Christ*, 3 vols., revised and ed. G. Vermes, F. Millar and M. Goodman, T&T Clark, Edinburgh, 1973. ***

Emil Schurer was anti-Semitic, but a great scholar. His compendium of source materials on our subject would be listed under the classics of early Judaism scholarship, except that it has been thoroughly updated by Vermes, et al. A resource book, not readable, this work catalogues all the literary and archeological resources on the subject.

Shanks, Hershel, ed., *Christianity and Rabbinic Judaism*, BAS, 1992. *
Picks up history where other books leave off, from first to sixth centuries. Nine top scholars of both faiths. Their prejudices are evident, and balance each other nicely. Mostly quite readable.

_____ , *Understanding the Dead Sea Scrolls*, Random House, NY, 1992. *
A collection of articles from the "Biblical Archaeology Review." This comprehensive book is the best and most interesting way to get intelligent information on scrolls scholarship and its implications for our understanding of the past.

_____ , *The Search for Jesus: Modern Scholarship Looks at the Gospels*, B.A.S., Washington D.C., 1994
Transcript of a presentation by three scholars. Doesn't go very deep, but you can catch up on the latest fads in the historical study of Jesus' life.

Sigal, Phillip, *The Halakah of Jesus of Nazareth According to the Gospel of Matthew*, University Press of Am., Lanham MD, 1986. ***
Scholarly thesis by a rabbi on the relationship between Jesus' teachings and rabbinic law.

Vermes, Geza, *Jesus the Jew*, Fortress Press, Phila., 1973. **
Classic study by a great scholar. Famed analysis of the different titles used for Jesus, and what they meant in his time.

_____ , *Jesus and the World of Judaism*, Fortress Press, Phila., 1983. **
Highly qualified scholarly treatment of the gospels, the "Son of Man" controversy, the Dead Sea Scrolls, and other topics of interest. Not as interesting to the general reader as Vermes' third book in his trilogy, see below.

_____ , *The Religion of Jesus the Jew*, Fortress, Minn, 1993. *
More readable than his previous works, this work by the famed Jewish scholar of the Dead Sea Scrolls and New Testament, like Klausner, reclaims Jesus for Judaism, this time on the basis of the most up-to-date scholarship. Whether or not you like his conclusions, his presentation is forthright and compelling.

Weiss-Marin, Trude, *Judaism and Christianity: the Differences*, Jonathan David, NY, 1948. *
Summarizes the more recent traditional-Jewish view of Jesus and Christianity emphasizing differences rather than similarities. Presents a "non-Jewish Jesus" from a Jewish perspective.

CLASSIC SECONDARY WORKS

Baeck, Leo, *Judaism and Christianity*, Jewish Publication Society, Phila, 1958. Especially essay "Romantic Religion." * *
Great German Jewish theologian explores the differences and similarities between the two religions. His defense of Judaism in the face of pro-Nazi university scholarship on religion.

Bickerman, Elias, *From Ezra to the Last of the Maccabees*, Schocken, NY, 1949, 1962. *
Concise, classic historical account of the early Second Temple period.

Bultmann, Rudolf, *Primitive Christianity*, Fortress Press, Phila., 1949, 1956, Fortress Edition, 1980. * *
Anti-Semitic; otherwise valuable. Bultmann was the father of the great form-critical school of New Testament interpretation.

Herford, R. Travers, *The Pharisees*, Beacon Press, Boston, 1924, 1962. * *
This text, along with Moore's *Judaism*, represents the appreciative school of Christian scholarship into Judaism in the time of Jesus.

_____, *The Ethics of the Talmud: Sayings of the Fathers*, Schocken, NY, 1945, 1962. *
Why bother reading Herford's big book when you can get the gist of his message in his delightful and edifying commentary to this beloved volume of ancient Jewish wisdom.

Jeremias, Joachim, *The Prayers of Jesus*, SCM Press, London, 1967. * *
This work dominated discussion of the historical Jesus for a period, under the influence of Jeremias' disciple Norman Perrin. The work is insulting to Judaism, and perhaps to all thinking people.

Klausner, Joseph, *Jesus of Nazareth*, Macmillan, NY, 1926. * *
The first great Jewish study on the life of Jesus. Presents the "Jewish Jesus" widely acknowledged by Jews to this day, who see Jesus as a loyal Jew, with a separate Christianity arising only later, in the time of Paul.

Moore, George Foot, *Judaism*, Cambridge, Harvard Univ. Press, 1946. 3 vols. * *
The classic and definitive pro-Jewish Christian account of Judaism in the time of Jesus, by a great historical scholar. Bends over backwards so far to undo centuries of anti-Semitic prejudice in historical scholarship that it becomes an uncritical paeon of praise to Pharisaic Judaism.

Sartre, Jean-Paul, *Anti-Semite and Jew*, Schocken, NY, 1948. * *

Modern philosopher explores the psychological and social roots of modern anti-Semitism.

Sandmel, Samuel, *We Jews and Jesus*, Oxford Univ. Press, NY, 1965. *
    Samuel Sandmel was a gentleman and a scholar, and one of the greatest Jewish scholars of early Christianity. This book features one of the best summaries of the search (and new search) for the historical Jesus, and a sensitive Jewish perspective on Jesus. See Sandmel's other books, too!

_____, *A Jewish Understanding of the New Testament*, University Publishers, NY, 1956. *

Schweitzer, Albert, *The Quest of the Historical Jesus*, MacMillen, 1968. ***
    Classic summary of 19th C. German Jesus scholarship. Wittily mocks view of Jesus as a liberal philosopher, and presents clear view of Jesus as an apocalyptic Jewish preacher—a person of his time, and not of modern times!

Tcherikover, Victor, *Hellenistic Civilization and the Jews*, Atheneum, NY, 1975. **
    Definitive, exhaustive historical study of Judaism in Greek period. Overwhelms you with information, but when it's all over you will know a lot.

Weiss-Marin, Trude, ed., *Jewish Expressions on Jesus: An Anthology*, Ktav, NY, 1977. **
    Contains many important materials, including Ben-Zion Bokser's famous Jewish analysis of the Sermon on the Mount, presenting a very "Jewish Jesus," and the famous essay by the Jewish theologian Martin Buber, "Two Types of Faith."

Yadin, Yigal, *The Message of the Scrolls*, Simon and Schuster, 1957. *
    Account by the Israeli general and archaeologist and, for many years, chief Israeli scrolls scholar, son of the Israeli professor Sukenik who first brought the scrolls to light.

Zeitlin, Solomon, *Who Crucified Jesus?*, Bloch, NY, 1964, 1975. *
    Great Jewish historical scholar responds to the anti-Jewish accusation of deicide. "The Romans did it!" The scholarship is somewhat eccentric.

Index

and Temple, 145
as associations, 145
as philosophical groups, 145
as political parties, 145
group identity, 144, 145
texts of, 105
writings of, 14
wrote Pseudepigrapha, 116
seder, 101
and Christian symbols, 102
Seleucus, 35, 36, 49
Sepphoris, 162
Septuagint, 39, 40, 104, 114, 115
Sermon on the Mount, 164, 173
Shammai, 137, 148, 151, 153,
    154
Shammai, House of, 136
Shavuot, 97-100
shekel, 91
Shema, 82, 86
Shemaiah, 148, 149, 154
Shemaiah and Avtalion, 71
Sheol, 60
Sicarii, 75, 77, 140, 146, 166
Siloam, 99
Simeon ben Gamaliel, 80, 185
Simeon the Just, 49
Simon bar Kokhba, 185, 186,
    192
Simon bar Shetah, 66, 68, 69,
    178
Simon Hasmoneus, 56, 63, 168
Solomon, King, 18
Son of Man, 173-176
source texts, 104
Stoics, 136, 145, 162
Sukkot, 65, 97-101, 177
supercessionism, 12, 95, 118,
    190
symposium, 102
synagogue, 86-88, 100, 142, 164,
    187

becomes house of prayer, 87
in Diaspora, 87
syncretism, 82, 192

Taanit, 177
tallit, 91
Talmud, 9, 14, 104, 142, 151,
    160, 186
tannaim, 110
Targum, 104
tax collectors, 75
Teacher of Righteousness, 121
Tefilah, 86
tefilin, 91
Temple, 18, 19, 21, 23, 30, 38,
    69, 70, 84, 85, 89, 91, 98,
    126, 139, 145, 166
and purity laws, 89
and theodicy, 191
attempt to rebuild, 195
destroyed by Romans, 73, 77,
    112
dues to, 91, 92
in Leontopolis, 55
in Mishnah, 109
Jesus cleanses, 129
rebuilt by Herod, 73
Temple
replaced by synagogue, 100
Temple Scroll, 121
Testament of the Twelve
    Patriarchs, 115
Testimonium Flavianum, 113,
    114
The Egyptian, 166
Theudas, 128, 166
Thomas, Gospel of, 105
Tiberius, City of, 71, 162, 186
Tiberius Julius Alexander, 115
Time Periods, 5
tithes, 91, 142, 143
Titus, 77, 78